CAESAR AUGUSTUS

CAESAR AUGUSTUS

SEVEN ASPECTS

EDITED BY
FERGUS MILLAR
AND
ERICH SEGAL

CLARENDON PRESS · OXFORD

Oxford University Press, Walton Street, Oxford OX2 6DP
Oxford New York Toronto
Delhi Bombay Calcutta Madras Karachi
Kuala Lumpur Singapore Hong Kong Tokyo
Nairobi Dar es Salaam Cape Town
Melbourne Auckland
and associated companies in
Beirut Berlin Ibadan Nicosia

Oxford is a trade mark of Oxford University Press

Published in the United States
by Oxford University Press, New York

First published 1984
Reprinted 1985

British Library Cataloguing in Publication Data
Caesar, Augustus.
1. Rome – Politics, and government – 30 B.C. –
68 A.D. – Addresses, essays, lectures, etc.
I. Millar, Fergus   II. Segal, Erich
III. Syme, Sir Ronald
937'09   DG277
ISBN 0-19-814858-5 Pbk

Library of Congress Cataloging in Publication Data
Main entry under title:
Caesar Augustus: seven aspects.
Papers presented at a colloquium held at Wolfson College, Oxford.
Includes index.
1. Augustus, Emperor of Rome, 63 B.C. – 14 A.D. Congresses.
2. Rome – History – Augustus, 30 B.C. – 14 A.D. –
Congresses.   3. Roman emperors – Biography – Congresses.
4. Syme, Ronald, Sir, 1903–   I. Millar, Fergus.
II. Segal, Erich, 1937–
DG279.C33   1984   937'.07'0924   83-20976
ISBN 0-19-814858-5 (pbk.)

Printed and bound in Great Britain by
Biddles Ltd, Guildford and King's Lynn

PREFACE

These seven essays were originally delivered as lectures at a colloquium organised by Wolfson College, Oxford, in April 1983, to honour the eightieth birthday of Sir Ronald Syme O.M. Hence the individual speakers and their titles were selected by the editors with a view to reflecting some of the areas of concern which inform *The Roman Revolution*.

The volume is not, however, intended as a *Festschrift*, a literary sub-species of which Sir Ronald is known to disapprove. Neither the editors nor the authors have set out to express either adherence to, or distance from, Sir Ronald's views. Nor has there been any attempt to eliminate differences of interpretation among the seven contributors. The only specific task assigned to each of the authors was to express his own views on a particular aspect of the complex phenomenon of Caesar Augustus.

We are deeply grateful to Sir Henry Fisher, President of Wolfson College, and to the staff of the College for their enthusiastic assistance in making the colloquium itself a memorable occasion. We would also like to thank the Oxford University Press for its support, and Mrs Elaine Matthews for preparing the index.

F.M.   E.S.
London
May 1983

CONTENTS

ABBREVIATIONS

AE	*Année Épigraphique*
AEA	*Archivo Español de Arqueologia*
AJA	*American Journal of Archaeology*
AJPh	*American Journal of Philology*
AMN	*American Museum Notes*
ANRW	H. Temporini (ed.), *Aufstieg und Niedergang der römischen Welt*
BCH	*Bulletin de Correspondance Hellénique*
BICS	*Bulletin of the Institute of Classical Studies*
BJ	*Bonner Jahrbücher*
BMC	*Catalogue of the Greek Coins in the British Museum*
CAH	*Cambridge Ancient History*
CIL	*Corpus Inscriptionum Latinarum*
CQ	*Classical Quarterly*
CP	*Classical Philology*
CRAI	*Comptes-rendus de l'Académie des Inscriptions*
DP	T. Mommsen, *Le droit pénal romain*
EJ	V. Ehrenberg, A. H. M. Jones, *Documents Illustrating the Principates of Augustus and Tiberius*[3]
FGrH	F. Jacoby, *Die Fragmente der griechischen Historiker*
FIRA[2]	S. Riccobono, *Fontes Iuris Romani Anteiustiniani*[2]
HRR	H. Peter, *Historicorum Romanorum Reliquiae*
HSCPh	*Harvard Studies in Classical Philology*
IG	*Inscriptiones Graecae*
IGR	*Inscriptiones Graecae ad Res Romanas Pertinentes*
IGUR	L. Moretti, *Inscriptiones Graecae Urbis Romae*
I.K.Eph.	*Inschriften griechischer Städte aus Kleinasien, Ephesos*
I.K. Kyme	*Inschriften griechischer Städte aus Kleinasien, Kyme*
ILLRP	A. Degrassi, *Inscriptiones Latinae Liberae Rei Publicae*
ILS	H. Dessau, *Inscriptiones Latinae Selectae*
IRT	J. M. Reynolds, J. Ward-Perkins, *Inscriptions of Roman Tripolitania*
JdAI	*Jahrbuch des Deutschen Archäologischen Instituts*

JOAI	*Jahreshefte des Österreichischen Archäologischen Instituts*
JRS	*Journal of Roman Studies*
MAAR	*Memoirs of the American Academy in Rome*
MEFRA	*Mélanges de l'École Française de Rome, Antiquité*
MH	*Museum Helveticum*
NSc	*Notizie degli Scavi di Antichità*
OGIS	W. Dittenberger, *Orientis Graeci Inscriptiones Selectae*
PIR²	*Prosopographia Imperii Romani²*
PBSR	*Papers of the British School at Rome*
POxy	*Oxyrhynchus Papyri*
REG	*Revue des Études Grecques*
REL	*Revue des Études Latines*
RE	Pauly-Wissowa, *Realenzyklopaedie der Klassischen Altertumswissenschaft*
RHD	*Revue historique de droit français et étranger*
RhMus	*Rheinisches Museum*
RPAA	*Rendiconti della Pontificia Accademia di Archeologia*
SCO	*Studi Classici e Orientali*
SDHI	*Studia et Documenta Historiae et Iuris*
SEG	*Supplementum Epigraphicum Graecum*
SIG³	W. Dittenberger, *Sylloge Inscriptionum Graecarum³*
TAPA	*Transactions of the American Philological Association*
ZPE	*Zeitschrift für Papyrologie und Epigraphik*
ZSS	*Zeitschrift der Savigny-Stiftung für Rechtsgeschichte*

I. THE *RES GESTAE* AND AUGUSTUS' PUBLIC IMAGE

ZVI YAVETZ

In introducing the theme of Caesar Augustus and our image of him, I shall concentrate on three questions: the first concerns Augustus' Autobiography, the second the *Res Gestae* and its intended audience, and the third the effect of Augustus' self-representation on history and historians.

I

A reconstruction of the Autobiography from the surviving fragments[1] is a vain labour.[2] Nor is a meticulous and rigid scrutiny of the authenticity of each of the fragments going to be any more fruitful. An East German scholar has recently attempted to distinguish between fragments quoted in direct and in indirect speech, between those quoted verbatim and those summarizing the content of a passage, only to reach the not very surprising conclusion that the work cannot be recovered: 'Im Endergebnis muss die Autobiographie des Kaiser Augustus als verloren gelten.'[3] However, even if one admits that most quotations which survive in ancient authors do not originate directly from the Autobiography, but rather from some obscure intermediate source (e.g. an anthology of *prodigia*), and even if the authenticity of some passages is to be completely rejected,[4] there is still enough room to establish two basic facts: that the Autobiography in thirteen books, which was dedicated to Maecenas and Agrippa,[5] was discontinued after the Cantabrian War;[6] and that conscious efforts, which are easily detectable, were made by Augustus to project a public image different from that which prevailed in his enemies' propaganda.

First, August defended himself against all those who attacked the ignobility of his family;[7] he admitted that his father was the first of his line to become a senator, but emphasized the fact that his equestrian family was old, wealthy, and respectable.[8]

Secondly, from an uncertain passage in Tertullian, combined with some passages in Suetonius, Plutarch, and Nicolaus of Damascus,[9] it is clear that Augustus intended to tell his readers that his great talents had already been recognized in early childhood. His adoption by his great-uncle was neither an accident nor due to the manipulations of his mother. Fate had great things in store for him.

The following pages of the Autobiography must have been dedicated to explaining his behaviour towards some of his previous allies (e.g. Cicero and Antonius), behaviour which could have been condemned not only as inconsistent but even as treacherous. Augustus probably stressed the fact that the end was to avenge his father's murder and to save the Republic.[10] In order to carry out these salient tasks all means had been justifiable.

To survive five civil wars, he had had to be firm and ruthless, but he must have found out to his distress that he had acquired a reputation as a cruel, vengeful, selfish, and treacherous youth.[11] This image had to be changed. It was not easy to alter public opinion, and he could not become a 'clementissimus' overnight; but slanders had to be refuted immediately. One example may suffice. His enemies had spread the story that once Octavian had suspected a praetor, Quintus Gallius, of having approached him with a sword concealed under his robe. Octavian had Gallius tortured like a slave, and ordered his execution, first tearing out the man's eyes with his own hands. Augustus must have felt that the story could not be ignored altogether, and a new version had to be produced. True, Gallius had been suspected of conspiracy, but he had been properly tried and sentenced to banishment; unfortunately, however, he had lost his life by some tragic accident on his way to exile.[12]

There was another set of rumours against which Augustus had to defend himself; these concerned his behaviour during the decisive battles of the civil war. Rumour had it that Octavian had behaved in a cowardly fashion on the battlefield, and that the palm for the victory should have been bestowed upon his aides. Indeed, at Philippi Octavian had been unable to participate actively in the preparations for the encounter because of sickness. This could be forgiven; but how to explain away the fact that he disappeared from his litter? The excuse was that one of his friends had been visited by a heavenly vision, telling Octavian to arise from his bed and depart from the camp.[13] Credulous and superstitious people might have swallowed this.[14] The conservative and old-fashioned Octavian himself did not disdain popular beliefs.[15] Elsewhere in his Autobiography Augustus admitted that on the day on which he was almost overthrown by a mutiny in the army he put his left boot on the wrong foot;[16] and in a letter to Tiberius he wrote that he dreaded the unlucky sound 'Nonis' ('you are not going'); and therefore never took up important business on the Nones.[17]

It is plausible to assume that in some other parts of the Autobiography Augustus was at pains to explain his not very distinguished performance at Actium.[18] But he had no difficulty in boasting of his previous brilliant successes against the Illyrian tribes: he had brought back those who revolted and compelled them to pay tribute; he had subjugated others who had been independent from the beginning; he had also conquered the tribes that inhabited the summit of the Alps, barbarous and warlike peoples who had often plundered Italy.[19]

Without going into too much detail, the apologetic, defensive, and occasionally polemical undercurrents are obvious in the surviving fragments of the Autobiography.[20] His enemies vilified his performance in war – he represented himself as a man of *virtus*. His enemies depicted him as cruel and savage – he emphasized his *clementia*. His enemies charged him with defiance of legal procedures – he paraded his *iustitia*. His enemies condemned his treacherous behaviour towards former friends, benefactors, and even members of his own family – Augustus stressed his loyalty. There were, of course, exceptions. He had been unable to tolerate Scribonia, and hoped that decent people would eventually understand and justify his behaviour when finally 'wearied by the perversity of her character': 'pertaesus . . . morum perversitatem eius'.[21]

But why did he stop writing his Autobiography after the Cantabrian War? Did he consider the second closing of the gates of Janus a suitable date? Perhaps, but so was the first closing. Was he afflicted by some disease which prevented him from writing? This is possible, but he recovered from his illness thanks to Antonius Musa's treatment.[22] Nevertheless, he did not take up his Autobiography again. A more convincing explanation is possible. After 23 BC Augustus reached the conclusion that further justification of his earlier career was unnecessary, and might even be counter-productive.

Let us imagine for a moment a novel about a Roman boy, born in 76 BC, whose uncle was killed in the Sullan proscriptions, whose father died in Spain fighting Sertorius, and who could still remember his mother's stories about Spartacus' atrocities. The news about his first cousin's death in Pompey's eastern campaigns reached him while Rome was afflicted by the Catilinarian conspiracy. In 59 BC the boy was seventeen, and in 58 BC he joined Caesar's army in Gaul. He excelled in battle and crossed the Rubicon in 49 BC. As a staunch supporter of Caesar he fought alongside him at Ilerda, Pharsalus, Zela, Thapsus, and Munda. He was thirty-two when Caesar was killed. His unit joined Caesar's heir without hesitation. He fought bravely at Mutina and Philippi, but he had chanced his luck too often: wounded at Philippi, he recovered all too slowly, and after twenty years of loyal and distinguished service he was honourably discharged and given a plot of land. He married; his wife gave birth to a son, but he hardly had the opportunity to rejoice. The day his son was born, his brother was killed at Actium. He loved his son and decided never to allow him to volunteer for army service, particularly if he might be involved in savage civil wars. If only someone could put an end to this senseless and endless killing and at last close the gates of Janus. He would adore him as almost super-human, and for the sake of peace transfer all authority to him. He was not sorry to sacrifice the long republican tradition. It meant very little to him. This, of course, is fiction – but is it pure imagination?

It was in this kind of atmosphere that Augustus might have thought that it would be superfluous to go on justifying his deeds, apologizing for irregularities, and trying to whitewash his character as he had done in his Autobiography. His *virtus* and *iustitia*, his *clementia* and *pietas* were beyond doubt, and, furthermore, they had been unanimously attributed to him by the Senate.[27] It was not, however, the case that from that moment on he felt strong enough to disregard evil words uttered against him, and contented himself with the power to stop anybody from acting against him. Gone were the days when action had been taken only against deeds, while words went unpunished. The statement that in the reign of Augustus no one suffered for exercising his freedom of speech should be taken with a grain of salt. Augustus may not often have abused his *auctoritas*, but now and then he did not hesitate to destroy vituperative pamphlets. The public burning of Cassius Severus' works and the exiling of the author to Crete only go to show that efficient means were at Augustus' disposal to combat invective. But defensive counter-publication was not one of them.[28]

It is more significant, however, that the esteem of his contemporaries was no longer enough; like many other Romans, Augustus started to think about posterity. So too Cicero had worried about the verdict history would pass on him 600 years after his death; he admits in a letter that he feared this verdict much more than the rumours and petty gossip spread by his contemporaries.[29] Equally, *laudationes* pronounced after the death of important Romans were not for contemporary consumption alone, and Hirtius completed Caesar's *Gallic Wars* to provide material for future historians: 'ne scientia tantarum rerum scriptoribus deesset'.[30] Augustus was no exception. As early as 36 BC he had his speeches written down and published as a booklet,[31] and in 13 BC he enumerated his achievements in writing and asked the quaestor to read out the manuscript to the Senate.[32] These steps have to be seen in the light of Augustus' own statement that he wanted his actions to be recorded as exemplary paradigms for posterity.[33] This aim could not be achieved by means of an autobiography. Hence it was discontinued, and instead his emphasis was laid on the writing and rewriting of the *Res Gestae*.

For the purpose of this essay it is not necessary to deal with the complicated problems of the various layers of the *Res Gestae* or to attempt to reconstruct the original version, an *Urmonument*.[34] Suffice it to assert that after 23 BC the main attention was focused on the *Res Gestae*, and that the document that has come down to us was carefully drafted and redrafted between 23 and 2 BC. The changes and additions alluding to events after 2 BC will not affect our discussion, since Augustus himself indicated that the title *pater patriae* conferred upon him in 2 BC constituted the climax of his career.[35] Historians have long since recognized that it was Augustus' main object to change his image from that of a ferocious tyrant to one of *pater patriae* (Gibbon), or from *dux partium* to *princeps civium* (Syme). To achieve this aim, Augustus did not underestimate the contribution of sympathetic historians, poets, sculptors, and architects. He did not even have to blush, like Cicero, while asking others to praise his deeds;[36] subtler means were at his disposal. Nor did he shirk the destruction of historical source material that might one day incriminate him,[37] thus making it even more difficult for his opponents to write against him: 'non est enim facile in eum scribere qui potest proscribere'.[38] However, Augustus refused to rely only on others. Without having read the sayings of his contemporary, the Jewish sage Hillel, he seems to have followed his advice: 'If I am not for myself, who is for me?'[39]

I should like to carry the argument one step further. As far as Augustus' self-representation is concerned, the relation between the Mausoleum Augusti on the one hand and the Augustus statue at Prima Porta on the other hand is similar to the relation between the unfinished Autobiography and the *Res Gestae*.

In his Autobiography Augustus was still reacting to slander and vituperation. The Mausoleum served a similar purpose. One does not have to believe that this huge edifice had been erected in contemplation of an early death, or to assume that as early as 28 BC the establishment of a royal dynasty was Octavian's prime concern. This may not have been the case even as late as 23 BC. It is, therefore, much more plausible to accept the argument that Octavian had fallen prey to his own propaganda, in which he vilified Antonius for *externi mores* and *vitia non Romana*, above all because of the latter's last wish to be buried in Alexandria. The building of the Mausoleum had thus begun in the second half of the 30s, and the immense structure was intended to remind everyone that, as opposed to Antonius, Octavian and his family were to be buried in Rome, between the Tiber and the Via Flaminia.[40] Therefore, as early as 28 BC he had opened the area round it as a public park: 'Circumiect-asque silvas et ambulationes in usum populi iam tum publi-carat.'[41] It is also possible that the so-called 'restoration of the Republic' on 13 January 27 BC was a reaction to Antonius' promise to restore the Republic to the Senate and the Roman people after the anticipated victory.[42]

As soon as he was securely holding the reins of government, he undertook to change his public image. No longer was a young Octavian represented on coins with his face encircled by a beard – an expression of grief for the assassination of Julius Caesar – but a new idealized image of a great man and a great warrior emerged. This was not intended to portray the real physical appearance of Augustus, as described in Suetonius – a rather short, occasionally limping fellow, his shoes somewhat high-heeled to make him look taller than he really was, with spots on his body and a few teeth, wide apart and decayed[43] – but an Augustus whose physique embodied a new political ideal.

The new Forum, dominated by the temple of Mars Ultor, was constructed from the proceeds of military spoils, and honoured the *summi viri* who had acquired new territories for Rome; it also gave a central place to the *quadriga* awarded by the Senate to Augustus in 2 BC, in which the *princeps* is shown as a triumphant general. In addition, Augustus appears on coins as the saviour of citizens' lives, and the Senate ordered that the magistrates, priests, and vestal virgins should perform an annual sacrifice before the Ara Pacis, which would com-memorate him as the father of the *pax Romana*.[44] But this was not all. Various surviving statues represent Augustus as a citizen offering sacrifice or performing some religious cere-mony, his toga drawn up to veil his head ('capite velato'), for he was proud to be *pontifex maximus* and to fulfil various priestly functions. It is a well-known fact that whenever sculptors or painters in antiquity wanted to carve or to paint forms of ideal beauty, which consisted not only of virility but also of purity and sanctity, they chose as their prototype Polyclitus' Doryphorus, depicted by Quintilian as 'vir gravis et sanctus'.[45] Therefore there can be little doubt that the statue of Augustus known to us from Livia's home at Prima Porta is more than merely an artistic creation.[46]

Augustus' new self-representation is established from the very first sentence of the *Res Gestae*: 'Exercitum privato consilio et privata impensa comparavi' is not an apologetic statement; it is not the language of an usurper, but that of a saviour. It recalls the principle traditionally attributed to L. Brutus the elder, who, in case of emergency, although a *privatus*, had carried alone the whole burden of government: 'In conserving the liberty of the citizens no one is a *privatus*'; 'In conservanda civium libertate esse privatum neminem.[47] No more vicious and insulting rumours about Augustus' cowardly behaviour in battle. The great protagonists of Philippi, Naulochus, and Actium were dead. Salvidienus had been conveniently disposed of, Agrippa was a faithful deputy, his other aides, each carefully picked, were loyal and efficient. Therefore, with sententious and oracular brevity: 'I was twice victorious in battle'; 'Bis acie vici'. There was no one left to contradict him.

II

Many important scholars (Mommsen, Dessau, Kornemann, and Hohl – to name just a few) have stated categorically that in his *Res Gestae* Augustus addressed himself primarily to the *plebs urbana* of Rome.[48] No one in Ancyra, Apollonia, or Antioch[49] could possibly have been interested in the boring enumeration of *largitiones* and *congiaria*, of games and of mimes performed in Rome. Mommsen stated explicitly that the *princeps* wrote down 'those things which he wished the whole *populus* and the plebs to believe about him'; and Syme mentioned in a footnote that Dessau's insistence that the inscription was primarily designed to be read by the plebs in Rome has not always been sufficiently regarded.[50] Many years ago, I myself adopted this view,[51] but have since given the problem more serious thought.

Three main arguments have been put forward to establish Dessau's view: first, Augustus had to conceal his *imperium proconsulare maius* cleverly because his military position could not have been popular with the city masses.[52] Secondly, Augustus emphasized his *tribunicia potestas* because he wanted to appear as champion of the common people. Thirdly, the tedious report in paragraphs 15–24 about *frumentum* and *congiaria*, games and circuses, distribution and allocation of land, was intended to instil into the minds of the plebs that the necessary funds came from the Emperor's own funds ('patrimonio meo'). These arguments are not convincing, and can be refuted one by one. *Imperium* had never been unpopular with the urban plebs.

For example, when Marcus Naevius the tribune accused Scipio Africanus of having received money from Antiochus III in order to conclude a peace favourable to the king, Scipio had to defend himself in a *contio*: 'I recall, fellow citizens, that this is the day on which in Africa in a mighty battle I conquered Hannibal, the most bitter enemy of your power ('imperio vestro inimicissimum') and I won for you a splendid peace and glorious victory.' Scipio suggested to the crowd that they should pay no attention to the mean accusations of a wretched tribune: 'Let us not be ungrateful to the Gods, but let us go at once to render thanks to Jupiter . . .' His charisma worked. The assembly, which had gathered to pass judgement on Scipio's irregularities, deserted the tribune, accompanied Scipio to the Capitol, and then walked home with him.[53]

Equally, in the reign of Augustus the *princeps* had no reason to conceal his *imperium*, his conquests, and certainly not his triumphs.[54] Cicero's statement that *gloria* and *laus* were approved alike by the testimony of *optimus quisque* and by that of the multitude[55] was still true in the time of Augustus. For Roman aristocrats in the middle and late Republic, warfare had become almost second nature, and most of them had to participate in several campaigns before running for political office.[56] *Rei militaris gloria* always enhanced the electoral chances of a candidate. The prayer of the censors for the expansion of the Empire[57] and the pride felt 'imperio amplificato, pace per orbem terrarum confecta'[58] seems to have echoed the attitudes of the upper classes to war and peace. On the other hand, some historians have suggested that ordinary citizens, i.e. those involved in the real fighting, were opposed to Roman imperialism,[59] and that military service became intensely unpopular during the republican era. There is indeed some evidence that citizens eligible for military service tried to avoid enlistment. But the opposite viewpoint has recently been argued by Hopkins and Harris, who urge the rejection of the presupposition that ordinary citizens were generally reluctant to serve.[60] May I suggest a more incisive distinction? *Imperium* was still popular in the time of Augustus. Otherwise he would not have honoured so greatly the memory of those heroes 'qui imperium P.R. ex minimo maximum reddidissent' by putting up their statues in two impressive colonnades of the Forum Augustum.[61] However, a clear distinction must be made between applauding conquests and participating in them, between cheering victorious generals and serving under them. Propertius would have loved to avenge Crassus' humiliation of Carrhae: 'Go forth and make fair the pages of Rome's story' he exhorts the soldiers ('ite, et Romanae consulite historiae'). However, he had no aspirations to enrich himself in war: 'be the spoils theirs whose toil has won it'. The poet is happy just to cheer the victors on the Via Sacra: 'Mi sat erit Sacra plaudere posse Via'.[62] Moreover, he assures us that none of his progeny will ever serve in the army: 'nullus de nostro sanguine miles erit'.[63]

This attitude was not the privilege of poets alone. The Roman plebs too applauded successful generals and were pleased to be informed of magnificent victories and a splendid peace. However, when it came to actual fighting, it seems that they were less enthusiastic. When trouble arose in Pannonia and Bohemia between AD 6 and 9, not enough *ingenui* were prepared to serve their country. Sons of freedmen and even slaves had to fill the ranks.[64] These combined attitudes allow us to understand paragraphs 25–34 of the *Res Gestae*. Augustus did not mention his *imperium*, either because he did not intend to write a treatise on constitutional law[65] or because it was obvious that all military successes had been achieved by his command and under his auspices. His *imperium* is implied already in his account of year 43 (1. 2–4), and later paragraphs leave no doubt: '*I* extended the territory of all those provinces of the Roman people on whose borders lay peoples not subject to our government'; '*My* fleet sailed etc.' (26); 'At *my* command and under my auspices ('meo iussu et auspicio') two armies conquered Ethiopia and Arabia'; 'When the Armenians rebelled, *I* subdued them'.[66] It was left to later historians to explain that Augustus' power consisted of 'legiones, classes, provincias, cuncta inter se connexa'.[67] Nobody in Rome would have imagined that all that had been achieved by someone *sine imperio*.[68]

Nor is the *tribunicia potestas* argument convincing. No one should deny Augustus' efforts to appear as a champion of the people (δημοτικός) or underestimate the esteem the tribunician power enjoyed with the lower classes. Its psychological effect was certainly more important than its legal one. But it may be suggested that Augustus found more effective ways to endear himself to the masses than by reminding them time and again that the *tribunicia potestas* was his. This was rather meant to remind the upper classes of what might happen should the *plebecula* be let loose on them. Only a man with *tribunicia potestas* could induce the people to yield to the authority of the *principes civitatis*. Thus the senatorial order would not be exposed to the open hatred of the masses. This fact was well known to the Roman nobles who embraced the *tribunicia potestas* as a necessary evil.[68]

The popular disturbances which took place between 23 and 19 BC clearly showed that Augustus was the only one who could save the upper classes, and keep the masses in check.[69] He could rein in the ambition of some Roman senators, and the fate of Egnatius Rufus should have served as an example to all those who might attempt, against his will, to gain the *favor plebis*. Ambitious young men had to be reminded that, just as all military achievements came about *suo iussu et auspiciis*, so he was the only one who could keep the lower classes *in bonis artibus* and take care that the plebs, corrupted by largesses and public supplies of corn, should be too busy to cause trouble to the state: 'uti plebs largitionibus et publico frumento corrupta, sua negotia habeat quibus ab malo publico detineatur.'[70]

It is doubtful if paragraphs 15–24 of the *Res Gestae (impensae)* were in fact intended to impress the *plebecula* with the fact that all the benefactions and donations which were lavishly squandered on the Roman masses came 'ex horreo et patrimonio meo'.[71] My contention is that the common people preferred to receive *largitiones* of all kinds rather than to read about them. Moreover, one would have to assume a very high percentage of potential readers among the *plebs urbana*. People who could just discern between a V for 'uti rogas' and an A for 'antiquo' cannot be considered literate; they could hardly have mastered the long and tedious inscription.[72] Cicero's testimony about some scathing edicts of Bibulus, which were so popular that one could not pass the place where they were posted up for the crowd of people reading them, must also be taken *cum grano salis*.[73] No one could tell whether everybody in the crowd was capable of reading the posters. It is just as plausible to assume that one knowledgeable man read them out to amuse the others.

For our argument it is enough to remember that slanderous posters were usually *short*, and generally aroused more curiosity than any inscription like the *Res Gestae*. The ancients knew that 'reckless wit gets bandied about more freely and is on everybody's lips'.[74] Did Augustus really have in mind the Roman *plebecula* picnicking after his death near the Mausoleum and reading for their recreation the *regina inscriptionum* incised upon tall bronze tablets?[75]

Augustus' ear was always sensitive to the hisses of the crowds and the murmurs of Italy, and he spared no effort to make this attitude well known to the masses. The news was deliberately spread that he had contemplated committing suicide after he had found out that the granaries contained supplies sufficient for three days only.[76] He used many other means to please the people; at popular performances he appeared with his wife and children and invited actors and even common circus clowns to his banquets.[77] He missed no opportunity to organize popular entertainments, and even the first shaving of his beard provided an occasion for a festival.[78]

It would, therefore, seem unlikely that such a connoisseur of the psychology of the masses (were they to be the potential readers of the *Res Gestae*) would tell them with pride that he had refused the consulship which was offered to him by the people for the rest of his life, and that he had rejected the dictatorship, even though the *plebecula* had urged him to accept it.[79] The urban plebs had no attachment to Cicero's definition of *libertas*, and republican niceties were not appreciated by them. But Augustus never intended to impress common people with written words; a long inscription, even one set up in an attractive park at the northern entrance of the Campus Martius,[80] could not enhance his popularity. They would remember him through statues and effigies, the Ara Pacis and the Forum

Augusti, and he genuinely believed that some day he would be considered as one of those who raised the Roman people to greatness, just as those heroes whose statues were set up by him in the niches of the colonnades around the Forum:[81] 'I have contrived this to lead the citizens to require me while I live, and the rulers of later times as well, to attain the standard set by those worthiest of old.'[82]

To conclude: written propaganda addressed to the masses would have to be short, like slogans on coins; it was common knowledge that the average man was more interested in daily news, and piquant gossip, than in the vast array of facts from the past.[83] Poetry and history, on the other hand, were designed to influence the upper and middle classes.[84] To secure his place in history, Augustus had to appeal to the more educated citizens, and it was they whom he told how he wished to be remembered.

He would never have denied the fact that he cared for the plebs, but he wanted posterity to know that he was much more than a προστάτης τοῦ δήμου, a champion of the people. He wanted his tact to serve as an example, and that everyone should remember how he succeeded in making every *honestissimus* his friend, how he won the affection of the humble without having lost the respect of their superiors.[85] He wanted to present himself as a *salubris princeps*,[86] who, like a good physician, took into his hands a disease-ridden body and succeeded in healing it.[87] His success was achieved through a *consensus universorum*, just as vague a concept as Cicero's *consensus omnium bonorum*. But, just as the latter refused to restrict *bonitas* to one social class ('sunt etiam libertini optimates'),[88] so did Augustus refuse to present himself as a leader of one stratum of the population. He wanted to be, and to appear as, *pater patriae*, and when the title was eventually bestowed upon him in 2 BC, he regarded this as the crowning achievement of his life.[89]

When the title was offered to him for the first time by a deputation of the plebs which came to see him at Antium, he declined the honour. Once, when he entered the theatre in Rome, the masses urged him to accept the title, but he declined again.[90] Augustus refused to be regarded as the darling of the plebs only – some kind of *parens plebis Romanae*, as Manlius had been.[91] Nor did the precedent of Sulla appeal to him, since the latter was acclaimed as *saviour* and *pater* by the most distinguished and influential citizens only.[92] By all traditional criteria he considered himself worthy of the title. He was a *conservator libertatis*,[93] he had put an end to a terrible civil war that had brought impious slaughter and intestine fury,[94] he was renowned for his *clementia*,[95] spared the downtrodden, had given quiet to the world and peace to his time,[96] reformed the *mores* of Rome,[97] and had the purity of the Roman family at heart. He expected everyone to recognize that and therefore only when the motion was initiated in the Senate by Messala, a former partisan of Brutus and Cassius, in accord with the people of Rome ('consentiens cum populo Romano') did he burst into tears: 'Having attained my highest hopes, Fathers of the Senate, what more have I to ask of the immortal gods that I may retain this same unanimous approval of yours to the very end of my life?'[98]

As far as Augustus' self-representation is concerned, chapter 35 of the *Res Gestae* (and not the much-debated chapter 34) is indeed the apex: 'Universus populus appellavit me patrem patriae,' and to emphasize the fact that he was not content with the routine formula *Senatus Populusque Romanus*, he added the sometimes forgotten *ordo equester*. He was pleased to accept the title 'Augustus' – *senatus consulto*. He was proud to receive the *corona civica* and the *clupeus virtutis* from the Senate and the Roman People. However, to become *pater patriae* he wanted the support of the people as a whole, and there was no *universus populus* without the *ordo equester*.[99]

III

Those who believe that the identity of the intended public of Augustus' *Res Gestae* is an irrelevant or unnecessary question should stop here. I myself believe that the issue is not without interest. Therefore, I submit a conjecture for further discussion.

It is not necessary to accept rigidly the three traditional parts of the *Res Gestae*: *honores*, paragraphs 1–14; *impensae*, 15–24; *Res Gestae*, 25–35. Mommsen had already remarked that Augustus followed this division 'sine scrupulosa anxietate'.[100] Indeed, in the first fourteen paragraphs Augustus tells us much more than about his *honores* alone. He asserts his unshaken loyalty to *mos maiorum*: i.e. he would never accept any office inconsistent with the customs of his ancestors (6), and he celebrates the fact that the new laws had passed on his initiative, by which be brought back into use many exemplary practices of the forefathers which had disappeared in his own days (8). In all his social and political legislation, it appears that he acted according to the principle once formulated by the censors in 92 BC, that no innovations should be made contrary to the usage and principles of the forefathers.[101]

Augustus' conservatism and traditionalism have long been recognized, and his alleged statement that a good man is one who does not intend to change the present state of things is considered to be genuine.[102] This conservatism expressed itself not only in his attitude to the patriciate, but also in his adherence to the old Roman religion.[103] One should, therefore, not be surprised by the fact that among his *honores* more emphasis is placed on his being *pontifex maximus, augur, quindecemvir sacris faciundis, septemvir epulonum, frater arvalis, sodalis Titius*, and *fetialis*, than on his *imperium proconsulare*.[104] Augustus recorded the fact that his name was inscribed in the hymn of the Salii by a decree of the Senate, and did not forget to stress the fact that an enormous number of people poured into Rome from all parts of Italy to celebrate his election as *pontifex maximus*. No wonder that he employed the ancient ritual of the Fetiales when declaring war on Cleopatra,[105] and boasted that he had built the temples of the Lares at the top of the Via Sacra, the temple of the Penates in the Velia, and the Aedes Iuventatis.[106] He considered himself not only a *conditor* but also a *conservator Romani nominis*.[107] These details leave no doubt that from a certain moment onward Augustus intended to present himself not only as *pater patriae* who cared for all the Roman *ordines* alike, but also as that ideal *vir gravis et sanctus*, who had put an end to the feud between social classes and political factions and to the hostile relations between Rome and external nations. The question, of course, arises: whom then did he intend to impress? It is essential to remember that the *Res Gestae* was intended as a record for future generations, to be put up in public only after his death.

Many years ago, Rostovtzeff, in his study of Roman lead

tesserae, reached the conclusion that in order to enforce his conservative policies, Augustus relied heavily on the *equites*, and especially on the young *equites*,[108] and took great interest in the organization of the *iuvenes*, not only in Rome but also in other Italian municipalities.[109] Rereading this rarely quoted work carefully, we can see a consistent pattern emerging. It would no longer seem strange that Augustus reviewed the *turmae equitum* at frequent intervals, thus reviving the custom of this procession after a long period of disuse;[110] that the Roman knights celebrated Augustus' birthday of their own initiative, by common consent and always for two consecutive days; and that he took great pride in the fact that the whole body of knights (*equites Romani universi*) both presented his grandsons Gaius and Lucius with silver shields and spears and hailed them as *principes iuventutis*.[111]

Following Mommsen, who had already pointed out the reorganization of the *equites* as a quasi-political corporation, especially with the appointment of the *seviri equitum Romanorum*,[112] Rostovtzeff emphasized the religious and pre-military aspects discernible in the organization of the youths belonging to the upper classes. The *iuventus*,[113] which included not only the young *equites*, but also sons of senators (theoretically till the age of thirty-five), enjoyed many privileges in the reign of Augustus. They filled the rows of the *cuneus iuniorum* in the theatre,[114] and as early as 28 BC Augustus made boys and men of the nobility participate in the circensian games.[115] At the shows he assigned special seats to boys under age, and the adjoining ones to their preceptors.[116] He sponsored frequent performances of the Lusus Troiae by older and younger boys, believing it to be a worthy custom that the flower of the nobility should become known in this way.[117] The Carmen Saeculare was sung by boys and girls from the leading families of Rome, and these were the same boys who paraded their horses in the solemn military review presided over by Augustus himself. He may have feared that a long period of peace and security might effeminate the youngsters and transform them into Sybarites, who would hate exposure to the sun on the Campus Martius, would be afraid to bathe in cold water, would not know how to handle a horse or throw a javelin, and be generally unfit to bear hardships.[118] Therefore,

Augustus reinstituted a custom which had once existed, but in his own days was obsolete, the *exercitatio campestris*.[119] He may have hoped thus to revive the 'race of hardy stock',[120] the manly breed of peasant soldiers – 'rusticorum mascula militum',[121] who had once defeated Pyrrhus, Hannibal, and Antiochus III. Dio must have understood all this when he put into Maecenas' mouth the following advice: 'When children turn into youths, they should turn their minds to horses and to arms and have paid public teachers in each. of these departments. In this way from their very boyhood they will have had both instruction and practice in all that they will themselves be required to do on reaching manhood, and will thus prove more serviceable to you.'[122]

Rostovtzeff concluded that the *iuvenes* provided a powerful prop for Caesarism: 'Die iuvenes waren eine mächtige Stutze des Caesarismus.'[123] More arguments can be presented to strengthen Rostovtzeff's argument, and thus clarify even further the self-representation of Augustus in his *Res Gestae*.

The Principate was not a *creatio ex nihilo*. Nor was it an automatic application of political ideas detectable in the writings of some earlier political thinkers. In 27 BC few alternatives were left. The restoration of the old regime of the *nobiles* was impracticable. The establishment of a dictatorship after the model of either Sulla or Caesar was hated or feared or both, and an absolute Hellenistic monarchy was out of the question.[124] But old traditions die slowly, and the few aristocrats and their sons who had survived the civil wars continued to believe that freedom did not mean serving a just master, but serving no master at all.[125]

Augustus was well aware that these diehards would never follow suit. But he may well have hoped that a new generation, less politically minded, would readily acquiesce. Already in the time of Cicero, there existed a class of people, especially in the Italian municipalities – tax collectors, money-lenders, and wealthy farmers – who had never been loyal to any political principle. Their main desire was to be left in peace, and they would never reject or fear a monarch, provided that they could be assured that he would not harm their interests.[126] The embarrassments caused to the Principate by the younger Crassus and Lepidus, Cornelius Gallus, Caepio, Primus,

Murena, and Egnatius Rufus, must have convinced Augustus more than anything that only a new, wealthy, and non-political class could become the backbone of his new regime. The loyalty of plebs and army was not enough; but the new class, though blessed with material wealth, lacked tradition.[127] Consequently, it must have occurred to Augustus that the best strategy for the introduction of a new tradition would be the revival of an old one. Realizing that the older generation would not be amenable to change, he took a strong personal interest in the education of the *iuventus*, caring not only for their physical fitness, but also for what he saw as their moral and spiritual well-being.[128] He forbade beardless teenagers to participate in the running at the Lupercalia, and at the Secular Games he would not allow young people of either sex to attend any entertainment by night unless accompanied by some adult relative.[129] In order to enable senators' sons to gain an earlier acquaintance with public affairs he allowed them to attend meetings of the Senate.[130] He established a library on the Palatine which contained books mainly on civil law and *liberalia studia*.[131] In a period of scarcity, when foreigners were expelled, the teachers among them were exempted.[132]

If anyone could have been attracted by his new image, it was the Roman *iuventus*, and it is possible that concomitantly with the *exercitatio campestris* they had to come to accept it. Constant repetition of simple ideas may have led them to acknowledge that Augustus' success had been due to his practical experience, historical knowledge, and human wisdom.

Acquaintance with tradition was thus to become an integral part of the education of Rome's future leadership, and grown-up men were supposed to know how life is interwoven with *mos maiorum*: 'To be ignorant of what occurred before you were born was to remain a child for ever.'[133] It is likely that Augustus became even more aware of the problems when it was a matter of the education of his own grandchildren. He taught them reading, writing, and swimming, he often dined with them and took them along on his journeys.[134] By that time Cicero in his eyes was no longer a political enemy, but a learned man and a great patriot.[135] The older he grew, the more Augustus might have felt, like Cicero, that it was the duty of the old and experienced to guide the young, and he too

could perhaps imagine no greater pleasure than to be surrounded by young people eager for knowledge.[136] In Roman
tradition there was no greater service that a man could render
to Rome than to instruct and train youth, especially in view of
the fact that young people had gone so far astray because of
moral laxity.[137] Hence the mental improvement and advance-
ment of the young was of prime concern to the *princeps*. Some
senators may have watched with anxiety and concern
Augustus' growing influence on the younger generation, but
they were helpless. The uncompromising Asinius Pollio,[138]
however, availed himself of an accident which happened to his
grandson during the Lusus Troiae (he broke his leg), and
complained bitterly in the Senate about the dangerous customs
introduced by Augustus.[139] It seems that Asinius Pollio's
opposition was not directed only against dangerous physical
exercises. The accident at the games presented him with an
occasion to raise his voice against Augustus. Eventually
Augustus had to give up this form of entertainment, but his
interest in youth did not slacken. His finest hour had, after all,
been the decision he took at the age of nineteen, and he never
ceased to boast of the *auctoritas* he had acquired at this young
age: 'Young men, listen to an old man, to whom old men
listened when he was young.'[140] It is not absurd to suggest that
he had the educated *iuventus* in mind when he wrote his *Res
Gestae*.

This was in keeping with Roman tradition. Cicero considered the publication of his speeches a debt which he must
not leave unpaid to the younger generation, and he expected
schoolboys to read them.[141] Horace, Tibullus, and Ovid sang
for the young,[142] and Virgil urged the youth never to start a
civil war again.[143] Augustus knew perfectly well that Roman
youngsters were best educated by *exempla* of noble deeds,[144]
that understanding of concrete detail was a characteristic
feature of the Romans,[145] and that they preferred to learn 'non
auribus modo verum etiam oculis' – as Pliny was later to
write.[146] When some *equites* complained about his marriage
laws, he did not preach to them, but simply asked them to
follow the example of Germanicus and his six children.[147]
Greeks believed in *praecepta*, Romans in *exempla*.[148] Young
men should be sent to the scene of action, see things with their

own eyes, rather than follow abstract precepts.[149] 'Longum iter per praecepta, breve et efficax per exempla'.[150] It seems that Augustus, like Trajan later, preferred setting an example rather than ruling by decree,[151] or, to quote Ovid: 'exemploque suo mores reget'.[152] His intention was to revive a traditional society in which the *exempla maiorum* would not only be respected but not even questioned.[153] He wanted to set an example for future generations, and was not satisfied with being *imperio maximus*. His goal was to become *exemplo maior*.[154]

He had dedicated his discontinued Autobiography to his friends Agrippa and Maecenas. Had a dedication for the *Res Gestae* survived, it might have read 'pro iuventute', because to them 'I transmitted exemplary practices for imitation.'[155] The *Res Gestae* would be much more impressive after his death: 'We hate virtue while it lives and mourn it only when snatched from sight.'[156]

The question remains: to what extent has his self-representation affected history and historians?

IV

At some periods in history the name of Augustus was criticized, condemned, and even vilified.[157] Tacitus would never have allowed a ruler to suppress history through his own *Res Gestae* and to direct posterity how and what to think of him, especially if critical contemporaries had been prevented from reporting the truth: 'Nam contra, punitis ingeniis, gliscit auctoritas', as he reports Cremutius Cordus claiming at his trial.[158] Should people be led astray by the fact that Augustus gave the civil-war-stricken generation some peace at last, they would be reminded by Tacitus that peace had been bought at a high price: 'pacem sine dubio post haec, verum cruentam', and that personal liberty had been restrained: 'acriora ex eo vincla'.[159]

Subsequently we encounter some criticisms of Augustus,[160] but by and large, and perhaps in comparison with later, less praiseworthy Emperors, Augustus' image as a 'circumspectissimus et prudentissimus princeps' prevailed.[161] In early modern Europe, however, the figure of Augustus was the object of dislike and sometimes even of hatred on the part of historians and political thinkers. For Machiavelli the destruction of the

Republic and the loss of freedom through the establishment of one man's rule was the beginning of the end. Eighteenth-century French writing was overwhelmingly anti-Augustan in tone. Montesquieu believed 'Auguste rusé tyrant, les conduit à la servitude',[162] and Voltaire considered Augustus to be 'indifférent au crime et à la vertue'. This devastating verdict may be quoted in full: 'Homme sans pudeur, sans foi, sans honneur, sans probité, fourbe, ingrat, avare, sanguinaire, tranquille dans la crime et qui dans une république bien policée aurait péri par le dernier supplice au premier de ces crimes . . . il est donc permis aujourd'hui de regarder Auguste comme un monstre adroit et heureux.' It was through his French masters that Edward Gibbon came to think that Augustus wished to deceive the people by an image of civil liberty.[163]

This negative approach to tyranny may go back as far as Savonarola: 'If personally the tyrant appeared friendly and mild-mannered, this was only a sign of his devilish cleverness. He transforms himself into an angel of light, to wreak greater damage.'[164]

However, these anti-Augustan appraisals are exceptions rather than the rule. The normal view under the Empire contrasted the misfortunes which afflicted Augustus' private life with his success in public affairs: 'Valida divo Augusto in rem publicam fortuna'.[165] History was kind to him, and even if sycophantic allusions in the Augustan poets are considered worthless adulation,[166] and even if the bitter criticism by Tacitus, who never mentions the *Res Gestae*, is fully accepted, one would still have to admit that on the whole Augustus enjoyed a 'good press' in subsequent historiography.[167] Augustus, and not Julius Caesar, became the accepted model for subsequent Roman Emperors; his actions were recognized as binding precedents,[168] and the name 'Augustus' was supposed to remind people of the man upon whom it was first bestowed.[169] Provincial writers would recall that Augustus healed the sicknesses common to Greeks and barbarians alike and that the title 'averter of evil' (ἀλεξίκακος) would suit him well.[170] To later Roman historians any regime other than monarchy would have appeared unthinkable and undesirable, and the ideal was 'felicior Augusto – melior Traiano'.[171] Christian historians were able to see the *pax Augusta* as a preliminary stage to the *pax Christiana*. Petrarch admired Augustus for his literary elegance, Dante for having established law and order after a period of anarchy,[172] and Erasmus praised him for his political wisdom, his clear-sightedness and sanity as opposed to monsters like Caligula, Nero, Domitian, and Commodus.[173] No wonder that Napoleon adored Corneille's panegyric of Augustus in his play, *Cinna* (severely criticized by Victor Hugo), and entertained his guests with it at Erfurth in 1808. It is not out of place to mention that Goethe considered Augustus a ruler who governed with 'Verstand und Macht', and translated the proverbial 'festina lente' as 'Eile mit Weile'.

In modern scholarship, however, Augustus' self-praise in the *Res Gestae* is, if not despised, at least not taken seriously. Mommsen uttered the warning that no sane man would seek the truth about the imperial government in such a document,[174] and for Syme the *Res Gestae* is 'no less instructive for what it omits than for what he says'.[175] Gaston Boissier professed that he could never read a passage in the *Res Gestae* without shivering, and K. Hannel declared solemnly in a *Festvortrag* that the Monumentum Ancyranum was anything but 'eine aufrichtige Lebensbeichte' – a frank confession of the character of his life.[176] Indeed, modern scholars have rarely used the *Res Gestae* as conclusive evidence; the Monumentum Ancyranum has tended to serve only as an auxiliary illustration, rarely as a prime source.[177] The consensus has been to reject the *Res Gestae* as a trustworthy source; very few would agree with Wilamowitz that whatever Augustus wrote was 'kurz und knapp, klar und wahr' – 'brief, concise, clear, and true'.[178] However, in spite of this explicit consensus, its presuppositions have in fact imposed themselves on modern scholarship. To illustrate the point, let me review briefly five major interpretations:

1. Some scholars have accepted at face value statements like 'imperium magistratuum ad pristinum redactum modum', and 'prisca illa et antiqua rei publicae forma revocata'.[179] Ferrero and Eduard Meyer agreed that Augustus, as opposed to the impulsive and tactless Caesar, was cautious and thoughtful, prudent and balanced. In contradiction to Antonius, who favoured Hellenistic and oriental ideas and practices, he sin-

cerely intended to restore the Republic, the authority of the Senate, and especially the old and traditional way of life.[180] This, so to speak, 'Roman' view does not rely mainly on suitable passages from the *Res Gestae* (e.g. 'rem publicam in libertatem vindicavi'), or on Augustus' statement, 'rem publicam ex mea potestate in senatus populique Romani arbitrium transtuli', but prefers more objective references, e.g. a passage from the *Fasti Praenestini*,[181] a statement of a survivor from the proscriptions, eulogizing a Roman matron,[182] or a coin from 28 BC with the legend LIBERTATIS P. R. VINDEX;[183] and even a line from Ovid's *Fasti* seems more appropriate.[184] There have been no lack of opponents to this view. They have implied that the session of 13 January, 27 BC might have been staged, that slogans like 'rem publicam . . . in libertatem vindicavi' meant very little, and that in Augustus' behaviour some hypocrisy might be detectable. They were all rebuked by Meyer's professorial authority: 'Es ist sehr billig hier von Heuchelei zu reden, aber auch sehr unhistorisch'; 'It is very reasonable from our standpoint to speak of hypocrisy – but also quite unhistorical.'[185]

2. Those who depict the regime of Augustus as a monarchy, on the other hand, clearly do not base their view on the *Res Gestae*. Some prefer Dio: 'The power of both people and Senate passed entirely into the hands of Augustus, and from his time there was, strictly speaking, a monarchy.'[186] Sceptics, who point out that Dio wrote a political and not a constitutional history, and that he admitted that it was not easy to write about the early principate because things were kept secret,[187] can instead rely on contemporary evidence. Nicolaus of Damascus never doubted Augustus' monarchical ambitions, and for Strabo he was an absolute ruler; 'His native land committed to him the foremost place of authority, and he became established as lord for life of war and peace.'[188] It is, of course, a gross over-simplification to speak in general terms of a monarchical theory,[189] and it is not my intention to survey the endless shades and subtleties prevailing in such a theory.[190] The most common definition of Augustus' system of government goes back to Gibbon, who thought that Augustus was a subtle tyrant, and his regime an absolute monarchy disguised

by the form of the commonwealth.[191] Many scholars have since formulated this view in different words,[192] but all have in common the study of the difference between form and fact, appearance and reality, or, as formulated by Ernst Hohl, 'Gegensatz zwischen Theorie und Praxis, zwischen republikanischem Schein und monarchischem Sein'; 'a contrast between theory and practice, republican appearance and monarchical reality'.[193] All of them have emphasized Augustus' efforts to establish a dynasty, his dependence on the army, and the promotion of the cult of his personality, particularly to the provinces. To substantiate these allegations, they have not used the *Res Gestae*, but looked elsewhere.

3. So did Mommsen. He never wrote a fourth volume of his *Römische Geschichte*,[194] and left his evaluation of the Augustan Principate for the *Staatsrecht*. A scrutiny of the *Res Gestae* led him to the conclusion that Augustus adroitly played the role of great man without being great himself; *arcana imperii*, as mentioned above, he could not find there.[195] Mommsen agreed with Tacitus that Augustus absorbed the functions of the Senate, the magistrates, and the laws, 'munia senatus, magistratuum, legum, in se trahere',[196] but rejected categorically the view that the Principate was a monarchy.[197] He invented the term 'Dyarchy', and the *princeps* was to him just another magistrate – no less and no more. He urged younger scholars not to rely on scattered quotations, apt and convenient as they might appear,[198] but rather to investigate the various institutions and the co-ordinated juridical and administrative competence of the *princeps* and the Senate. Those who followed his advice could do without the *Res Gestae*.

4. As far as the notion of a Dyarchy is concerned, Mommsen remained in splendid isolation, and even V. Gardthausen, his staunchest supporter, followed him with some reservations.[199] As early as 1898 the young Julius Kaerst doubted whether it was possible to understand the Principate purely in juridical terms.[200] Henceforth a number of studies were published, which focused on the slow but steady flow of Greek philosophical ideas into Roman political life.[201] To these historians of ideas, the *Res Gestae* were, of course, of secondary importance only.

5. Another reaction to Mommsen's juridical approach expressed itself in the study of the social history of the Roman Principate.[202] In his *Wesen und Werden des Prinzipats*, Anton von Premerstein deplored the fact that so much emphasis had been put on legal procedures, and so little attention paid to social developments. Premerstein devoted over a hundred pages to the sociological foundations of the Principate, carefully studying the patron–client relationship. Syme too was not convinced by Reitzenstein or Weber, and argued that Romans, instructed in a long tradition of law and government, did not need to take lessons from theorists or from aliens. He was interested in a process, not in an event, in groups of people, not in a biography, in a history of acts that could be verified, not in a history of ideas. He thought that it would be more instructive to discover the identity of the agents of power than to speculate upon the subtleties of legal theory. The *Res Gestae* would offer little assistance if one wanted to identify the diplomats and soldiers, engineers and financiers, who constituted Augustus' power base; instead, Syme used a diversity of sources to explore the intricacies of Augustus' Principate. In 1939 he must have felt that his book might shock the inveterate admirers of Augustus; anticipating criticism, he explained that it was not necessary to praise political success or to idealize men who win wealth and honour by civil war. He believed in a more sceptical approach, and wrote elsewhere: 'The present epoch, having been impelled to admit darker conceptions of power and politics than that obtained in a previous age of relative innocence should not be in danger of underestimating the testimony of Cornelius Tacitus, 'vivid, solemn and suitably ambiguous.' '[203] In vain. Thirty-five years after *The Roman Revolution* appeared, Hans Erich Stier remained unappeased: 'Für Syme schrumpft die Gestalt des Octavian zu einem revolutionaren 'Führer' zusammen;'[204] 'for Syme the figure of Augustus dwindles to that of a revolutionary "Führer".' He could forgive modern historians for having evaluated Syme's work as the most marvellous analysis of the Roman revolution, but he was stunned by the fact that even ancient historians were impressed – 'die Fachwelt sich beeindruckt zeigte.' What Stier did not grasp was Syme's professed intention not to depreciate Augustus, but rather to

reveal his ability and greatness all the more sharply by an unfriendly presentation.

Yet it may be that even the Augustus of the *Res Gestae* would not have objected to Syme's approach. Augustus would not have wished to have his soul searched and his motives scrutinized, however many scholars have been preoccupied by the problem as to whether his intentions were sincere or not. Hammond is a good example: 'whether Augustus was a clever but hypocritical politician or a sincere statesman of genius is a question of fundamental importance.'[205] I suspect that Augustus would have gloated over the frustration of twentieth-century scholars, still at pains to understand his enigmatic personality, and finding him 'puzzling, elusive, baffling and inscrutable'[206] – like the Sphinx engraved upon his signet ring.[207] Syme however preferred cheerfully to abandon such topics, and to leave them to moralists and casuists: people should be judged by their deeds and not by alleged intentions.

This is precisely the image which Augustus presented when he wrote his *Res Gestae*: he conveyed his achievements and not his feelings. Had the writings of a Cremutius Cordus or an Asinius Pollio, of a T. Labienus or a Cassius Severus survived, they would undoubtedly have thrown dark shadows on Augustus' character and would have disclosed the not very immaculate means by which he had reached his goal. But could they have altogether denied the fact that at a certain moment a vast majority in Rome felt like Favonius, who had to admit that civil war was worse than an illegal monarchy?[208] Even Timagenes – had his work survived – would not have been able to obliterate this simple truth.[209] Augustus would not necessarily have objected to a historical work which depicted the Principate as absolute. All he wanted to convey in the *Res Gestae* was the fact that his rule was not arbitrary, but founded on law.[210] *Mutatis mutandis*, he would have gladly accepted a Guicciardini's appraisal of a Lorenzo Magnifico:[211] he may have been a tyrant, but it would have been impossible to find 'Un tiranno migliore e più piacevole' – 'a better and more pleasant tyrant'.

NOTES

1. 'Imperatoris Caesaris Augusti de vita sua' in H. Peter, *HRR* II (1906), 54–64; H. Malcovati, *Imperatoris Caesaris Augusti operum fragmenta*⁵ (1969), 84–97. Both rely heavily on A. Weichert, *Imperatoris Caesaris scriptorum reliquiae* (1846). All quotations in this paper follow the edition of Malcovati, unless otherwise stated.

2. The most elaborate attempt is still F. Blumenthal, 'Die Autobiographie des Augustus', *Wiener Studien* 35 (1913), 113 ff. ; 36 (1914), 84 ff.

3. H. Hahn, 'Neue Untersuchungen zur Autobiographie des Kaisers Augustus', *La Nouvelle Clio* 10–12 (1958–62), 137 ff. I have not been able to consult his unpublished dissertation 'Untersuchungen zur Autobiographie des Kaisers Augustus' (Diss. Leipzig 1957). Among other studies concerning the Autobiography the following may be mentioned: G. Misch, *Geschichte der Autobiographie*³ (1949); Th. Vaubel, *Untersuchungen zu Augustuses Politik und Staatsverfassung nach den Autobiographischen Schriften und der zeitgenössischen Dichtung* (Diss. Giessen, 1934). See also the brief and trenchant remarks of Eduard Schwartz in a footnote, *Hermes* 33 (1898), 208–9.

4. e.g. fr. 13 = App. *BC* V, 42–5. Appian himself admits that he had difficulty in translating the speeches from Latin into Greek.

5. Fr. 8 = Plut. *Comp. Dem. cum Cic.* 3. 1.

6. Fr. 1 = Suet. *Aug.* 85. 1.

7. Attacks echoed in Suet. *Aug.* 2. 3.

8. Fr. 3 = Suet. *Aug.* 2. 3.

9. Fr. 4 = Tert. *De anim.* 46; cf. Suet. *Aug.* 94. 9; Plut. *Cic.* 44. 2. Reliance on dreams and superstitions should not appear strange where Augustus is concerned. See below, n. 15.

10. Fr. 9 = Plut. *Cic.* 45. 5; 46. 1. Fr. 10 = Plut. *Brut.* 27. 1.

11. e. g. Tac. *Ann.* I. 10; Suet. *Aug.* 13

12. Fr. 11 = Suet. *Aug.* 27. 4. According to Appian, Quintus Gallius asked for the command in Africa, but plotted against Octavian; in consequence he was stripped of his praetorship, the enraged people tore his house down, and the Senate condemned him to death. Octavian however tried to spare his life. He ordered him to depart to his brother, Marcus Gallius, who was serving under Antonius. Quintus took ship and was never seen again: Appian, *BC* III. 95. For the theme of his *clementia* see also fr. 18 = *Dig.* XLVIII. 24. 1: 'Ulpianus Libro Nono De Officio Proconsulis: corpora eorum qui capite damnantur, cognatis ipsorum neganda non sunt. Et id se observasse etiam divus Augustus Libro Decimo de Vita sua scribit.' On Augustus' cruelties after the Perusian War, see Suet. *Aug.* 15.

13. Fr. 12 = Plut. *Brut.* 41. 5.

14. See esp. Polyb. VI. 56. 6–12., cf. Cic. *de div.* 148; *de nat. deor.* II. 28.

15. Fr. 4 = Tert. *de an.* 46; fr. 6 = Pliny, *NH* II. 93; fr. 7 = Serv. *Auct. ad. Verg. Buc.* IX. 46.

16. Fr. 20 = Pliny, *NH* II. 24. This was not an unusual phenomenon; even an enlightened man like Julius Caesar would repeat a spell three times before entering a carriage to prevent accidents. Pliny, *NH* XXVIII. 21.

17. Suet. *Aug.* 92. 2. See A. Momigliano's apt remark: 'a touch of charismatic self display may well have been a feature of early Roman autbiographies' in his *The Development of Greek Biography* (1971), 94. cf. Suet. *Aug.* 94. 4.

18. Fr. 17 = Plut. *Ant.* 68. 1.

19. Fr. 15 = App. *III.* 14.

20. On the basis of the surviving fragments one cannot agree with Vaubel that

'Augustus wünschte zu zeigen, dass die Republik fortbestehe', and that no constitutional changes had been introduced by him (see Vaubel, op. cit. (n. 3), 26, n. 3) nor with Blumenthal, op. cit. (n. 2), 113: 'seine politische Tätigkeit zu rechtfertigen und die Wiederherstellung der Republik als gelungen zu erweisen.'
21. Fr. 14 = Suet. *Aug.* 62. 2.
22. Dio LIII. 30; Hor. *Ep.* I. 15. 2–5. Suet. *Aug.* 81. 1; 59. 1; *Tib.* 11; for details see A. Esser, *Caesar und die julisch-claudischen Kaiser in biologischen, ärztlichen Blickfeld* (1958), 59 ff. During the next seventeen years Augustus was healthy, and felt some weakness only when he reached the age of fifty-six.
23. Z. Yavetz, *Caesar in der öffentlichen Meinung* (1979). 207–8 =*Julius Caesar and his Public Image* (1983), 206–7. On rumours in general cf. *Ad Herenium* II. 12.
24. Compare similar reactions by Frederick the Great, who found it demeaning for kings to polemicize: 'Es genüge für die Herrscher ihre Streitigkeiten mit den Waffen zum Austrag zu bringen, ohne sich vor der Welt durch Schriften zu prostituieren, die für die Hallen, nicht für die Throne, passten', quoted by Misch, op. cit. (n. 3), 282–3.
25. K. Scott, 'Octavian's Propaganda and Antony's "de sua ebrietate" ', *CP* 24 (1929), 133.
26. The outbreaks of joy at the end of the civil wars appear to have been genuine, e.g. Virg. *Aen.* I. 291; VIII. 717–22; Ovid, *Fasti* I. 709–22, etc.; cf. *Anth. Pal.* IX. 285.
27. *RG* 34; cf. Hor. *Car.* III. 2–6.
28. Tac. *Ann.* I. 72; cf. IV. 34–5.
29. Cic. *Att.* II. 5. 1.
30. *Bell. Gal.* VIII. *praef.* 2.
31. App. *BC* V. 130.
32. Dio. LIV. 25. 5.
33. *RG* 8. See pp. 19–20 above, and notes.
34. e. g. Kornemann, *Mausoleum und Tatenbericht des Augustus* (1921). For a full discussion see J. Gagé, *Res Gestae Divi Augusti³* (1935), 16 ff.
35. Suet. *Aug.* 38. 2.
36. Cic. *Fam.* V. 7; V. 12; *Att.* II. 1. 2.
37. App. *BC* V. 132: καὶ γραμματεῖα ὅσα τῆς στάσεως σύμβολα ἔκαιε. Dio. LII. 42. 8; Suet. *Aug.* 31.
38. Macr. *Sat.* II. 4. 21.
39. R. Travers Herford, *Pirkè Aboth: the Tractate 'Fathers' from the Mishnah, commonly called 'Sayings of the Fathers'* (1945), 33–4.
40. Plut. *Ant.* 58: ἐπεφύετο δὲ τῶν γεγραμμένων μάλιστα τῷ περὶ τῆς ταφῆς. This was forcefully and convincingly argued by the late Konrad Kraft, 'Der Sinn des Mausoleum des Augustus', *Historia* 16 (1967), 189 = *Gesammelte Aufsätze zur antiken Geschichte und Militärgeschichte* (1973), 29.
41. Suet. *Aug.* 100.; see Strabo V. 3. 8. (236).
42. Antonius blamed Octavian: ὑμῶν μοναρχῆσαι ἐπιθυμεῖ (Dio L. 22. 4), and promised τὸ πᾶν αὐτῆς κράτος τῇ τε γερουσίᾳ καὶ τῷ δήμῳ ἀποδώσειν (Dio L. 7. 1).
43. Suet. *Aug.* 79–82, esp. 73; 'Calciamentis altisculis ut procerior quam erat videretur'.
44. *RG* 12. 2. See G. Moretti, *Ara pacis Augustae* (1948); Erika Simon, *Ara Pacis Augustae* (1967); A. H. Borbein, 'Die Ara Pacis Augustae, Geschichtliche Wirklichkeit und Programm', *JOAI* 90 (1975), 242.
45. Quint. *Inst. or.* V. 12. 20–2. I owe this reference to Professor P. Zanker; see also his *Forum Augustum: Das Bildprogramm* (1968); and *Studien zu den Augustusporträts (der Actium-typus)* (1972).
46. K. Virneisel and P. Zanker (eds.), *Die Bildnisse des Augustus* (1979), 45. On

Augustus' awareness of the importance of his appearance in public see Suet. *Aug.* 99: just before his death he asked for a mirror and had his falling jaw set straight. See also D. J. Boorstin, *The Image* (1978), e.g. 185 ff.

47. Cic. *Rep.* II. 46; cf. *Phil.* III. 5; V. 28; 43.

48. Th. Mommsen, *Res Gestae Divi Augusti* (1883), v–vi; H. Dessau, 'Mommsen und das Monumentum Ankyranum', *Klio* 22 (1929), 278; E. Kornemann: *RE* XVI. 1, esp. col. 224; E. Hohl, 'Zu den Testamenten des Augustus', *Klio* 30 (1937), 323.

49. I have no explanation for the strange coincidence that the only three known copies of the *Res Gestae* were found in different districts of a single province.

50. R. Syme, *The Roman Revolution* (1939), 523, n. 4. But Syme was more incisive than Dessau: 'the inscription was primarily designed to be read by the plebs of Rome, very precisely the clients of the princeps.'

51. Z. Yavetz, *Plebs and Princeps* (1969), 56. n. 2.

52. For a typical example see J. Kaerst, *Studien zur Entwicklung und theoretischen Begründung der Monarchie im Altertum* (1898), 82: 'Von dem alleinigen militärischen Imperium, dem wichtigsten Bestandteile der kaiserlichen Gewalt, ist . . . charakteristischerweise nicht die Rede.'

53. Aul. Gell. *NA* IV. 18. 3.

54. There were of course occasions in which he had to conceal the fact that his success depended on force and pressure of arms. e.g. Dio. XLVI. 45. 5. But this is not the case in the *Res Gestae*.

55. Cic. *Phil.* I. 29.

56. P. A. Brunt: 'Laus imperii', in P. D. A. Garnsey and C. R. Whittaker (eds.), *Imperialism in the Ancient World* (1978), 159 ff. See especially Pliny. *NH* XXXV. 23. for the relevance of military glory to electoral success.

57. Val. Max. IV. 1. 10: 'quo dii immortales ut populi Romani res meliores amplioresque facerent rogabantur.'

58. *CIL* I². 2. 2500 (the Lex Gabinia de Delo Insula), lines 19–20: 'imperio am[pli]-ficato [p]ace per orbe[m terrarum confecta]'. For readings and interpretation see C. Nicolet *et al.*, *Insula Sacra. La loi Gabinia Calpurnia de Délos (58 av. J.–C.)* (1980).

59. e.g. A. J. Toynbee, *Hannibal's Legacy* II (1965), 95–6.

60. K. Hopkins, *Conquerors and Slaves* (1978), 30–1; W. V. Harris, *War and Imperialism in Republican Rome* (1979), 46.

61. Suet. *Aug.* 31. 5.

62. Prop. III. 4. 10 and III. 4. 22.

63. Idem, II. 7. 14.

64. For shortage of manpower see Pliny, *NH* VII. 149: 'Servitiorum delectus, iuventutis penuria'. Cf. Suet. *Tib.* Dio. LVI. 23. 1–3.

65. P. A. Brunt and J. M. Moore: *The Res Gestae Divi Augusti* (1967), 40.

66. Paras. 26 and 27; for references to all Augustus' "mosts" and "firsts" see W. Ensslin, 'Zu den Res Gestae Divi Augusti', *RhMus* NF 81 (1932), 335 ff., esp. 363, and M. Reinhold, 'Augustus's Conception of himself', *Thought* 55 (1980), 36. It is therefore not appropriate to characterize Augustus' performance as a *Rückgriff* rather than a *Neubeginn*, e.g. W. Hoffman, 'Der Widerstreit von Tradition und Gegenwart im Tatenbericht des Augustus', *Gymn.* 76 (1969), 17 ff., esp. 31

67. Tac. *Ann.* I. 9. cf. R. Syme, *RR*, 521.

68. cf. *CIL* V. 7817 = *EJ* no. 40 (p. 62): 'Eius ductu auspiciisque gentes Alpinae omnes quae a mari supero ad infernum pertinebant sub imperium p. R. sunt redactae.' See Cic. *Leg.* III. 24–5, cf. Dio. LIII. 17. 9.

69. cf. Dio LVI. 43. 4. For further details see Yavetz, op. cit (n. 51), 54–7 and 91–5.

70. [Sallust.], *Ep. ad Caes.* I. 7, 2; cf. *Ep. ad Caes.* II. 5 8.
71. *RG* 18.
72. See E. E. Best, 'Literacy and Roman Voting', *Historia* 23 (1974), 428 ff. I am indebted to Dr N. M. Horsfall who has enlightened me on problems of literacy in the ancient world and has drawn my attention to the relevant literature. See also F. Millar, *The Emperor in the Roman World* (1977), 252 ff. and the article 'Nachrichtenwesen' in *RE* XVI. 2, cols. 1496–1540.
73. Cic. *Att.* II. 21. 4.
74. Sen. *de ira*, III. 23. 4: 'Magis enim circumfertur et in ore hominum est temeraria urbanitas.'
75. For a description of a plebeian picnic in ancient Rome, which does not suggest literary interests, see Ovid, *Fasti*, III. 523–4: 'Plebs venit ac virides passim disiecta per herbas potat et accumbit cum pare quisque sua.' See esp. J. Griffin, 'Augustan Poetry and the Life of Luxury', *JRS* 66 (1976), 99. On the beauty of the area see Strabo V. 3. 8 (236); cf. Platner – Ashby, *A Topographical Dictionary of ancient Rome*, s.v. 'Mausoleum Augusti'. In a forthcoming article N. M. Horsfall will discuss the height of the inscription, which must have entailed problems of legibility.
76. *Epit. de Caesaribus* I. 29 cf. Pliny, *NH* VII, 149.
77. Suet. *Aug.* 45. 1; cf. 74.
78. Dio XLVII. 34. 3.
79. *RG* 5. 1–3. It must have been common knowledge that Augustus rejected the dictatorship: 'dictaturam magna vi offerente populo genu nixus, deiecta ab umeris toga, nudo pectore, deprecatus est' (Suet. *Aug.* 52).
80. Strabo V. 3. 8 (236); Tac. *Ann.* III. 9.
81. Ovid, *Fasti* V. 552–70; Aul. Gell. *NA* IX. 11; Hor. *Carm.* IV. 8. 13. According to Dio LV. 10. 3, the statues were of bronze; cf. *HA. Sev. Alex.* 28. 6, speaking of marble.
82. Suet. *Aug.* 31. 5; cf. Dio. LV. 10. 3–5.
83. Juv. *Sat.* VII. 98–100. W. Schubart, *Das Buch bei den Griechen und Römern* (1907), does not deal with these problems.
84. Syme, *RR*, 468.
85. Well put in Pliny, *Epp.* IX. 5.
86. Suet. *Aug.* 42. 1.
87. Dio LVI. 39. 2.
88. Cic. *pro Sest.* 97. For its importance in the time of Augustus see H. U. Instinski: 'Consensus Universorum', *Hermes* 75 (1940), 265; contra A. von Premerstein, op. cit. (n. 202), 64.
89. Suet. *Aug.* 58.
90. Ibid.
91. Livy VI. 14. 5.
92. Plut. *Sulla*, 34. 1–2: ἐνδοξότατοι καί δυνατώτατοι τῶν πολιτῶν.
93. e.g. Cic. *Rep.* II. 46–7; *Phil.* III. 11.
94. Hor. *Carm.* IV. 5, 19; III. 14, 14. No wonder that in 36 BC he was honoured with a statue bearing the inscription 'peace long disturbed he established by land and sea'; App. *BC* V. 342. At the end of his life some sailors from Alexandria declared that it was thanks to him that they could sail peacefully and enjoy their freedom and their fortunes; Suet. *Aug.* 98. 2.
95. Sen. *Clem.* I. 10. 3.
96. *Octavia* 473–5: 'Consulere patriae, parcere afflictis, fera caede abstinere, tempus atque irae dare, orbi quietem, saeculo pacem suo.' Cf. A. Alföldi, *Der Vater des Vaterlandes in römischen Denken* (1971); E. Skard 'Pater patriae: Zum Ursprung einer religiös-politischen Idee', *Festschrift H. Koht* (1933), 42.

97. Pliny, *Pan.* 53. 1; Dio LVI. 9. 3.
98. Suet. *Aug.* 58. Nor does Ovid forget to mention the *equites*: *Fasti* II. 127–9: 'Sancte pater patriae, tibi plebs, tibi curia nomen hoc dedit, hoc dedimus nos tibi nomen, eques; res tamen ante dedit.' cf. Dio LV. 10. 10.
99. e.g. *ILS* 139. 1. 12; *ILS* 140. line 54; For 'omnes ordines', Suet. *Aug.* 57. 1.
100. Mommsen, op. cit (n. 48). More recently M. A. Levi, 'La Composizione delle Res Gestae Divi Augusti', *Riv. di filol.* 25 (1947), 189. It is not pertinent to try once more to classify the *Res Gestae* in terms of its literary genre. Some have called it a 'Grabinschrift' (Bormann and Nissen); others a 'Rechnungsbericht' (Wölflin) or a 'Rechenschaftsbericht' (Mommsen), or 'Tatenbericht' (Kornemann). Was it Augustus' political testament (Hirschfeld); a 'Rechtfertigung der Apotheose'; (Wilamowitz); or an 'elogium' composed by Augustus himself, transcending in its scope, size, and importance the various earlier ones; thus, recently, E. W. Gray, *ZPE* 6 (1970), 229, n. 5. See also F. Hampl, 'Denkwürdigkeiten und Tatenberichte aus der alten Welt', in *Geschichte als kritische Wissenschaft* (1979), 202–20.
    One should agree with Mommsen that it is as futile to classify the *Regina Inscriptionum* as it is pointless to classify a *Faust* or the *Divine Comedy*. Th. Mommsen, 'Der Rechenschaftsbericht des Augustus',.*Ges. Schr.* IV. 247.
101. Aul. Gell. *NA* XV. 11. 2; Cic. *De Imp. Cn. Pomp.* 60. Desiring to revive the ancient fashion of dress he directed the aediles not to allow anyone to appear in the Forum or its neighbourhood unless wearing a toga; Suet. *Aug.* 40. 5.
102. Macrob. *Sat.* II. 4. 18; cf. Dio LIII. 10. 1: τοὺς κειμένους νόμους ἰσχυρῶς φυλάττετε καὶ μηδένα αὐτῶν μεταβάλλετε.
103. The nomination of new patricians was indispensable for the perpetuation of traditional institutions; see Dio LII. 42. 5. For further discussion see E. J. Salmon; 'Augustus the patrician', *Essays on Roman Culture*, ed. A. J. Dunston (1976), 3.
104. *RG* 7. Cf. R. M. Ogilvie, *The Romans and their Gods in the Age of Augustus* (1967).
105. For Augustus as an archaic type: R. Heinze, 'Kaiser Augustus', *Hermes* 65 (1930), 385. Dio L. 4. 4: Suet. *Aug.* 40, 5.
106. *RG* 19–21. A total of eighty-two temples. For details see Zanker, op. cit. (n. 45). He made the sons or the descendants of original dedicators of temples responsible for their upkeep and restoration; Dio LIII. 2. 4. The restoration of temples was meant to deliver sons from their ancestors' sins; Hor., *Carm.* III. 6. 1, cf. Livy III. 20. 5; VI. 41. 8. For the title 'founder or renewer' of all temples', see Livy IV. 20. 7.
107. Vell. Pat. II. 60. 1.
108. M. Rostovtzeff, *Römische Bleitesserae* (1905). He referred to his conclusions once more in his article 'Augustus', *University of Wisconsin Papers in Language and Literature* No. 15 (1922).
109. See Suet. *Aug.* 38. 3; cf. 57. 1; Dion. Hal. VII. 72. See also S. Weinstock, *RE* VIa. 2, cols. 2178–87; P. Veyne, 'Iconographie de la "transvectio equitum" ', *REA* 62 (1960), 100.
110. Suet. *Aug.* 38. 3. Augustus was passionately eager ('flagrantissime cupiverat') that they should be thus titled. For illustrations see M. L. Vollenweider, 'Princeps iuventutis', *Gaz. Num. Suisse* 13/14 (1963–4), 76.
111. *RG* 14. cf. Tac. *Ann.* I, 3.
112. Mommsen, *Staatsrecht* III. 14, III. 1, 476 ff., esp. 525.
113. For a good summary of the various definitions of 'iuventus' see the recent dissertation by G. Phister, *Die Erneuerung der römischen Iuventus durch Augustus* (1977). For earlier views see L. R. Taylor, 'Seviri equitum Romanorum and Municipal Seviri', *JRS* 14 (1924), 158 ff., esp. 160. M. Jaczynowska, 'Les collegia iuvenum et leurs liaisons avec les cultes religieux au temps du haut-

Empire romain', *Zeszyty Naukowe Uniwersyteta M. Kopernika in Torunin, Nauki hum.-spol. 32, Historia* IV, ed. M. Wojciechowski (1968), pp. 23 ff.; eadem, 'Les organisations des iuvenes et l'aristocratie municipale au temps de l'empire romain', in *Recherches sur les structures sociales dans l'antiquité classique,* ed. C. Nicolet, (1970), 265 ff. The view adopted here is that *iuventus* is identical with *turmae equitum.*

114. Tac. *Ann.* II. 83.
115. Dio LIII. 1. 4.
116. Suet. *Aug.* 44. 2.
117. Suet. *Aug.* 43. 2. '. . . edidit frequentissime'; cf. Dio XLVIII. 20. 1; LI. 22. 4; Virg. *Aen.* V. 550; 575; Ovid. *Trist.* III. 12. 7–22. For his grandsons' participation, Dio. LIV. 26. 1; LV. 10. 6.
118. Hor. *Carm.* I. 8. 1; III. 24. 51; III. 2. 2; *Sat.* II. 2. 9.
119. Cic. *Cael.* 11; Hor. locc. citt.
120. Virg. *Aen.* IX. 603. cf. VII. 162–9.
121. Hor. *Carm.* III. 6. 37.
122. Dio LII. 26. 1.
123. It is impossible to take up here the controversy concerning the definition of *eques Romanus* in the early Principate, and whether the conferment of the rank by the Emperor was identical with the grant of the public horse: *FIRA* ² II. 271: 'ut is ad imperatorem lato clavo vel equo publico similive honore honoretur'. C. Nicolet thinks that all imperial *equites* were *equo publico:* see his *L'Ordre Équestre à l'époque républicaine* I (1966), 177 ff. His view is not shared by P. A. Brunt, 'The equites in the late Republic', in *2nd Conf. Inter. of Ec. Hist. 1962* (1965), 117–49, reprinted in R. Seager (ed.), *The Crisis of the Roman Republic* (1969), 83. For the best discussion of this controversy, see T. P. Wiseman, 'The Definition of "Eques Romanus" ', *Historia* 19 (1970), 76, and the remarks of F. Millar in *The Emperor in the Roman World* (1977), 279. For our purpose it is enough to stress that Augustus revived the ceremonial of the annual parade (*transvectio*), and that he carried out the censorial function (without being censor) of the examination (*recognitio*) of the *equites* at the parade.
124. Thus an alternative emerged from the presupposition 'nec vitia nostra nec remedia pati possumus', a situation depicted by Christian Meier as 'Krise ohne Alternative', see *Res Publica Amissa*² (1980), 301 ff.; *Enstehung des Begriffs Demokratie* (1970), 143 ff.; *Die Ohnmacht des allmächtigen Dictators Caesar* (1980), esp. 225–87. I find myself in full agreement with him.
125. Cf. Cic.*Rep.* II. 43; Dio XLV. 18. 2.
126. Cic. *Att.* VII. 75.
127. On the gross and scandalous fortunes of the great politicians see Syme, op. cit. 381. Augustus, however, introduced into the Senate and relied mainly on 'omnem florem ubique coloniarum ac municipiorum, bonorum scilicet virorum et locupletium'; *ILS* 212, col. II. 3.
128. Emphasis on premilitary education in M. Rostowzew, 'Principes Iuvenum', *Röm. Mitt.* 15 (1900). 223; see also L. R. Taylor, 'Seviri equitum Romanorum and Municipal Seviri', *JRS* 14 (1924), 158; M. de la Corte, *Iuventus* (1924); and more recently W. O. Moeller, 'The Riot of A.D. 59 at Pompeii', *Historia* 19 (1970), 86. Denying the military aspect, S. L. Mohler, 'The Iuvenes and Roman Education', *TAPA* 68 (1937), 442. R. MacMullen, *Soldier and Civilian in the Later Roman Empire* (1963), 135, n. 52.
129. Suet. *Aug.* 31. 4.
130. Suet. *Aug.* 38. 2.
131. Schol. Iuv. I. 128 'bibliothecam iuris civilis et liberalium studiorum in templo Apollinis Palatini dedicavit Augustus'; Ovid, *Tristia* III. 1. 63.

132. Suet. *Aug.* 42. 3.
133. Cic. *Or.* 120: 'Nescire autem quid antea quam natus sis acciderit, id est semper esse puerum. Quid enim est aetas hominis, nisi ea memoria rerum veterum cum superiorum aetate contexitur?'
134. Suet. *Aug.* 64. 3.
135. Plut. *Cic.* 49. 3.
136. Cic. *Off.* I. 122–3; *De sen.* 28.
137. Cic., *De div.* II. 4: 'Quam si docemus atque erudimus iuventutem'.
138. Cic. *Fam.* X. 31. 3: 'Ita si id agitur ut rursus in potestate omnia unius sint quicunque is est ei me profiteor inimicum.'
139. Suet. *Aug.* 43. 2.
140. Plut. *Mor.* 207 E. = *Apoph. Aug.* 21.
141. Cic. *Att.* IV. 2. 2; cf. II. 1. 3; *Qu. fr.* III. 1. 11.
142. Hor. *Carm.* III. 1. 2–4, cf. IV. 6. 31; Ovid, *Ars. Am.* II. 9; II. 733; *Tristia*, III. 7; Tibull. I. 4. 79–80.
143. Virg. *Aen.* VI. 832. On attitudes to youth I have learned a great deal from W. Steidle, 'Einflusse römischen Lebens und Denkens auf Ciceros Schrift de oratore', *Mus. Helv.* 9 (1952), 10, and W. Stroh, *Taxis und Taktik* (1975), 52 ff. I am indebted to Professor Stroh for having discussed with me the relevant passages.
144. Hor. *Ep.* II. 1. 130–1: 'Recte facta refert, orientia tempora notis instruit exemplis'.
145. W. Staidle, *Sueton und die antike Biographie* (1963), 113; H. Kornhardt, *Exemplum* (Diss. Göttingen, 1936), 26.
146. *Ep.* VIII. 14. 4.
147. Suet. *Aug.* 34. 2.
148. Quint. XII. 2. 30.
149. Pliny, *Ep.* VIII. 14. 5.
150. Sen. *Ep.* I. 6. 5.
151. Pliny, *Pan.* 45–6: 'Nec tam imperio nobis opus est quam exemplo. Melius homines exemplis docentur.'
152. Ovid, *Met.* XI. 834.
153. Cf. e.g. Cic. *De nat. deorum* III. 6: 'A te enim philosopho rationem accipere debeo religionis, maioribus autem nostris etiam nulla ratione reddita credere'; *Phil.* IX. 3: 'Non igitur exempla maiorum quaerenda, sed consilium est eorum a quo ipse exempla nata sunt explicandum'; *De Imp. Cn. Pomp.* 60: 'Nequid novi fiat contra exempla atque iustitia maiorum.'
154. Vell. Pat. II. 126. 4: 'nam facere recte civis suos princeps optimus faciendo docet, cumque sit imperio maximus, exemplo maior es.'
155. *RG* 8.
156. Hor. *Carm.* III. 24. 31–2: 'Virtutem incolumem odimus, sublatam ex oculis quaerimus invidi.'
157. For typical criticisms see Tac. *Ann.* I. 10; Suet. *Aug*; 4. 2; 7. 1; 10. 4; 16. 1–2; 68–70; Sen. *Clem.* I. 9. 1.
158. Tac. *Ann.* II. 35.
159. Tac. *Ann.* I. 10. III. 28.
160. e.g. Julian, *Caesares* 309 A–C.
161. Suet. *Tib.* 21. 3.
162. Montesquieu, *Considérations sur les causes de la grandeur des romains et de leur décadence* (Paris, 1948), p. 71.
163. Voltaire, *Dictionnaire philosophique* (1820), and E. Gibbon, *Decline and Fall of the Roman Empire*, ed., J. B. Bury, I (1896), 12.
164. Quoted in F. Gilbert, *Macchiavelli and Guicciardini* (1965), 111.
165. For the contrast between public success and private misfortune, see *RG* 14; Suet. *Aug.* 65; Tac. *Ann.* I. 3; Pliny, *NH* VII. 147.

166. Compare the praise of Augustus uttered by trained parrots; see *Anth. Pal.* IX. 562 = A. S. F. Gow, D. L. Page, *Greek Anthology: The Garland of Philip* (1968), Crinagoras xxiv.
167. e.g. Tac. *Ann.* I. 9; Suet. *Aug.* 13; 98. There is, unfortunately, no Gundolf (*Geschichte seines Ruhmes*, 1924) for Augustus. For a rapid orientation (far from exhaustive) see K. Hönn, *Augustus im Wandel zweier Jarhtausende* (1938). See also, R. Urban, 'Die Res Gestae divi Augusti', *Gymnasium* 86 (1976), 16.
168. e.g. the Lex de Imperio Vespasiani; see P. A. Brunt, *JRS* 67 (1977), 95.
169. Pliny, *Pan.* 88. 10: 'nomine Augusti admonemur eius cui primum dicatum est'.
170. Philo, *Leg. ad Gaium*, 144–5.
171. Eutrop. VII. 2.
172. Dante, *De monarchia* I. 16.
173. Erasmus, *Collected Works* IV (1977), 377–81.
174. *Res Gestae Divi Augusti, iterum edidit Theodor Mommsen* (1883), vi.
175. Syme, *RR*, 523.
176. K. Hannel, 'Kaiser Augustus', *Gymnasium* 78 (1971), 196.
177. For a typical example see A. Hohl, 'Augustus', *Das Altertum* 2 (1956), 224.
178. U. von Wilamowitz-Möllendorf, 'Res Gestae Divi Augusti', *Hermes* 21 (1886), 625.
179. Vell. Pat. II. 89.
180. G. Ferrero, *Grösse und Niedergang Roms* IV (1909), 259; E. Meyer, *Kleine Schriften* (1924), 425–574; the same line is, roughly speaking taken by F. B. Marsh, *The Founding of the Roman Empire* (²1927; repr. 1959); M. Hammond, *The Augustan Principate* (1933; ²1968). With some serious reservations, O. Th. Schulz, *Das Wesen des römischen Kaisertums der ersten zwei Jahrhunderte* (*Studien zur Geschichte und Kultur des Altertums* VIII. 2, 1916).
181. *CIL* I², 231; *Ins. It.* XIII. 2, p. 113: '[Quod rem publicam] p(opulo) R(omano) rest[it]u[it]'.
182. *ILS* 8393, II, line 35; 'Pacato orbe terrarum, res[titut]a re publica'.
183. C. H. V. Sutherland, C. M. Kraay, *Catalogue of the Coins of the Roman Empire in the Ashmolean Museum* I: *Augustus (c. 31 BC–AD 14)* (1975), 3.
184. Ovid, *Fasti* I. 589: 'Redditaque est omnis populo provincia nostro'.
185. Eduard Meyer, op. cit. (n. 180), 459. See also J. Béranger, 'Le refus du pouvoir', *Mus. Helv* 5 (1948), 178 = *Principatus* (1975), 165; cf. Ovid *Ex Ponto* IV. 13, 25–9. Vell. Pat. II. 124. 2.
186. Dio LIII. 17. 1; cf. LI. 1. 1; LII. 1. 1; LIII. 11. 4. For Maecenas' speech as Dio's own concept of monarchy with the co-operation of the best see E. Gabba, 'Sulla storia Romana di Cassio Dione'. *Riv. Stor. It.* 71 (1959), 361.
187. F. Millar, *A Study of Cassius Dio* (1964), 83 ff. See Dio, LIII. 19. 3–4; LIV. 15. 1–3; LV. 28. 2; LVI. 31. 1.
188. Strabo VI. 4. 2 (288), and esp. XVII. 3. 25 (840), with Mommsen's comment, op. cit. (n. 174), 146: 'Liberius enunciat non rerum speciem sed rem ipsam.'
189. For some of the most outspoken versions of this view, see e.g. E. Kornemann, *Mausoleum und Tatenbericht des Augustus* (1930): W. Kolbe, 'Von der Republik zur Monarchie, aus Roms Zeitwende', in Otto Immisch (ed.), *Das Erbe der Alten*, Zweite Reihe, Heft XX (1931), 39; H. Dessau, *Geschichte der römischen Kaiserzeit* (1924); V. Ehrenberg, 'Monumentum Antiochenum', *Klio* 19 (1925), 207; E. Kornemann, *Doppelprinzipat und Reichseinteilung im imperium Romanum* (1930).
190. e.g. for Kolbe the year 27 symbolized the restoration of the Republic; 23 was already a semi-monarchy: op. cit. (n. 35), 39–65; by contrast Otto Schönbauer, 'Untersuchungen zum römischen Staats-und Wirtschaftsrecht', *ZSS* 47 (1927), 264 depicted the Principate as a mixture of republic, monarchy, and dyarchy.

191. E. Gibbon, *Decline and Fall of the Roman Empire*, ed. J. B. Bury, I (1896), 7.
192. e.g. L. R. Taylor, *Party Politics in the Age of Caesar* (1949), 180: 'Caesarism was not the frank monarchy of Julius . . . It was veiled in Catonism'; F. B. Marsh, *The Reign of Tiberius* (1931), 16: 'A complex and delicately adjusted system where the realities were carefuly disguised by elaborate legal fictions'; A. H. M. Jones, *Augustus*, (1970), 167: 'he disguised his absolute powers in constitutional wrappings'; M. Gelzer, in *Meister der Politik*, as adopted by R. Heinze, 'Kaiser Augustus', *Hermes* 65 (1930), 386 = *Vom Geist des Römertums*³ (1960), 163: 'Militärmonarchie mit republikanischer Scheinfassade'; E. Hohl, 'Augustus', *Das Altertum* II (1956), 236: 'Das republikanisch drapierte Prinzipat des Augustus ist im Grunde eine Militärmonarchie'; K. Hannel, 'Kaiser Augustus', *Gymnasium* 78 (1971), 191: 'Eine maskierte Monarchie' – and many others.
193. E. Hohl, 'Das Selbstzeugnis des Augustus über seine Stellung im Staat', *Mus. Helv.* 4 (1947), 107.
194. Some scholars thought that Mommsen himself might have reached the conclusion that he had exaggerated Caesar's greatness in his Roman history and could therefore find no way to explain the success of Augustus (e.g. E. Meyer). Others thought that Mommsen never understood Augustus properly: e.g. E. Kornemann, 'Augustus, der Mann und sein Werk', *Breslauer historische Forschungen* IV (1937), 1.
195. 'Magni viri personam apte gesserit; ipse non magnus'; op. cit. (n. 174) vi.
196. Tac. *Ann.* I. 2; 11. 5.
197. 'Die neue ordnung staatsrechtlich keineswegs als Monarchie, auch nicht als eine beschränkte', *Staatsrecht* II. 2. 748.
198. Ibid. 749.
199. V. Gardthausen, *Augustus und seine Zeit* (1889–1904).
200. J. Kaerst, *Studien zur Entwicklung und theoretischen Begründung der Monarchie im Altertum* (1898), 80; 'Es ist vor allem unmöglich, auf einen staatsrechtlich bestimmten Ausdruck zu bringen' – see esp. p. 86.
201. To name just a few: R. Reitzenstein, 'Die Idee des Principats bei Cicero und Augustus', *Nachr. Gött. Ges. d. Wiss.* 1917, 399; A. von Domaszewski, 'Die philosophischen Grundlagen des augustäischen Prinzipats', *Festgabe für Gotheim* (1925), 63; J. Kaerst, 'Scipio Aemilianus, die Stoa und der Prinzipat', *Neue Jahrb. f. Wiss*, 5 (1929), 653; M. Pohlenz, *Antikes Führertum* (*Neue Wege zur Antike* II. 3, 1934), 1. A. Alföldi, 'Die Ausgestaltung des monarchischen Zeremoniells am römischen Kaiserhofe', *Röm. Mitt.* 4 (1934), 1 = *Die monarchische Repräsentation im römischen Kaiserreiche* (1970) 3; V. Pöschl, *Römischer Staat und griechischer Staatsgedanke bei Cicero* (*Neudeutsche Forschungen, Abh. Klass. Phil* Bd. 5, 1936); H. Wagenvoort, 'Princeps', *Philologus* 99 (1936), 206 ff.; 223 ff.
202. A. von Premerstein, *Vom Werden und Wesen des Prinzipats*, Abh. der bayer. Ak. der Wiss, phil.-hist. Abt., NF, 15 (1937); Syme, *RR* (1939).
203. R. Syme, 'History or Biography: the case of Tiberius Caesar', *Historia* 23 (1974), 481, on p. 496.
204. H. E. Stier, 'Augustusfriede und römische Klassik', *ANRW* II. 2 (1975), 3 = *Kleine Schriften* (1979), 383.
205. M. Hammond, 'The Sincerity of Augustus', *HSCPh* 69 (1965), 152, or cf. R. Heinze op. cit. (n.192), 386.
206. J. Firth, *Augustus Caesar and the Organization of the Empire* (1903), quoted in M. Reinhold, 'Augustus' Conception of Himself', *Thought* 55 (216) (1980), 36.
207. Suet. *Aug.* 50.
208. Plut. *Brut.* 12: χεῖρον εἶναι μοναρχίας παρανόμου πόλεμον ἐμφύλιον. Note also that when Cato the younger decided to commit suicide he bade his son go to Caesar, Dio XLIII, 10. 4–5, an action which perhaps symbolizes the lack of any alternative.

209. Compare the report that when conflagrations occurred in Rome, Timagenes claimed to feel regret only because the Romans would put up better buildings than those which had been destroyed. Sen. *Ep*. 91. 13. For his relations with Augustus, Sen. *Controv*. X. 5. 22.
210. Cf. e.g. Ovid, *Fasti* II. 141: 'vis tibi grata fuit, florent sub Caesare leges'.
211. Quoted in F. Gilbert, op. cit. (n. 164), 116.

I would like to express my gratitude to Professors Chr. Meier, W. Stroh and P. Zanker for having enabled me to present my views to their excellent students at a seminar on Augustus which we held jointly at the University of Munich during the winter semester 1982/83. I would also like to thank Dr M. Wörrle, who kindly allowed me to use the library facilities of the Kommission für alte Geschichte und Epigraphik. None of them should be held responsible for the views expressed in the paper.

II. STATE AND SUBJECT:
THE IMPACT OF MONARCHY

FERGUS MILLAR

In 26 or 25 BC, as a new Greek inscription records, a citizen of Ephesus was responsible for 'the setting up of the *Sebastos* and the dedication of the sanctuary'.[1] The reference appears quite casually in a list of holders of priesthoods; but the very casualness of the allusion has a lot to tell us about how people in a Greek city saw the world in the 20s BC. *Sebastos* was of course to be the established Greek equivalent for *Augustus* and was to reappear on thousands of inscriptions throughout the imperial period. But when this statue was erected it was only one or two years since the name Augustus, never before used for a personal name, had been thought up in Rome, and solemnly voted by Senate and People in 27; voted, that is, as the new additional name of the thirty-five-year-old victor of the civil wars, 'Imperator Caesar divi filius', whom we call Octavian. The victory itself, the battle of Actium in which the forces of Antonius and Cleopatra had fled, was only five or six years in the past. Antonius himself had been in Ephesus in the winter of 42/1 BC and again in 33/2; and on one of these occasions one of the other six men named in the list of priests had acted as ambassador to him.[2] Then, immediately after the battle, Octavian also had arrived in Ephesus. Chance has preserved the letter which he then had occasion to write to the almost totally insignificant city of Rhosos on the coast of Syria. His words reflect a relationship which must have been formed at the same moment with scores, perhaps hundreds, of other Greek cities:

The ambassadors sent by you . . . having come to me at Ephesus, addressed me on the matters on which they had instructions. On receiving them I found them to be patriotic and good men, and accepted the honours and the gold crown. When I come to those parts I will do my best to be of service to you and to preserve the privileges of the city . . .[3]

Ephesus had thus been for a moment the political focus of the Graeco-Roman world, and no one there could have been unaware that power had just changed hands. But the vote taken in Rome in 27 BC was also known in Ephesus, and *Augustus/Sebastos* was already so common a term that 'the *Sebastos*' could mean a statue – already ordered, made and ceremonially installed. Associated with that was a sanctuary (*temenos*); new elements have entered the communal activity, the religious life and the visible topography of the city.

By implication what I have been saying is that one way to try to approach that crucial turning-point which is the reign of Augustus is to look at how the world was represented, or mirrored, in hundreds of communities round the Mediterranean; for there really was a revolution, above all a revolution of consciousness, but it was not only a Roman one. Of course, if we do look, we can only see what there is to be seen. From cities in the Greek world, in North Africa, Italy, or southern Gaul there are written documents, architectural remains, statues, coins. Elsewhere there may be literally nothing, or at best a tale of conquest, seen from the outside.

So all we can do is to examine the inherent logic when Augustus is represented, in word or symbol.[4] Sometimes there is aid from unexpected quarters, for instance a red cow named Thayris. This hitherto unknown constituent of the early Roman Empire stepped into the light of history in the pages of the *Journal of Egyptian Archaeology* of 1982; a papyrus published there records that she was leased out in 26 BC by the slave of a Roman citizen resident in Egypt. We know the date because it was 'the fifth year of the dominion (*kratesis*) of Caesar, son of a god'.[5] Forty years later those citizens of Rome who took a stroll round Augustus' Mausoleum would be able to read in the *Res Gestae* (27) that he had added Egypt to the *imperium* of the Roman people. There is a certain contradiction here, and one which neither can be nor should be resolved. But the words in which two people in Egypt dated the purchase of a cow constitute a fact in themselves. So do the words which the lamplighters of Oxyrhynchus had used in taking an oath four years earlier, in 30/29 BC. This document is particularly important, for it takes us to a level of society which our evidence elsewhere systematically fails to reach; two at least of the four lamplighters, three with Egyptian names and one with a Graeco-Egyptian one, were illiterate. They swore to supply oil for the temple lamps for the current first year of Caesar 'in accordance with what was supplied up to the 22nd year which was also the 7th' (*POxy* 1453). Life and its obligations went on; but one monarch, Cleopatra, had given place to another, called Caesar.

It is easy to object that, however the world was construed in Egypt, the only major Hellenistic monarchy to pass directly into the 'dominion' of a single Roman ruler, this is not how things will have seemed in Rome. This view has some truth; but only some. Cornelius Nepos, concluding his biography of Atticus, recorded Atticus' awareness that Octavian and Antonius each desired to be *princeps*, 'not just of the city of Rome but of the whole world' (*Att.* 20. 5). This dispassionate neutrality, clearly shared by Nepos himself, was to be perfectly matched in the attitudes shown by one of the common people of Rome when Octavian returned in 29 BC, two years after Actium. As Octavian approached Rome, among the crowd which came out to meet him there appeared a man with a crow, which duly called out 'Ave Caesar Victor Imperator'. Suitably impressed, Octavian bought the dutiful bird (*officiosa avis*) for 20,000 sesterces. It was then that the man's partner reported the existence of a second crow, which when produced emitted the words 'Ave victor imperator Antoni' (Macrobius, *Sat.* II. 4. 29). The story has a lot to tell us. First, the established ritual of greeting important persons could be easily applied to the new situation. Secondly, the single victor who was due to appear could be expected to distribute largesse when honour required it; the sum which the man's partner failed to share is described as a *liberalitas*.

But there is also a much more important message to be gained from this anecdote. What the man exhibits is loyalist *behaviour*, of a sort which he believes to be both appropriate in a public context, and advantageous to himself. But in his case, and perhaps in his case alone, we know that he did not feel loyalty, that he was indeed quite indifferent. It is important therefore to stress that in looking at rituals, cults, public expressions of gratitude, the erection of statues, and all those other visible forms of symbolism, we should not ask what people really felt, because we do not know (and in almost all cases cannot in principle know). Some two centuries after Augustus' death, Tertullian was to point out to the pagan world that all their loyalist rituals showed precisely nothing about their real feelings; if (he imagines) their hearts were covered with some transparent material, you would be able to look in and, just as they were acclaiming one Emperor, you would see the image already formed there of his rival and successor distributing largesse (*Apol.* 35, 7). There is not, and cannot be, any such privileged view into the hearts of Augustus' subjects. We cannot know either that they felt, or for that matter that they did not feel, the reverence, loyalty, and gratitude whch they so lavishly expressed. But we can study the logic of their public actions, and of their words, artefacts and buildings.

Or, to be more precise, we can study the logic of these things provided both that the communities concerned did once speak, act, or create artefacts and that these, or some reflections of them, have survived. Equally, if we try to look at the actions of Augustus or the Senate in order to see how these actions were represented by their subjects, we can only do so, once again, by courtesy of those whose perceptions have left some trace. The conception we gain is thus bound to be partial. But I would insist that in speaking of perceptions or representations we are talking about an essential aspect of what the Roman Empire 'was'. First, the emergence of a single ruler from within the Roman republican system had created a constitutional situation which seems to us inherently ambiguous. The symbols and words used in the provinces to represent the new situation thus acquire a particular importance. Secondly it was because they were internally self-governing political communities that the provincial cities could and did respond to changes of power at the centre. They were both free, and yet also obliged, to choose the correct symbols and responses, precisely because they were typically neither garrisoned by Roman troops nor supervised by any Roman official who was permanently present among them. The civil wars had indeed meant for many places within the Empire, at least at certain moments, that Roman forces and officials might be present as an active, violent, and oppressive force. Whether or not their brutalities and exactions had any serious economic effects, which is not easy to say,[6] the ending of all that after Actium and the conquest of Egypt was a moment which did not pass without notice. Plutarch's great-grandfather, for instance, used to recount how the citizens of Chaeronea had been forced into service to carry down to the sea sacks of grain for the forces of Antonius at Actium. Lashed by the whip, they had already carried one consignment when news came of Octavian's victory. Antonius' agents and soldiers promptly fled, and the citizens shared out the grain (*Ant.* 68). If we want to try to imagine what the blessings of the Augustan peace really amounted to, we could always start by remembering these resilient Greeks digesting the supplies which had come their way.

Within a very few years at the most, there were no Roman legions at all in what became in 27 the province of Achaea, that is most of present-day Greece; and the same was true of many other areas. The single governor of each province, with his staff, might appear from time to time to give justice, but only in the main centres; smaller places therefore would never actually see him at all. Being a subject community of the Roman Empire therefore consisted, first of all, in a symbolic, or diplomatic, adhesion, and secondly in the obligation to pay tribute. But here too the direct weight of Roman agents was no longer felt in the same way as it had been previously. For the contractors (*publicani*) who had collected the tribute up to the late Republic now disappear, at least from most areas, leaving the communities (as it seems) to pay it themselves.[7] Thus we can actually see the Roman Empire changing shape before the eyes of its subjects if we simply take the example of complaints about taxation. Some time in the late Republic, as a new inscription shows, the cities of Asia, leagued together in their *koinon*, made such a complaint; its subject was oppression by the *publicani* who were active in the province, and the step taken was to send an embassy to speak before the Senate in Rome.[8] In 29 BC, however, two years after Actium, the whole pattern had changed. When the people of the small Aegean island of Gyaros decided to ask for a reduction of their minute annual tribute, they sent an ambassador to make a petition before Octavian, then at Corinth on his way to Rome. The sum concerned was 150 drachmas, or 600 sesterces, a mere fraction of the amount which Octavian was soon to give for a talkative crow (Strabo, *Geog.* 485).

The islanders' perception of where power now lay must be regarded as having been significant in itself, even if it had been wrong; even if, that is, Octavian will have told them to make their appeal to the Senate. But I rather doubt whether he did. For while we do not know what happened to the fisherman from Gyaros, we do know exactly what Octavian or Augustus wrote, probably some time between 31 and 20 BC, to the much larger Aegean island of Samos. We know it because they requested him to grant them freedom, including freedom from tribute, and he refused, and in doing so made an unfavourable comparison to Aphrodisias in Caria. The city of Samos, we can safely assume, did not inscribe this reply. But the city of Aphrodisias did. It is therefore worth noting the exact words of this reply, first published in 1982:[9]

You yourselves can see that I have given the privilege of freedom to no people except the Aphrodisians, who took my side in the war and were captured by storm because of their devotion to us. For it is not right to give the favour of the greatest privilege to all at random and without cause. I am well-disposed to you and should like to do a favour to my wife who is active on your behalf, but not to the point of breaking my custom. For I am not concerned for the money which you pay towards the tribute, but I am not willing to give the most highly prized privileges to anyone without good cause.

If freedom had been granted to Samos, we cannot prove that the constitutional machinery of a vote by the Senate would not have been used; indeed it had been used in precisely the grant to Aphrodisias, in 39 BC, which Octavian/Augustus refers to as if it had emanated solely from his own will.[10] None the less the implication and logic of the reply is unmistakably that the effective decision belongs to the speaker, and has been determined by considerations which are entirely personal to himself. The reference to Livia is also highly important, as we will see. What is significant for the moment is the clear expression of the unqualified right and determination of the speaker to decide a matter which affected the revenues due to be paid to the Roman state; and the effort to explain the principles upon which his decision is based.

I should like to dwell on this point for a moment. In the event, so I believe, the reign of Augustus turned out to have inaugurated almost three centuries of relatively passive and inert government, in which the central power pursued few policies and was largely content to respond to pressures and demands from below.[11] In this, the revolution of consciousness to which I have referred played a crucial part; that is the consciousness that there was an individual ruler, whose name and image appeared everywhere (or everywhere that words were written or images made) and to whom appeal could be made. The step taken by the fisherman of Gyaros embodies exactly that perception. But in the reign of Augustus there is also something else, which to me recalls not the relative torpor of the intervening centuries, but the moralizing and reforming zeal of the tetrarchic period, of Diocletian and Constantine. From the emphasis on victory, to the use of members of an extended imperial family in military and governmental roles in different parts of the Empire, the obsession with large-scale building projects, the reform of the basis of taxation or the level of moralizing self-justification addressed to the people, a whole series of features unites the two periods. Another feature, which looks forward to the restless journeyings of the tetrarchic courts, is the active movement round the Empire which distinguishes the first part of Augustus' reign; of the eighteen years after Actium he was in Rome for about seven.[12]

On one of these journeys, in Gaul in 27 BC, Augustus took a census of the people. Our total evidence on this event, the Epitome of Livy (134) and Dio (LIII. 23. 5) hardly says more than that; nor does either source make clear that no *provincial* census, numbering persons and recording property, had ever been taken before. It is of course only the author of Luke's Gospel who actually states both that there was a universal census and that it was promoted by an edict from Augustus: 'It happened in those days that an edict went out from Caesar Augustus that all the inhabited world should be censused. This was the first which took place, while Quirinius was governor of Syria' (2:1). As Professor Brunt has reminded us, we should not deduce from the scattered and defective nature of our evidence that Luke was simply wrong.[13] At the most he has compressed into a single moment a process spread over many years in different places. As it happened, a census was going on in Syria anyway, under Quirinius, when in AD 6 the rule of Herod's son Archelaus was ended, the province of Judaea came into existence, a census was imposed, tribute was demanded, and resistance flared up, never finally to die away until it led to the great revolt and the destruction of the Temple in AD 70.[14] Luke's allusion reflects the reverberations of that first census. So of course did the questions about tribute which were put to Jesus in Jerusalem. 'The coin of the census', 'of whom is this image and the inscription?', 'give to Caesar the things which are Caesar's' – the language used perfectly reflects a perceived association between census, tribute, coinage, and Emperor.[15] In principle, if indeed people in Judaea did believe that they were paying their tribute 'to Caesar', it is quite certain they were wrong. Even Egypt, as Augustus claimed, was added 'to the *imperium* of the Roman people'.[16] But this mistake, like various others which we shall look at, is illuminating just because it is a mistake. Whether tribute did indeed have to be paid in what Matthew calls 'the coin of the census', and which all three Gospels identify as a *denarius* – that is specifically in Roman coins – we, as it happens, do not know. But the image and inscription had been there for all to see since before Actium.

We accept too easily, without surprise, almost without notice, the change which had come about within a very few years in the coinage of the Mediterranean world. Let me just recall the facts in outline. Up to 44 BC, thirteen years before Actium, there is no certain case of a living Roman being portrayed on a Roman coin. The precedent was set by Julius Caesar in 44, followed by Octavian, Antonius, and Lepidus, in the triumviral period. But all this time there were other coin issues which did not portray any living person.[17] Then from 31 BC onwards almost every single issue of official Roman coinage, in gold, silver, and bronze, portrays Octavian–Augustus.[18] The story of the non-Roman coinage of the Empire is if anything more dramatic.[19] Before 31 BC there may have been a few contemporary portrayals of Pompey and Caesar on city coinages; there were a few of Marcus Antonius, and perhaps one of Octavian. But between 31 BC and AD 14 portrayals of Augustus are known from 189 different places.

Though some cities (such as Tyre, a free city) continued to mint without the head of Augustus, and other places produced some coins with and some without his portrait, we should not minimize the colossal change which had come over the symbolic character of the coinage, both Roman and non-Roman. The term 'propaganda', often used of coin-types and legends, seems to me unhelpful; we know neither who decided these matters nor what reactions they evoked. What we have is once again a set of visible and uncontrovertible examples of how people construed the world in which they lived; or, to put it another way, of the symbols which they thought it appropriate to display publicly. In this light it is therefore of some importance that both Roman and civic coinages of Augustus' reign may also portray other members of his family, Livia, Agrippa Postumus, Gaius and Lucius, and Tiberius.[20] Gaius and Lucius, together or separately, appear on the coins of more than thirty cities.[21]

That fact has its own importance, since, as we will see, it is clearly reinforced by other evidence. For the moment it is enough to say that if provincials on the streets of Jerusalem, or anywhere else in the Empire, imagined their payment of tribute as 'giving to Caesar that which was Caesar's, it was a forgivable mistake, and a highly significant one. In fact even the tribute of the imperial provinces did not actually belong to Caesar, whatever some confusing modern theories may have claimed. But with that we have to turn to the division of the provinces in 27 BC. Here too we will come round in the end to a significant mistake or misconstruction, this time embodied in a major contemporary document. We will also, looking at the new structure created in 27, see more examples of positive, reforming government from the centre, by Augustus; I think, or at least I hope, that I have not been the only person not to see the accumulated weight of this evidence, some of it quite new.

In January 27 BC, three and a half years after his victory, Octavian appeared before the Senate and formally offered to lay down his powers. What exactly those powers had been, either as Triumvir down to the end of 33 BC or in the intervening period, it is perhaps better not to enquire, since the question presents insoluble problems.[22] But his only formal office was that of consul, as it had been since 31, and would remain until 23. The response of the Senate, followed by the People of Rome, was to vote him the new, unheard-of name 'Augustus' and various other honours, and to establish a new arrangement for the appointment of provincial governors. If we look at all of this from the angle of the provinces, the new name was very soon current, at least in the major centres. As for the new form of government, we have only one detailed contemporary picture of it, in the last paragraph of Strabo's *Geography* (840): 'For when his native country entrusted to him the care of the government, and he was established for life as master of war and peace, he divided the entire territory [of the Empire] into two and allotted one to himself and one to the People.' To anyone accustomed to the intricacies of that familiar topic 'the Augustan constitution' these words will seem wrong, either a blatant over-simplification or, if taken literally – i.e. as referrring to the actual words of a constitutional enactment – just false. But, once again, we do have to remember that Strabo was a member of a prominent family in Pontos whose contacts with the leading Romans went back to the time of Lucullus; and that he himself had been in Rome and in the twenties had sailed up the Nile in the entourage of the then Prefect of Egypt, Aelius Gallus.[23] If this was how he saw the change in 27 BC, that is a historical fact in itself; if his words are misleading, they constitute, again, a significant error. Note also that to Strabo the division was not between Augustus and the *Senate*, but between Augustus and the People. The content of the division was that the People 'sent' governors of consular or praetorian rank to its provinces, while Augustus sent both governors of consular or praetorian rank (i.e. senators) and also ones of equestrian rank to his provinces. The division, therefore, in Strabo's eyes consisted in the method of appointment of provincial governors. He could not have failed to know, but does not make it clear, that senatorial governors in the People's provinces bore the republican title of 'proconsul', while those appointed by the Emperor bore a title which explicitly referred to their dependence on him, namely *legatus*, or deputy. He could not have failed to know, for the obvious reason that these titles appeared everywhere on public inscriptions. He might perhaps not have known, what Cassius Dio was later to explain so clearly (LIII. 13–14), that, while the

THE IMPACT OF MONARCHY

legati were appointed by Augustus, and served until he chose to replace them, the proconsuls were chosen by the ancient system of the lot, and served for a year only. In their case therefore the right to submit their name to the lot was one which came to them automatically five years after holding the elected office of praetor or consul. The government of these provinces *was* thus conferred by the vote of the people, even if indirectly, and imperial patronage played no part. But *legati* were appointed by imperial patronage, and their public title proclaimed this fact.

Whereas under the Triumvirate, or so it seems, all governors had been appointees, now a man could once again become proconsul of the great and rich province of Africa or Asia, while owing nothing to anyone's patronage. Was this however always clearly perceptible to the class of educated Greeks who, like Strabo, accepted the fact of Roman dominance and ran their own cities within its framework? It does not seem so. One of the most famous of Augustan documents is the great dossier which records how in 9 BC the cities of Asia celebrated the new era by agreeing to start all their separate annual calendars from Augustus' birthday, 23 September.[24] The proposal, indeed instruction, for this had actually come from the proconsul of Asia himself, Paullus Fabius Maximus, the descendant of a prominent Republican family.[25] In response to his sycophantic epistle the *koinon* of Asia duly passed a decree making the new arrangements; in it they alluded to their proconsul in the following terms: 'the proconsular benefactor of the province, sent by his [Augustus'] right hand and judgement.'

So here is another significant mistake; even this distinction, between appointees and non-appointees, could vanish from the perspective of the leading citizens of a rich and civilized province. However, I have so far expressed myself as if this division in the method of appointment of governors, together with the new name 'Augustus', were all that there was, from a provincial point of view, to the settlement of 27 BC. That is indeed exactly what I think; the idea that there were ever two separate spheres of authority or administrative activity, that of the Emperor and that of the Senate, in relation to the provinces is just a modern fiction.[26] Indeed it is even more of a fiction than I once thought. For I did for a time suppose that while the Emperor from the beginning gave a set of instructions (*mandata*) to the *legati* whom he sent out, he did not do so for proconsuls until about the end of the first century AD. They therefore, on this view, preserved a certain functional independence.[27] But Dio states quite clearly that Augustus began to issue instructions to proconsuls, as well as to his own appointees, already in 27 BC (LIII. 15. 4). Recent evidence strongly suggests that Dio was right. A recently re-edited letter of Domitius Corbulo, as proconsul of Asia under Claudius (*AE* 1974, 629), refers to the *entolai*, 'instructions', which must surely be those of the Emperor; and that is confirmation enough.[28] Beyond that, two other new items of evidence, of the greatest importance, illustrate the way in which codes of instruction from Augustus, issued to provincial governors or officials, filtered down to affect the lives of communities and individuals in the provinces.

The first is the bilingual edict of Sextus Sotidius Strabo Libuscidianus, issued when he was *legatus* of Galatia early in Tiberius' reign.[29] It is indeed clear that he had been appointed as *legatus* by Augustus, and had continued in office after the Emperor's death and deification in AD 14. The subject matter of the edict is the local application, to the city of Sagalassus and its surrounding region, of an immensely complex set of rules relating to the right of official travellers to requisition transport at fixed prices, and to demand free accommodation up to specific limits. The governor's dependence on the rules drawn up by the Emperor is heavily stressed in his opening paragraph:

It is the most unjust thing of all for me to tighten up by my own edict that which the Augusti, one the greatest of gods [Augustus], the other the greatest of Emperors [Tiberius], have taken the utmost care to prevent, namely that no one should make use of carts without payment. However, since the indiscipline of certain people requires an immediate punishment, I have set up in the individual towns and villages a register of those services which I judge ought to be provided, with the intention of having it observed, or, if it shall be neglected, of enforcing it not only with my own power but with the majesty of the best of princes [in Greek the 'Saviour *Sebastos*', namely Augustus] from whom I received instructions (*entolai/ mandata*) concerning these matters.

Behind the confused and self-deprecating language it is evident that a positive code of rules had been drawn up by Augustus, had been embodied in the *mandata* which the *legatus* had originally received, and had been confirmed by Tiberius. There is every reason to suppose that similar instructions were issued by Augustus to governors of all types.

Another code of instructions issued by Augustus was the *Gnomon*, or handbook, for the Roman official in Egypt who was in charge of the *Idios Logos*, the 'private account', which absorbed vacant or confiscated properties. We know it best from a selection of its most commonly applied clauses, found on a papyrus of the mid-second century. The preamble of this text runs: 'A summary of the *gnomon* which the deified Augustus delivered to the administration of the *idios logos* and of the additions made from time to time by Emperors or Senate or the Prefects or *idioi logoi* of the time . . .' The code imposed very detailed regulations concerning personal status, the rights of the Emperor to vacant property, and the confiscation of property after condemnation. If this text seems far away from Augustus himself, we come a great deal closer (once again) with a newly published papyrus which contains extracts from the code, and was written before the middle of the first century AD (*POxy* 3014).[30]

If we think of status, and the rules relating to it, we must inevitably think of the citizenship. By what seems to be a paradox, but is in fact typical of the Imperial system, it was precisely imperial patronage which was the instrument which opened the Roman citizenship to the provinces. In that sense the citizenship provides a perfect example of that ambivalent relationship analysed by Andrew Wallace-Hadrill, in which statuses and ranks in the republican system themselves provided the content of patronage by the Emperor.[31]

As regards Augustus and the citizenship there are three points to make. First, the disposal of the citizenship by Caesar and Augustus served to distribute around the provinces individuals with the Roman *nomen* Julius, living symbols of the unseen Emperor's influence. Secondly it was Augustus, in the third of his edicts inscribed in the market-place of Cyrene, who laid down the all-important principle that gaining Roman citizenship would not of itself affect a man's obligations to his home community; it was precisely this principle which was to determine the political and social structure of the Empire for the next two centuries.[32] Thirdly, there is yet another new document, the bronze tablet from Banasa in Morocco. For it is this which reveals that Augustus, with what we can begin to see as an obsession with documentation (compare Suet. *Aug.* 101), had started an archive (*commentarius*) which was to record the names and details of every single person granted the Roman citizenship by himself and (as it turned out) subsequent Emperors, at least up to Marcus Aurelius.[33]

The citizenship could thus be exported to the provinces, and the details recorded. But so too could existing citizens. We perhaps do not emphasize sufficiently that the age of Caesar, the Triumvirs, and Augustus is not merely the first, but the only period in Roman history which saw the state engaged in active and large-scale settlement of citizens outside Italy. The scale and the geographical range of the establishment of veteran colonies makes this one of the important direct effects ever achieved by government in the ancient world; as Augustus claims in the *Res Gestae*, 120,000 men were already in the colonies by 29 BC, and the *coloniae* themselves were by the end to be found in Africa, Sicily, Macedonia, Spain, Achaea, Asia, Syria, Gallia Narbonensis, Pisidia, and Italy itself (*RG* 15; 28). Once again, these complex human movements and rearrangements did not just happen. They were subject to direct supervision by Augustus himself. Our evidence that detailed plans, and records of grants of land (significantly called the *liber beneficiorum*), remained in the imperial archives 'subscribed by the hand of the founder' must relate in the first instance to Augustus himself. Edicts of Augustus attempted to regulate the consequences of the immense disturbances to property and legal rights which were inevitably caused: 'There are also certain *edicta* of Augustus, by whch he indicated that wherever he had taken lands from the territories of other cities and assigned them to the veterans (i.e. of a particular colony), nothing else pertained to the jurisdiction of that colony except what had been given and assigned to the veterans.' All this information comes from that invaluable, but obscure and complex source, the writings of the Roman land-measurers.[34] Each individual colony might also get letters of instruction;

giving judgement over disputed land in AD 82, Domitian was to recall: 'The letter of the deified Augustus, a most diligent *princeps* and most indulgent towards his *quartani* [the veterans of the fourth legion settled at Firmum], in which he advised them to make a record of, and sell, all their unassigned plots.' 'I do not doubt', Domitian concludes, 'that they obeyed such salubrious advice.'[35]

In Italy, so Suetonius records (*Aug.* 46), the twenty-eight colonies, once founded, used to be visited by Augustus, who would equip them with buildings and public revenues. Elsewhere the imperial will could still be felt at a distance. Another new document, from the colony of Alexandria Troas, refers to 'the works carried out in the *colonia* by the order of Augustus', as well as to the levy conducted by him and Tiberius in Rome, and to military decorations granted by Germanicus (*AE* 1973, 501). We should not treat as banal the fact that a Latin inscription from the north-west corner of Turkey should recall specific actions on the part of three different members of the imperial house.

Even outside the *coloniae* we come across many traces of both individual decisions and general rules issued by Augustus and affecting the cities of the Empire: in the western Mediterranean, for instance, various *beneficia* granted to the obscure community of the Vanacini in Corsica, or revenues (*vectigalia*) to the equally obscure Saborenses in Spain.[36] The apparent source of authority for general rules had changed also. I say apparent authority, because we can rarely be quite certain whether or not some constitutional processes did not precede, or perhaps follow, pronouncements by Augustus. For an example of that problem we may look again at the famous document from Kyme in Asia, first published in 1958.[37] What I think is certain about this much-debated text is as follows. First, Augustus and Agrippa, as consuls in 27 BC, issued some form of general pronouncement ordering the restitution of sacred or public properties which were illegally in private possession. Secondly a man from Kyme approached the proconsul of Asia and demonstrated that a shrine in Kyme was illegally in private possession. Thirdly the proconsul wrote to the magistrates of Kyme to say that the shrine was to be restored in accordance with the order (*iussum*) of Augustus, and was to have an inscription saying 'Imperator Caesar Divi filius Augustus has restored [it]'. The document has a much wider significance than the tedious debates about it have allowed. First, if it really does reflect a general pronouncement concerned with sacred and public property in all provinces, then it seems to be the earliest attested case of such an intervention in the history of Roman rule outside Italy. Secondly if (as many have argued) a *senatus consultum* or some other collective constitutional act preceded and authorized the pronouncement by Augustus and Agrippa, then it has vanished, even from the perspective of the proconsul himself. What is more, Agrippa, who really did have some role, has also vanished. The more constitutionalist one's assumptions about the original process, the more striking is the concentration by the proconsul on the figure of Augustus: 'Imperator Caesar Divi filius Augustus has restored it.'

The inscription is also an example of how an imperial ruling could have its effect not by direct enforcement but being known and being used by an interested party. Both the man in the street and the proconsul act on assumptions which reflect a new map of the world. Above and behind the governor is the unseen figure of the Emperor, whose word, if known, can be used to enforce local effects.

How, or if, the Emperor's word would become known to his subjects is a monstrous problem, still too little discussed. One way, of course, in those areas where at least some were literate, was the public inscription. But it was not the Roman state or its agents which normally created these, but any city which felt moved to do so. This is the case even with the most general, the most reformist and the most clearly propagandist pronouncement of Augustus which we have, namely the last of the five edicts inscribed in Greek in the market-place of Cyrene. The procedure involved, namely the passing of a *senatus consultum* under Augustus' influence, aptly reflects the uneasy collaboration of Emperor and Senate; the aim, to establish a simpler process for gaining restitution of money improperly acquired by governors, is typical of Augustus' reforming and moralizing spirit. The tone of paternalistic propaganda addressed to the people might belong to Diocletian. The preamble runs:[38]

Imperator Caesar Augustus, Pontifex Maximus, holding the *tribunicia potestas* for the 19th time, says:

The decree of the Senate passed . . . with myself being present and being named jointly as author, being relevant to the security of the allies of the Roman people, I have decided, so that it may be known to all of whom we have the care, to send to the provinces and to subjoin it to my own edict, from which it will be clear to all who dwell in the provinces how much concern is exercised by myself and the Senate that none of those subject to us should endure any improper injury or exaction.

This is in fact the earliest known Roman pronouncement which explicitly addresses itself to the attention of all the inhabitants of the Empire. Though the body of the document is a decree of the Senate, it is Augustus' name and titles which occupy the first two lines, and Augustus' words which make up the first paragraph. Those who could read would read them first. Those who could not, could have seen a statue of the Emperor; the second edict records that the removal of such a statue, along with others, from public places had already been the subject of accusations within the city (*SEG* IX. 8. ii).

With that we come back to our starting-point, the symbolic presence of the Emperor, in word and physical representation, in the provincial community; or rather in those Greek or Latin cities where the 'epigraphic habit', as Ramsey MacMullen has called it,[39] was entrenched, and where statues were made. That should bring us in its turn to the imperial cult, or to the confusing nexus of different acts and ceremonials which go under that heading. But the evidence is too complex, and anyway may well evoke 'tedium and distaste'. Let me therefore make a few brief points.

First, the notion that the cults directed to Emperors evolved from those for Hellenistic kings is hardly even a half-truth. There is nothing anywhere to suggest that the *scale* of cult-acts for Hellenistic kings had ever approached that which immediately appeared for Augustus. Few cults of deceased Hellenistic kings still lingered on, and only a modest range of evidence attests cults or games or shrines for even the major Roman figures of the late Republic. The sudden outburst of the celebration of Octavian/Augustus was a new phenomenon.[40] Nicolaus' remarks on the temples and sacrifices for Augustus by cities and provinces (*FGrH* 90 F 125) are all the more important because written in the 20s BC (p. 62 below). It was new first in its wide diffusion at the city level and above all in the creation, from 30/29 BC onwards, of provincial cults, with common temples of Roma and Augustus, common annual games associated with them, and annual High Priesthoods. Everyone knows that these arrangements were formally permitted to the provinces of Asia and Bithynia by Octavian in 30/29 BC (Dio LI. 20. 6–9). What deserves equal emphasis is the fact that he subsequently took a detailed interest in the practical arrangements. For instance, in the early days of the provincial cult in Asia a choir assembled to sing hymns to the Emperor; I am not sure whether I wish that a text of such a hymn had survived. At any rate Augustus subsequently laid down arrangements for the expenses of the choir to be shared by the cities of the province.[41]

In Syria there is nothing to suggest that a provincial league already existed, as it had in Asia, or that there were any surviving cults of the Seleucids. Indeed, until a few years ago there was no evidence even of the existence of a provincial cult in Syria under Augustus. But now we know there was, and that the first High Priest was a man personally honoured by the Emperor. This is how the man, Dexandros, appears in an inscription from Apamea in honour of his great-grandson: listing distinguished ancestors, the inscription continues 'And above all Dexandros, the first man to have been priest of the province, his great-grandfather (who) by the decree of the deified Augustus, because of his friendship and loyalty to the Roman people, was inscribed as a friend and ally on bronze tablets on the Capitol'.[42] The inscription shows the honours given to a local notable associated with the cult of the Emperor; and it is also another example of the use by Augustus of the apparatus of the Roman *res publica*.

The provincial cult was not, even in Asia, a natural development from a long tradition, but an organized novelty, soon exported, as we now know, to Syria, and also, as has always been known, to Gaul. At the level of the city also, the dossier of 9 BC from Asia can simply assume that there will be *Kaisareia* at least in the assize-centres, and 'Caesarean' games apparently everywhere; city cults of Augustus are in fact attested in thirty-four places in Asia, a figure never again approached in the case of any later Emperor.[43] Once again the reign of Augustus can be seen not only as a beginning, but as a phase in itself. Equally distinctive is the scatter of cults for other members of the imperial family, matching their appearance on both Roman and civic coins (p. 45 above). For example, an inscription published in 1962 revealed a priest of Augustus, Gaius, and Agrippa on Samos,[44] and one of 1972 a priest of Agrippa Postumus and Hermes at Iasos in Caria (*AE* 1974, 628).

But we do not need these passing allusions to perceive the importance of the imperial family in the new political system. We can go back to the long-known oath of Gangra in Paphlagonia, the same oath which was being sworn in the country districts at the *Sebastea* and at Neapolis in the *Sebasteon*, at the altar of the *Sebastos*. The opening words were 'I swear by Zeus, Ge, Helios, all the gods and goddesses and the Sebastos himself to be loyal to Caesar Sebastos *and his children and his descendants* . . .'[45] Perhaps these are after all just ignorant Greeks from the interior of Asia Minor, accustomed to royal dynasties. So let us take the inhabitants of the Roman *colonia* of Narbo in Provence – by now called in full Colonia Iulia Paterna Narbo Martia – and the exact words of the *votum* which they took in AD 11; 'That it should be good, fortunate, and auspicious for Imperator Caesar divi filius Augustus, Pater Patriae, Pontifex Maximus, holding the *tribunicia potestas* for the 34th time, *and his wife and children and his family* and the Senate and People of Rome and the *coloni* and *incolae* of the *Colonia*.' Even on an altar to the *numen* of Augustus, erected in recognition of his settlement of divisions in the town, they did not have to select just these elements, in that order.[46]

If we turn to yet another new document, we can see that the emphasis on the imperial family could seem appropriate, not just to provincial communities but to a senatorial official fulfilling a public role in his province. Thus the town of Messene passed a decree to honour the *quaestor pro praetore* of Achaea, Publius Cornelius Scipio, who 'being filled with unexcelled good will to Augustus *and all his house*' had conducted the *Kaisareia* in lavish style and, learning the news of Gaius Caesar's campaigns in the East, had carried out a public sacrifice for his safety (*SEG* XXIII. 206 = *AE* 1967, 458). When Gaius died, what significance was to be attached to the event? We can judge best from the second of the two famous inscriptions from Pisa, or rather the 'Colonia Obsequens Iulia Pisana', a place already equipped with an Augusteum and a Flamen Augustalis:[47]

when the news was brought that Gaius Caesar, the son of Augustus, Pater Patriae, Pontifex Maximus, guardian of the Roman Empire, and governor (*praeses*) of the whole *orbis terrarum*, grandson of the deified . . . had by a cruel fate been seized from the Roman people, when already designated as a most just *princeps* and closest to the qualities of his father, and the only protector of our *colonia*'.[47]

We ought to recall, listening to these words, that those who composed them came from precisely that Italian middle class which Jones once supposed to have been the group most attached to the republican constitution.[48]

New documents allow us to hear more and more of the words which people felt to be publicly appropriate under Augustus, or which he uttered to them. We should not brush these words aside as insincere (which we cannot know and in any case is irrelevant) or as misapprehensions of some privileged reality which is knowable in some other way. For these public expressions *are* a significant part of what we can know of the reality of the Roman Empire for those who lived in it. Instead we should be impressed by the suddenness and extent of the creation of a symbolic relationship between the new source of power and the provincial communities. It is possible to see entire town centres, say at Athens, or at Lepcis Magna,[49] which were transformed under Augustus by the erection of buildings related to the Emperor and his household.

I have concentrated on provincial towns, and the rituals, images, and words in which they represented the imperial power; on the role of senatorial governors in reinforcing that same message; and on the relatively active role of Augustus himself in addressing his words to the people. But in fact there was nowhere where the impact of monarchy was more emphatic than in Rome itself. There is no need for a catalogue of buildings. Let us take one of our best examples of the continued functioning of *res publica*, namely the law passed in 9 BC to define offences against the acqueducts: 'The Consul,

T. Quinctius Crispinus, duly put the question to the people and the people duly passed a vote in the Forum, before the Rostra of the temple of the deified Julius on the thirtieth day of June. The Sergian tribe was to vote first . . .'[50]

The consul spoke from the new rostra, decorated with the spoils of Actium, and placed in front of the temple of Julius Caesar; completed in 29 BC, the temple occupied a central point in the old Forum, blocking off the Regia from the large open space including the Comitium. The temple therefore rose behind the consul as he had the law read out; if the doors were open, the crowd would have been able to see the statue of the deified Caesar within. To the right, some at least of the crowd could see the new arch of Augustus dedicated in 19 BC. If they looked further round to the right they could see the Basilica Iulia, begun by Caesar and completed by Augustus. Directly behind them stood the old Rostra, shifted to a new position by Julius Caesar. Those at the back, if a large enough crowd had come, could see on their left the new Senate house, the Curia Iulia, begun by Caesar and finally dedicated by Octavian in 29 BC, which was attached to the outside of one of the porticoes of the vast new Forum Iulium.[51] From further over to their left they might have been aware of work going on to complete the Forum of Augustus with the temple of Mars Ultor; as yet, however, they had been spared its programmatic re-reading of Roman history in terms of legendary ancestors and kings, together with historical *summi viri*, that is to say those *duces* whose individual achievements had brought the *imperium* of the Roman people from insignificance to greatness.[52]

If they were still unclear as to what symbolic message was being delivered, they could always have taken a walk to the north end of the Campus Martius, past the Saepta and Pantheon built by Agrippa, past the Ara Pacis, dedicated in January of that very year (9 BC); and parallel with it – probably dedicated at the same time – the monstrous sundial marked out by Augustus over some 150 metres of the Campus, its shadow provided by an obelisk brought from Heliopolis, which stood, with its base, some 30 metres high.[53] They could then have contemplated the hideous mass of Augustus' Mausoleum;[54] at some 88 metres across the base, it was the largest Roman tomb so far known, begun perhaps in the late 30s or at the latest in 28 BC, that is just before the chance was solemnly offered for Senate and People to exercise their *arbitrium*. By 9 BC the Mausoleum already contained the remains of two members of the imperial family, Marcellus and Agrippa, and would very soon receive those of Drusus. A quarter of a century later, once Augustus' ashes had also been placed there, the passer-by was to have the chance to read his *Res Gestae*, inscribed on bronze tablets attached to pillars standing in front of it. Unlike modern scholars, this passer-by could also, from time to time, lift up his eyes from the text and observe, at a height of some 40 metres above where he was standing, the bronze image of Caesar Augustus which rose over the tomb. Returning to the text, he was probably not clever enough to read it as a republican document.

NOTES

1. *SEG* XXVI. 1243; *AE* 1975. 799; now *I.K.Eph.* III. 902: ὃς καὶ προενοήθμ τῆς καθιδρύσεως τοῦ Σεβαστοῦ καὶ τῆς καθιερώσεως τοῦ τεμένους.
2. Ibid., lines 8–10: Περικλῆς Ἡρακλείδου φύσει δὲ Χαροπίνος, ἱερονείκης ἀπ[ὸ] συνόδου, certainly to be identified with the Charopinos of Ephesus of R. K. Sherk, *Roman Documents from then Greek East* (1969), no. 57.
3. *IGLS* III. 718: Sherk, op. cit., no. 58, doc. iii.
4. I am much indebted throughout to the methodology of S. R. F. Price, 'Between Man and God: Sacrifice in the Roman Imperial Cult', *JRS* 70 (1980), 28, and to his *Rituals and Power: the Roman Imperial Cult in Asia Minor*, to be published by CUP in 1984.
5. See J. R. Rea, 'Lease of a Red Cow named Thayris', *JEA* 68 (1982), 277.
6. See F. Millar, 'The Mediterranean and the Roman Revolution: Politics, War and the Economy', *Past and Present* 102 (1984), 3.
7. See E. Badian, *Publicans and Sinners* (1972); for the problems about the ending of the *publicani* system for direct taxation see P. A. Brunt *ap.* A. H. M. Jones, *The Roman Economy* (1974), 180 f. But cf. Nicolet, pp. 101–3 below.
8. The inscription from Aphrodisias originally published by K. T. Erim, *PBSR* 37 (1969), 92, has been re-edited by T. Drew-Bear, *BCH* 96 (1972), 443, and J. Reynolds, *Aphrodisias and Rome* (1982), doc. 5.
9. Reynolds, op. cit. (n. 8), doc. 13. Miss Reynolds is inclined to date the reply earlier, because of the reference to the war, which she argues to have been that of Labienus. But while, for the reasons she gives, the presence of the name Αὔγουστος is not significant for dating, the reference to Aphrodisias having taken 'my side' (τὰ ἐμὰ φρονήσας) seems to me to reflect the situation after Actium. Compare the cases of Sparta and Mantinea which also took Octavian's side (see p. 169 below). The date must in any case be before Samos successfully gained freedom in 20/19 (Dio LIV. 9. 7).
10. Reynolds, op. cit. (n. 8), doc. 8.
11. See F. Millar, *The Emperor in the Roman World (31 BC–AD 337)* (1977).

12. Return to Rome, 29 BC; Gaul and Spain, 27–24 BC; in the Greek East, 22–19 BC; in Gaul, 16–13 BC.
13. See P. A. Brunt, 'The Revenues of Rome', *JRS* 71 (1981), 161, on pp. 163 f. Note also T. D. Barnes, *The New Empire of Diocletian and Constantine* (1982), 226 f.
14. See E. Schürer, *History of the Jewish People*, ed. G. Vermes and F. Millar, I (1973), 381–2; 399–427. For the continuity of the resistance movement, M. Stern, 'Sicarii and Zealots', *World History of the Jewish People*, First Series, VIII (1977), 263. Census in Syria: *ILS* 2683.
15. Mark 12: 13–17; Math. 22: 17–22; Luke 20: 21–6. For the significance to the population of the representation of the Emperor (as opposed to that of any short-term information – or propaganda – content of coin-types), see M. H. Crawford, 'Roman imperial coin types and the formation of public opinion', in C. N. L. Brooke, I. Stewart, J. G. Pollard, T. R. Volk, *Studies in Numismatic Method Presented to Philip Grierson* (1983), 47.
16. *RG* 27; cf. *CIL* VI. 702: 'Aegypto in potestatem populi Romani redacta' (from the base of the obelisk used for Augustus' sundial, see p. 57 of this paper); cf. Vell. Pat. II. 39. 2.
17. See M. H. Crawford, *Roman Republican Coinage* (1974), 734 f.; for the gold statue portraying Flamininus, not a *Roman* issue, see p. 544.
18. For the most complete account, C. H. V. Sutherland, C. M. Kraay, *Catalogue of Coins of the Roman Empire in the Ashmolean Museum* I: *Augustus (c. 31 BC–AD 14)* (1975).
19. For a very useful survey of the civic coin portraits of Augustus see S. Walker, A. Burnett, *Augustus: Handlist of the Exhibition and Supplementary Studies (British Museum Occasional Papers* 16, 1981), 23 f.
20. See e.g. C. H. V. Sutherland, *Coinage in Roman Imperial Policy 32 BC–AD 68* (1951), ch. iv, for the representation of different members of Augustus' families on Roman coinage.
21. Walker and Burnett, op. cit. (n. 19), 57 f.
22. For the author's views, which remain controversial, see F. Millar, 'Triumvirate and Principate', *JRS* 63 (1973), 50.
23. On Strabo see G. W. Bowersock, *Augustus and the Greek World* (1965), 127–9.
24. The fullest discussion of the various texts is U. Laffi, 'Le iscrizioni relativi all' introduzione nel 9 a. C. del nuovo calendario della provincia d'Asia', *Stud. Class. e Or.* 16 (1967), 5. See lines 44–5: ὁ ἀνθύπατος τῆς ἐπαρχήας εὐεργέτης ἀπὸ τῆς ἐκείνου δεξιᾶς καὶ [γ]νώμης ἀπεσταλμένος.
25. *PIR²* F 47; see R. Syme, *History in Ovid* (1978), ch. viii.
26. See F. Millar, 'The Emperor, the Senate and the Provinces', *JRS* 56 (1966), 156; see also W. K. Lacey, 'Octavian in the Senate, January 27 BC', *JRS* 64 (1974), 176.
27. Millar, op. cit. (n. 26), 157–8; op. cit. (n. 11), 314–17.
28. G. P. Burton, 'The Issuing of Mandata to Proconsuls and a New Inscription from Cos', *ZPE* 21 (1976), 63.
29. Published by S. Mitchell, 'Requisitioned Transport in the Roman Empire: a New Inscription from Pisidia', *JRS* 66 (1976), 106; *AE* 1976, 653; *SEG* XXVI. 1392.
30. S. Riccobono, *Il Gnomon dell'Idios Logos* (1950); see Millar, op. cit. (n. 11), 159.
31. A. Wallace-Hadrill, 'Civilis Princeps: between Citizen and King', *JRS* 72 (1982), 32.
32. See F. Millar, 'Empire and City, Augustus to Julian: Obligations, Excuses and Status', *JRS* 73 (1983), 76 .
33. First published by W. Seston, M. Euzennat, 'Un dossier de la chancellerie romaine: la *Tabula Banasitana*, Étude de diplomatique', *CRAI* 1971, 468; see e.g. A. N. Sherwin-White, *JRS* 63 (1973), 86; *AE* 1971, 534.
34. *Corpus Agrimensorum Romanorum* I, ed. Thulin, pp. 165–6 and 82–3; Millar, op. cit. (n. 11), 263–4.

60   THE IMPACT OF MONARCHY

35. *CIL* IX. 5420; *FIRA*² I, no. 5.
36. *FIRA*² I. 72; 74.
37. *SEG* XVIII, 555; Sherk, op. cit. (n. 2), no. 61; *I. K. Kyme* no. 17 (with restorations which seem to me ill advised). See most recently N. Charbonnel, 'À propos de l'inscription de Kymé et des pouvoirs d'Auguste dans les provinces au lendemain du règlement de 27 av. n.è.', *RIDA* 26 (1979), 177.
38. *SEG* IX. 8. v; Sherk, op. cit. (n. 2), no. 31.
39. R. MacMullen, 'The Epigraphic Habit in the Roman Empire', *AJPh* 103 (1982), 233.
40. See esp. K. Tuchelt, *Frühe Denkmäler Roms in Kleinasien* I: *Roma und Promagistrate* (1979), and Price, op. cit. (n. 4).
41. F. K. Dörner, *Der Erlass des Statthalters von Asia Paullus Fabius Persicus* (1935), col. viii, lines 11–19; *I. K. Ephesos* Ia, nos. 17–19, 18d, lines 11–19.
42. J. P. Rey-Coquais, 'Inscriptions grecques d'Apamée', *Ann. Arch. Arab. Syr.* 23 (1973), 39, no. 2; *AE* 1976, 678; see *BE* 1976, 718.
43. Price, op. cit. (n. 4), ch. 3.
44. P. Herrmann, 'Die Inschriften römischer Zeit aus dem Heraion von Samos', *Ath. Mitt.* 75 (1960, app. 1962), 68, no. 1, part B.
45. *IGR* III. 137; *OGIS* 532; *ILS* 8781; cf. P. Herrmann, *Der römische Kaisereid* (1968), esp. 96 f.
46. *ILS* 112. See P. Kreissel, 'Entstehung und Bedeutung der Augustalität. Zur Inschrift der *ara Narbonensis* (*CIL* XII. 4333)', *Chiron* 10 (1980), 291.
47. *ILS* 140. See e.g. A. R. Marotta d'Agata, *Decreta Pisana* (*CIL XI, 1420–21*) (1980).
48. A. H. M. Jones, 'The *Imperium* of Augustus', *JRS* 41 (1951), 112 = *Studies in Roman Government and Law* (1960), 1.
49. See T. L. Shear, 'Athens: from City-State to Provincial Town', *Hesperia* 50 (1981), 356; E. Smadja, 'L'inscription du culte impériale dans la cité: l'example de Lepcis Magna au début de l'Empire', *Dial. d'hist. anc.* 4 (1978), 171.
50. Frontinus, *de aquae ductu* II. 129. Loeb trans.
51. See P. Zanker, *Forum Romanum: die Neugestaltung durch Augustus* (1972).
52. See P. Zanker, *Forum Augustum: das Bildprogramm* (1968); A. Degrassi, *Ins. It.* XIII. 3: *Elogia* (1937). See S. R. Tufi, 'Frammenti delle statue dei summi viri nel Foro di Augusto', *Dial. di Arch.* 3 (1981) 69. For the *duces*, Suet. *Aug.* 31: 'memoriae ducum . . . qui imperium populi Romani ex minimo maximum reddidissent'.
53. See E. Buchner, *Die Sonnenuhr des Augustus* (1982).
54. For the Mausoleum see e.g. R. A. Cordingley, I. A. Richmond, 'The Mausoleum of Augustus', *PBSR* 10 (1927), 23; K. Kraft, 'Der Sinn des Mausoleums des Augustus', *Historia* 16 (1967), 189 = *Gesammelte Aufsätze zur antiken Geschichte und Militärgeschichte* (1973), 29 (for the view that building began in the late 30s and was complete by 28 BC); J.–C. Richard, ' "Mausoleum": d'Halicarnasse à Rome, puis à Alexandrie', *Latomus* 29 (1970), 370. See J. M. C. Toynbee, *Death and Burial in the Roman World* (1971), 144 f.

I am very grateful to Michael Crawford and Simon Price for corrections and comments.

III. THE HISTORIANS AND AUGUSTUS

EMILIO GABBA

PREFACE

I should like to begin with one particularly relevant item from the varied range of ancient historical writing on Augustus.[1] It is reliably reported that he was present at a reading of the work of Cremutius Cordus, despite the fact that it lavished praise on the murderers of Caesar and heaped obloquy on the authors of the proscriptions. Needless to say, the implicit approval of one Emperor did not suffice to save the historian from the attentions of the next.[2] Again under Augustus, admiration for Brutus and Cassius in Livy did not stand in the way of friendship with the Emperor, who merely teased Livy for his Pompeian sympathies.[3] It was cunning of Josephus, with a view to avoiding unnecessary risks, to submit his *Bellum Judaicum* for the advance approval of Titus and King Agrippa II. Their written endorsement guaranteed the reliability of the narrative and ensured the safety of the historian.[4] Despite the attractive and sympathetic picture which Marguerite Yourcenar has painted of Hadrian, I cannot quite imagine him listening with open approbation to a reading of the first book of the *Annales* of Tacitus. I do not of course presume to rival any of the historians I have named, and it is just as well that Sir Ronald Syme is not a Roman Emperor.

I

The *Life of Augustus* by Nicolaus of Damascus opens with a preface designed to explain its meaning and purpose.[5] The name of Augustus, and the honours and cults spontaneously conferred on the Emperor by the whole of humanity, simply recognized the extent of his virtue and the magnitude of his services. A leader of outstanding wisdom, at the head of the greatest empire ever known, Augustus had extended the frontiers of the Roman world and had provided a framework for the existence and the consciousness of Greek and barbarian alike, initially by force of arms, then by a process of persuasion and reconciliation. The greatness of the Empire was demonstrated by the fact that it had conquered peoples of whom previously no one had ever heard; but the dominant elements in Nicolaus' universalist vision of the Empire are its humane ideals, the more than human wisdom with which it was ruled, the peace which it brought. The vision of Nicolaus naturally emphasizes the benefits which the Empire as a whole conferred on the diverse peoples who lived in it or on its borders. In marked contrast, as we shall see, to Tacitus, Nicolaus held that the theme was suitable for a competition between historians, as to who should excel in the presentation of such dramatic developments. Though he went too far, Nicolaus rightly insisted on the education and culture of his hero, which underlay the wisdom and justice with which he ruled the world.

Nicolaus' view of the Roman Empire and of the position of Augustus is important not only in a historiographical context, and it is not simply the product of oriental or Hellenistic political values. For it formed the basis of Nicolaus' cultural activity and of his political role as adviser of King Herod:[6] it was he who suggested how the king should behave towards Augustus and Agrippa; it was he who understood and expounded their eastern policy in his *Universal History*, preserved for us with some changes of emphasis in the *Antiquitates Judaicae* of Josephus. In other words, Nicolaus' view of the Roman Empire is presupposed by the way in which, as an outsider, he grasped the nature of its administration and made use of his knowledge.

It is now generally agreed that the *Life of Augustus* is to be dated to 25–20 BC. The fragment which survives is thus our oldest historical source directly concerning Augustus, and it is for that reason that I have begun with Nicolaus. The date of the work raises the problem of its relation to the *De vita sua* of Augustus, published after 25 BC. It is reasonable to suppose that the *Life* was a free paraphrase of Augustus' work, adapted to the point of view of the eastern part of the Empire. Nicolaus will have drawn therefrom the essence of Augustus' account of his seizure of power and his relationship with Antonius. The presence of a full account of the murder of Caesar is an argument in favour of an early date for the *Life*. Although no doubt modified, the inclusion of this section may be explained in terms of the need to counter hostile propaganda current until recently. Nicolaus' harping on the themes of peace and stability, guaranteed by the new regime and dependent on the superhuman virtues of Augustus, belongs in the context of a universalist ideology, the values of which were deliberately fostered by the imperial power, specially in the provinces. One has only to recall the edict of Paullus Fabius Maximus, a relative of the imperial family, in which he invited the provincial *koinon* to consider the introduction of a new calendar for the province of Asia, based on the birthday of Augustus; the reasoning of the edict centres on the themes of general renewal and the good of humanity, and is picked up in the decree of the *koinon*.[7] Elements of this ideology are to be found also in Velleius Paterculus, and at the end of the *Life* of Suetonius, with the episode of the sailors from Alexandria.[8]

II

This view of the Roman Empire and its founder, for which Nicolaus is probably our earliest evidence, remained politically relevant, as well as historiographically important. For it satisfied the longing for order and peace of the upper classes in the provinces. In due course, the notion became an indispensable element in the Christian view of the Roman Empire, which saw it as called into existence by providence in order to make possible the birth and spread of Christianity.[9] Fifty years after Nicolaus, we find a full account of the notion in Philo of Alexandria.[10] Augustus is someone who with all his virtues has vanquished human nature; who has deserved the name by reason of the extent of his power and the nobility of his behaviour. He has saved the world by bringing it peace; he has restored order throughout the world; he has brought freedom to the cities; he has civilized the barbarians; he has ensured the freedom of the seas for maritime trade. Above all, he has added new Greek lands to those already existing and has brought about the Hellenization of the barbarian world by the harmonious distribution of his favours and the distribution of all the good things of the world to everyone. The superiority of a monarchical regime emerges from its role as benefactor and from its outstanding success in the field of government.[11]

So enthusiastic a view of the monarchy of the Roman Empire is the result of the fact that all the subject peoples form parts of a harmonious whole; first and foremost, the Jewish people, who in the vision of Philo actually form a stabilizing element in the Roman Empire. Within the whole, there coexist different historical and cultural traditions, all assured of freedom to express themselves as they will.[12] The near-divine honours granted to the Emperor are only appropriate to the extent of his power; for a single centre of power is essential, to guarantee peace, social and political stability, the distribution of favours, freedom of trade, justice for everyone. The man who has brought all this about stands in sharp opposition to the era of the civil wars; he is not their consequence or their heir, as in most contemporary works of history in Latin. Only intellectuals in ivory towers could object that universal peace had put an end to creative internal conflict or stimulating competition between states, and brought about political servitude and cultural conformism.[13] It was only after the tragic experience of the fall of Jerusalem that Josephus countered the optimistic account of Philo with a more realistic version, composing of the Roman Empire a bitter description worthy of Tacitus: an empire built on force and terror which destroyed every trace of independence among the subject peoples.[14]

On the other hand, to see the Roman Empire as a force for peace and unity involves seeing it as a political form which has created new types of relationship, in substance equal, between the ruling Roman element and the other peoples of the Empire. An interpretation along these lines starts from the premiss, visible in Nicolaus and explicit in Philo, that the fundamental element in the harmonious whole is Greek culture.

III

The historical vision of the Empire which we have been discussing attaches a central importance to the political and administrative mechanisms of the state, their actual functioning, as seen and judged by the subject peoples. This approach characterizes all historical writing about the Empire in Greek down to Cassius Dio. It is of course obvious that the origins of this approach can already be traced in Polybius, for instance in the preface to Book III and in Book VI, and also in Posidonius. Strabo's awareness of the civilizing mission of Rome does not simply result from his acceptance of the ideology of the Augustan age; rather it derives from independent reflection on the new dimensions of historical and geographical knowledge, which were the result of the expansion and consolidation of Roman rule; others had already thought along similar lines in the Hellenistic period. At the same time, a single centre of power was essential for the maintenance of civilized life and was a guarantee of peace and well-being. The Roman creation of new and better forms of life was evident in recently conquered barbarian lands, such as Gaul and Spain; it was indeed in historical terms the justification of the act of conquest.[15]

The pre-eminence of Greek culture, recognized by Nicolaus and Philo, recalls the political and cultural interests of Dionysius of Halicarnassus and their historical expression. According to the view expressed in the preface of *De antiquis oratoribus*,[16] the consolidation of Roman rule and the support given to the right-thinking upper classes of the Greek cities meant the end of Asianic culture, popular and debased, and the renascence of classical Greek culture, as represented by the great orators of the fourth century BC, and of the high political and moral ideals of which this culture was the standard-bearer. Classical culture, by its very nature élitist, was to form the basis of the new social and political order of the Roman Empire, for Greek city and Roman élite alike.

These developments were the prerequisite for a new administrative order, soundly based, in which the upper classes of the Greek world could envisage a role for themselves. It is in this context that the *Roman Antiquities* makes sense. There were of course negative aspects, such as moral and political corruption and the civil wars, and there was no need to accept the whole of the Augustan ideology; but the hegemony of Rome was legitimated by her Greek origins and by the high ideals and real virtues which had marked and indeed brought about her rise. Dionysius rejects hostile stories about the origins of Rome and unfavourable versions of her history.

Early Rome is presented as a model and a source of assurance for present and future alike. The policy of assimilating the conquered and the outsider of merit, in particular those of high birth, was a constant element in the history of Rome. On this basis it was possible for a Greek intellectual to move on from the role which had been typical of the first century BC, that of an adviser fawning on a Roman general, to a real political function in the new order of things.

The fact that Dionysius took up once more the notion of a mixed constitution in its original sense naturally meant in essence that he accorded a central role to the educated upper classes; for it is not really possible to see the Augustan system in terms of a mixed constitution.[17]

IV

With the history of Dionysius, we are in the middle of the age of Augustus. Indeed, despite the content of his narrative, we are far removed from the political interests and historio-graphical approaches of the senatorial upper class with its republican traditions. Rather, we are at the beginning of a political and cultural tradition which tended ever more to accept the existence of the imperial system and sought to integrate the upper classes of the Greek world into it. This tradition is one of the most important elements in the history of the first two centuries of the Empire. The attitude of Philo may of course in part be explained in terms of the position of his family; but without understanding the intellectual aspects of the attitude it is impossible to understand the policy of Tiberius Julius Alexander. The political and cultural horizons of Strabo are the same as those of Dionysius. In the middle of the first century AD, a Platonic philosopher, Onasander, actually dedicated a monograph on generalship to a Roman consul and army commander; in it, he unhesitatingly inserted motifs from Greek history of the fourth century BC, in order to show that Roman military success was dependent on the use of Greek techniques.[18] Arrian, a Roman magistrate and a Greek historian, possessed of course a quite different level of know-ledge and held a quite different position; but he combined the writing of the history of Alexander and the Successors with the writing of technical military treatises and accounts of contemporary history. There were of course other approaches, but they were in the minority. Plutarch was opposed to the process of integration, for instance, and did not envisage the possibility of going beyond a stage of limited co-operation between Romans and Greeks, even if he recognized that the two peoples had common interests and accepted the essential equality of their histories and cultures.[19]

V

It was Aelius Aristides who provided a theoretical account of the process of integration which I have described and of the historical developments associated with it; this theoretical account was intended to serve as the basis for a rethinking of history. The results are presented, for instance, in the speech *To Rome*.[20] The position of Aristides is the opposite of Romano-centric and the relationship between principate and freedom consequently means nothing to him. He is not concerned with Roman national ideals, because *Romanità* is now a matter of culture. Aristides deals with the Empire from the point of view of the Greek cities which form part of it, and quite consciously picks up the ideals of the Greek cities of the classical period: the Empire is as it were a city, with every element in harmony. It is the administration of this city-empire and the various forms which this administration takes that characterise the structure of the state. In contrast to the primitive and capricious despotism of the Persians, the Roman administrative system is seen, and of course idealized, as a model of efficiency, control, smooth functioning, with no room for dangerous individual initiatives. There is a general hierarchical structure, with the Emperor at its head, and with magistrates and officials endowed with the role of acting as intermediaries between the head and the population as a whole. Existing social differences of course find their place in this framework, but there is also a fundamental equality between all subjects, and overall liberty. The Empire is a true world democracy; it guarantees peace and security. Indeed, the ultimate aim of Roman rule is the creation of a universal state covering the entire civilized world.

Liberty and peace exist together under the Empire; Tacitus had taken a rather different view shortly before. In the world as seen by Aristides, everyone is a citizen or may become one. The policy of grants of citizenship, of assimilation, of an administration open to talent was naturally applied to the better element among the subject peoples and in particular to the Greek cities; the policy was also implemented in the context of the army. We are faced with a concept of liberty which is clearly not that of the Republic. Equally, Aristides' view of the monarch, in whose eyes all are equal, safe in the enjoyment of their freedom under the Empire, has very little to do with those views of a *princeps* which were principally concerned with how far his position could be reconciled with political liberty of a traditional kind; yet it was such views which had occupied the minds of a large part of the senatorial class during the first century AD, both in the sphere of politics and in that of history.

The administrative system forms in fact the meeting-point between the central authority and the subject population. It is not the bureaucratic aspects of the administration which are idealized, but its capacity to bring the various elements of society into a harmonious relationship with each other, in freedom and under the rule of law. In a sense, Aristides finally resolves a problem which had been left open by Polybius in the preface to Book III: Roman rule was to be judged by the manner in which it dealt with those subjected to it. Polybius never dreamt of a monarchic system which was to convert subjects into partners, sharing equally with Romans the responsibility for running properly a state which conferred such benefits on its members. One may go on to observe that Aristides' account of the administrative practice of the Empire replaces Polybius' account of the political system of the Republic.[21]

VI

Aristides' analysis, with its attempt to provide an integral account of the whole, is fundamental to an understanding of Appian and Dio; both were members of the Roman ruling class, as Arrian was earlier; and it was they who provided a historical presentation of the universalist interpretation which we have been considering, or perhaps rather provided a historical account of the origins and development of an empire seen in this way. Precisely because they shared in the exercise of power, both men, and in particular Dio, found themselves faced with the need to defend their position and that of the class to which they belonged against the growing claims of the monarchy, which had evolved in a way not foreseen by Aristides.

Appian's preface opens with a detailed geographical description of the Empire, and includes an encomium of the monarchic system, which has brought concord, order, security, and lasting peace to all the peoples of the Empire.[22] All that is necessary to demonstrate the superior qualities of the Roman system is to engage in the standard comparison with the earlier empires of the Mediterranean world. The actual history of Rome was dealt with partly in books devoted to the different regions where the Romans had fought wars of conquest, partly in books devoted to specific themes. To the second group belonged the lost book which dealt with the composition of the armed forces and with the income– and expenditure–account of the Roman Empire.[23] I think that this is the only known case of a historian in antiquity including in his work an independent account of administrative matters. Short digressions, related specifically to the narrative, occur of course in Fabius Pictor, Polybius, Josephus, and Dio. Appian, who was perhaps an imperial administrator, must have given a quantified account of the fiscal base of the Roman Empire and indeed probably also described its historical evolution. By including this material in his history Appian necessarily also regarded it as relevant to his evaluation of the Empire. If there is any precedent, it lies in the attempt to present a balanced picture of the Empire which Augustus himself made when he drew up his *rationarium* and *breviarium totius imperii*,[24] and when he wrote the *Res Gestae* and included the list of his expenses.

The importance attached to administrative processes is in fact a corollary of belief in the inevitability of the monarchic system, which had conferred on the inhabitants of the Empire precisely that peace and tranquillity which mattered to Appian, and which he defended against the attacks of popular philosophers seeking to disturb the peace. It was to make clear the benefits of monarchy that Appian provided a detailed description of the disasters and the endless ills which were the consequences of the civil wars.[25] Appian knew perfectly well that the last of the party leaders had succeeded in establishing and handing on despotic power, and that this was the origin and basis of the Imperial system.[26] In any case, the account of the civil wars from 63 to 36 BC is in no way favourable to Caesar or to Octavian. The loss of the *Aegyptiaca* means that we cannot know how Appian, a Greek from Egypt who makes no attempt to hide his nostalgia for the kings who once ruled his land, saw the final battle at Actium. One may even suppose that to a certain extent he accepted the standard division of the life of Octavian into two phases, and that he placed the turning-point after 36 BC, with the first attempts at the restoration of peace and a return to legality.[27] In fact, in describing the Illyrian campaign of Octavian in his *Illyrica*, Appian certainly followed the account which Augustus himself gave in his *De vita sua*. But the hypothesis that Appian accepted the notion of a turning-point after 36 BC remains a hypothesis. What is clear is that Appian sometimes followed traditions favourable to Augustus, sometimes the opposite, without attempting to harmonize them; and that this fact is to be explained in terms of a complete indifference to political events and decisions and ideologies which belonged to the distant past. One is reminded of the well-known passage in the *Annales* of Tacitus dealing with the Punic Wars.[28] Whatever political significance the distant past may have had was now irrelevant to the handling of the quite different problems which concerned an imperial administrator of Greek origin of the middle of the second century AD, turned historian.

VII

The problem of interpreting Dio, a much greater historian, whose work is fundamental to an understanding of the Augustan Principate, is strictly analogous.[29] There are still some modern scholars who wonder where the original thought of Dio is to be found. The answer seems obvious, namely first and foremost in the speeches; these are usually placed at particularly critical moments and are sometimes to a certain degree at odds with the narrative sequence. The original thought of Dio is also to be found in the sections describing institutions or administrative problems, in which he shows a special interest. In the course of the straightforward narrative of historical events, one sometimes comes across unresolved problems or passages which have not been adequately related to their context. The sheer scale of Dio's *History* from the origins of Rome down to his own day, the difficulty of mastering a large number of sources, the failure to rethink the data which they provided, the adoption of the attitudes of the sources, the consequent juxtaposition of opposite points of view – all this may be explained in terms of Dio's limited interest in events of the distant past. Instead, he preferred to intervene directly and expound his own point of view in the speeches and the technical digressions. Naturally, the period close to, or contemporary with, the historian poses different problems. Speeches and digressions are here the elements which offer an analysis as opposed to a purely descriptive narrative.

There are of course divergences in the ways in which Octavian and Augustus are represented and assessed, but they should not be exaggerated. Hostile stories and analyses of Octavian, recognition of Augustus' hypocrisy and lack of scruple, none of this serves to modify Dio's basically favourable judgement of the first Emperor, as is clear from the funeral oration pronounced by Tiberius in Book LVI. Furthermore, a decisive element for the understanding of Dio is the sometimes explicit, but usually implicit comparison between the age of Augustus and his own day. The past is important in so far as it survives in the present. To show how the monarchic system of the Empire came into being, to expound the hypocrisy, the cruelty, the danger associated with the exercise of power, to locate in the age of Augustus a theoretical account of conspiracy against the Emperor – all of this is an approach to explaining the present and to understanding Septimius Severus.[30]

Some central concepts stand out clearly throughout the work of Dio, above all the necessity of monarchy. A monarchic system is imposed by the size of the Roman state and by the variety, and, in some cases, the importance of the peoples who belong to it. There are in Tacitus occasional passing references to this line of argument, but there is no urge to elaborate it.[31] In Dio, on the other hand, the approach is argued through with full documentation, and related to the specific ways in which the state functioned. The equation of a republican or a democratic system with a small state and of a monarchy with a vast territorial state was of course a *locus classicus*. The important part of the problem was how to prevent monarchy ending up as despotism. Monarchy is thus for Dio, for reasons which are almost automatic, a matter of fact which is not worth discussing. It follows that the argument that the only way to obtain peace after the civil wars was to grant sole power to one man has no particular importance for Dio. Where the idea does exist, it provides evidence for nostalgic longing for the past and a reluctant sacrifice of political liberty and democracy; the idea is prominent in history writing by senators down to Tacitus. But Dio can have had no regrets whatever for the Roman Republic. The republican arguments placed in Agrippa's mouth in the debate in Book LII are interesting for the economic and fiscal observations which accompany them; but they are no more than a necessary record of points of view which were relevant in 29 BC, and are not accepted by Dio. One may even say that by placing the debate of Book LII precisely in 29 BC, Dio aimed to capture the moment when the secular argument over the choice between monarchy and republic ceased to have any historical significance.[32]

Sheer necessity put an end to the Roman Republic. Dio repeats again and again that it was necessity which conditioned the actions of Octavian during the period of the civil wars. The first Emperor could only show himself in his true political colours after 31 BC, when he was no longer under the iron constraint of necessity.[33] In this way, the standard division of the life of Octavian into two phases is carried further and placed in the context of an overall historical vision.

According to Dio, Augustus realized that although he was obliged to make his innovations within the framework of a claim to restore what had been destroyed, and had to take account of existing political forces, the Roman state needed to rationalize the ways in which the central authority and the subject population related to each other and to adjust its administrative machinery. Augustus is described by Dio as the man who established a complex of administrative norms and practices, which of course then evolved over time. This is the point of the speech of Maecenas in Book LII, with Dio's specific comment that the suggestions not immediately adopted by Augustus were put into effect later.[34] The speech of Maecenas, and indeed the whole of Book LII, are barely intelligible without Book LIII, as is made clear by the references from one to the other.[35] In Book LII, Maecenas lays down guide-lines on major political and administrative issues, intended to be valid over a long period. In Book LIII, Dio inserts in his narrative the description of the practical applications of the general principles just enunciated; as Dio states explicitly on several occasions, here as in Book LII, the framework of reference goes beyond the strict chronological limits of Augustus' reign.[36] Likewise the list of legions at LV. 23–4, goes beyond the reign of Augustus; it forms an introduction to a treatment of financial problems in relation to army pay, the *praemia militiae*, the introduction of the *aerarium militare*, and the empirical search for financial resources.[37] The lost book of Appian dealt with precisely these problems.

In Dio's analysis of the Empire, the Emperor has a more active and less idealized role than in Aelius Aristides' speech *To Rome*. A senator from Bithynia, Dio had a very different career, and knew very well that the decision-making power of the Emperor was indispensable; he also knew from his own experience the range over which imperial power was exercised.[38] The fundamental problem is thus to see how the imperial power was established and legitimized, both at its origin and in the framework of the Empire as a whole. For this reason, as indeed with Aelius Aristides, Dio's aim is to achieve a realistic characterization of the position of the ruling class of the Empire in the political, administrative, and social life of the state. The ruling class, according to Dio, must be chosen from the upper classes of the whole Empire, as was indeed increasingly the case.[39]

For Dio, the senatorial class and to a lesser extent the *equites* serve the Emperor by acting as intermediaries between the central authority and the population as a whole. Dio's defence of the two groups, and in particular of the senatorial class, has nothing whatever to do with the nostalgia for the political power of the Roman aristocracy that we find in the first century AD and in Tacitus. Dio belongs in the tradition of Aelius Aristides and sees the imperial system as the realization of a true world democracy, in which every group and social class has its fixed and proper position, with its own rights and duties, and hence with its proper degree of freedom. We have come a long way from any notion of a mixed constitution. In Dio's hierarchically organized world, the population as a whole is expected to know its place, which is quite different from that of the armed forces, despite the fact that these were recruited from it. The advantages in social and political terms of a professional army, separate from the rest of the body politic, are described with great clarity. It seems not impossible, though one cannot be certain, that the splendid pages of Adam Smith on the social and economic significance of a standing army, seen as evidence of progress since it reflects a division of labour, draw on the arguments of Dio and Aristides.[40]

The central position of the senatorial class in the arguments and proposals of Maecenas is directly related to the dangerous and uncertain position in which it found itself in the age of Severus. Dio makes no attempt to hide the fact that conspiracies against the Emperor usually originated among the upper classes, and that the motives of those involved were lofty.[41] In concrete terms, the economic considerations advanced in the speech of Maecenas (and indeed also in that of Agrippa) are linked with a need for greater economic independence for the senatorial class and hence also for guarantees of its position. This independence was indispensable for the continuation of the role envisaged for the senatorial class by Dio.

The creation of the new imperial system by Augustus had involved the reorganization of the army and of the administration of the provinces; it had, however, had little effect on the precarious financial situation of the Empire, which was a permanent source of worry for an Emperor. The three chapters in the speech of Maecenas which deal with this problem offer detailed proposals for reviving the economy and restoring agriculture; the chapters in question provide a perfect example of the relationship between Dio's treatment of the Principate of Augustus and contemporary concerns, which are of real and immediate interest to him.[42] Some misrepresentation of the first Emperor is inevitable; but the power of tradition, the constant reappearance of the same problems and the continuity of imperial policy will have ensured that the area of choice under Augustus and under Severus was much the same. Dio provides a historical account, from Augustus to his own day, of the emergence of the imperial system. Administrative problems are dealt with from the point of view of the functioning of institutions and from that of the participation of the upper classes. Dio is just as interested in the prerogatives of his class as Tacitus had been; that class, however, was very different from what it had been in the age of the Flavians and Trajan. Dio sees the Empire as a whole, in which senators, Equites and upper classes in general fulfil the role of intermediaries between Emperor and people; by contrast Tacitus had still in the traditional manner identified the state and its well-being with the ruling class to which he belonged.

VIII

In dealing with the reign of Augustus, Tacitus and Dio alike had for the most part used the accounts written in the first century AD; in these accounts there were no doubt already differing interpretations of Augustus.[43] Both historians obviously followed those versions which best fitted their overall political vision. For Tacitus, monarchy was the only way out of the civil wars; for Dio, it was in absolute terms the best possible form of government for a state of his own day and the guarantor of true liberty.

The distance between the two historians is enormous. One example must suffice. In Book LIII. 19 Dio explains why it is that it was less possible to know about imperial history than about republican. The reasons are technical and do not give rise to a hostile political analysis. The power of decision-making now belongs to the Emperor, and not collectively to public bodies. The absence of public knowledge means that motives and processes of causation must remain uncertain; there is also the fact that the ruling power reveals what it chooses and in the way it chooses. Dio in fact in no way disapproves, since he has already, at LII. 15, placed in the mouth of Maecenas the recommendation to Augustus to reserve to himself the right to make political decisions. A more important factor is the sheer size of the Empire, which makes it difficult to know everything that is going on inside and outside the frontiers; the result is that the attention of a historian tends to be concentrated on the narrow field of Rome and the court.

Tacitus approaches the same problem in quite a different way in the prefaces of his major works and elsewhere. The difficulty of knowing what happened, and hence the thankless task of a historian of the Empire, derives from the political situation, involving the loss of freedom. The deformation of the truth in one direction or another is the result. For the Elder Seneca, the writing of history suffered from diminished attention to the truth with the civil wars, perhaps from 49 BC.[44] Tacitus at the beginning of the *Historiae* treats Actium as the dividing line. The fact that historians play no part in decision-making and hence in the running of the state means that they lack experience; this defect in a historian is just as grave as a party spirit. This harsh general judgement seems to include Livy.[45] Tacitus obviously starts from the premiss that a historian should still, as under the Republic, be a politician, directly responsible for political affairs and hence capable of understanding them; in fact, under the Empire, a historian was entirely excluded from the political process, which was the prerogative of the Emperor and the court. At the beginning of the *Annales*, Tacitus appears to be more optimistic than in the *Historiae*, and seems to trace the beginning of the decadence of history writing to the reign of Tiberius, even if the age of Augustus had already seen a decline in the political position and moral authority of the class which might produce historians. In *Annales* IV. 32–3, before the debate on Cremutius Cordus in the Senate, Tacitus offers a theoretical account of the transition from a richly textured narrative history, to one of no importance in which nothing happened, in fact to a sort of psychological history. History and the writing of history are directly related to the political system of the time; with the arrival of despotism, analysis of the behaviour of the Emperor and of senators in relation to him provides bitter confirmation of the view that a knowledge of history is useful.

IX

Tacitus' theoretical account of the relationship between access to knowledge and the truthfulness or otherwise of works of history, together with the role assigned to political freedom, necessarily implies a critical view of Augustus and of the Empire. A view of this kind had been generously tolerated during the reign of Augustus, and even later it was possible to hold it, except perhaps under Tiberius.[46] To hold such a view did not automatically imply opposition to the imperial system or to a particular Emperor, or a desire to restore a senatorial Republic. The good, or at any rate reasonable relations between Augustus and Asinius Pollio are no objection to the hypothesis that the unfavourable tradition on Octavian followed by Appian in Books IV and V of the civil wars may derive from Pollio.[47] The plausibility or otherwise of the hypothesis must be assessed in other ways.

In any case, Latin historiography on the origins of the Principate and on Augustus is the sphere of authors belonging to the senatorial class. The Principate is portrayed, rightly, as the outcome of the civil wars. Augustus is seen as the last of the great revolutionary military leaders. Any biography, or indeed autobiography, of the first Princeps must explain his behaviour during the civil wars. The civil wars, indeed, determined the pessimistic tone of Latin historiography from Sallust to Tacitus. The last phase of the free state is also involved, at least from 60 BC; but one could of course trace the political and moral roots of the problem further back, to 146 BC, or at least to Sulla.

But the civil wars continued to be a real historical and political problem even after 31 BC, as Livy shows, because only their causes allow one to judge their outcome, in whatever way one does so. Such judgements are closely related to political attitudes. Many historians had belonged to the losing side or were close to it for ideological or class reasons. In any case, we know of a wide variety of opinions, which the Augustan regime had no intention of suppressing. This was so not least because it would have been extremely difficult to suppress unwelcome interpretations of so recent a past. Only the passage of time and the death of the protagonists will have allowed in due course the emergence of a pattern of censorship, because at that stage the revival of republican sentiments might appear spontaneous and dangerous.

Latin historiography on the origins of the Principate preserves the propagandist motifs of the period, often defamatory; the propaganda had of course been a weapon in the various battles between politicians on different sides; its content was gradually toned down as it came to form the basis of historical judgements. Material of this kind is woven into Suetonius' biography of Augustus in large quantities, though here it seems to have lost all historical significance. It is in this context that the *De vita sua* of Augustus belongs;[48] it is very different, even if the content·in some cases overlaps, from the later *Res Gestae*. The rich supply of memoirs of the early imperial age was the work of the protagonists in the civil wars, faced with the need to explain and defend political decisions, changes of position, their entire role in the unfolding of the story of those years.

In this context, the standard motifs of imperial ideology – *clementia, pax, res publica restituta* – cannot but seem useful fictions, called into being to mask or legitimate a policy of suppression of liberty. Caesar Augustus managed to emerge victorious from the civil wars after resorting to political compromises of every kind, which could not simply be forgotten, even if his later career could be seen as belonging to a different historical period. Octavian's need to manoeuvre his way by devious means through the storm of the civil wars was recognised even by historians favourable to him; for those who were hostile or unsympathetic, the man who held sole power was always and necessarily a hypocrite.

The themes of security, tranquillity, and peace propagated by the regime could be turned to unfriendly ends. Peace was the result of the enforced and regretted loss of liberty in order to achieve a greater good. It was provincials in particular who appreciated the benefits of peace, the pursuit of which was the proper aim of any holder of supreme power and the principal basis of his legitimacy. Furthermore, as I have already remarked, peace can even be seen as a symptom of decline or of psychological and cultural stagnation, as the result of the loss of moral and political verve. In this context a biological theory of history is fundamentally pessimistic; the arrival of Empire is a stage in the decline of Rome.[49]

X

The authors of histories in Latin belonged in general to the senatorial class, which was deprived by the new regime of its earlier role at the head of affairs. It is these historians who identified republican freedom with their own pre-eminent position; it is they who linked playing a part in decision-making with freedom of opinion and the ability to write history truthfully; these were men, in fact, accustomed to make and to write history. This was the class which was the loser in the civil wars. In much the same position, naturally, are those who clung to an idealized vision of republican history, even if they did not go so far as to identify with the nostalgia of the senatorial class and did not care to pander to the tastes of those who continued to be fascinated by the civil wars. Livy is a case in point.[50] His reconstruction of the early Republic involved acceptance of the aristocratic ideology of the senatorial class and of its values. It is for this reason that Augustus regarded him as a Pompeian; it is also for this reason that he ended up being critical of Cicero. Late in the day, Livy took over the myth of early Rome and he remained fascinated by it; he contrasted it with the present, precisely at the moment when the myth was disappearing into the mist.

Livy's preface belongs in an early phase of the conception and composition of the work; it can be dated to 27–25 BC. It is thus slightly earlier than the *De vita sua* of Augustus, the *History* of Pollio and the *Life* of Nicolaus. The moral and material consequences of the civil wars are still very much present. The present and the immediate future are far from clear or secure. But temporary flight to and refuge in the early history of Rome is not an indication of an unwillingness to face the present; rather it is for Livy a quite deliberate distancing of himself from the present, a placing of himself in deliberate opposition. It involves an ideological choice just as much as does the decision to write on the civil wars. But Livy's pessimism does not appear only in the preface. His awareness of a moral decline and a loss of religious sense is ever present;[51] one cannot suppose that Livy had any trust in the programme of Augustus to restore moral values and religious belief.[52] Livy is aware that the sheer size of the Empire is a source of weakness;[53] he documents the depopulation of regions of Italy once full of people and sources of manpower;[54] he implicitly concludes that the decline in Italian manpower is at the root of the military weakness of the Augustan Empire. The apogee of Roman power is placed in the period of the Hannibalic War, the peak of Roman virtue in the age of the Samnite Wars.[55]

It may be that in his account of the recent past and of contemporary affairs Livy faithfully followed the version of events and their interpretation provided by the *princeps*; but it is clear that in the books which survive Livy is doubtful or outright sceptical of the reality of the moral revival claimed by the regime. One is forced to ask whether Livy can even in part be regarded as Augustan. As far as his attitudes and sentiments are concerned, he seems to belong to a category of losers.

XI

Within the senatorial class there were of course those to whom the traditions of the republican aristocracy were alien and who had never shared in the senatorial monopoly of the writing of history. Their traditions were different and it was precisely the civil wars and the Principate which had allowed them to move from the middle classes, or even lower, to the highest levels of society. Their social ambitions were entirely legitimate and they were skilful at inserting themselves in the new order. They did not idealize the past and they were entirely satisfied with the new regime. Tacitus does not even allude to them, unless perhaps he includes them among the group cursorily condemned in *Annales* I. 2 – 'ceteri nobilium, quanto quis servitio promptior, opibus et honoribus extollerentur ac novis ex rebus aucti tuta et praesentia quam vetera et periculosa mallent.' Velleius Paterculus belongs in this category.[56] Of a pro-Roman Italian family, he records with satisfaction his ancestors, and speaks readily of himself, because he is aware of his meteoric rise.[57] It is perhaps for this reason that he turned to the writing of history, to provide a cultural context for his own person. Velleius is interested in the cause of the *socii Italici* in the Social War,[58] less interested in republican liberty. The battle for *libertas* is not his problem, but in the appropriate historical context he speaks with respect of Cicero – against Antonius – and in due course also of Brutus and Cassius.[59] Velleius is an optimist, where Tacitus is a pessimist. He resembles in some ways Marcus Aper in the *Dialogus de oratoribus*, a man of similar origins, proud of his own rise, untouched by aristocratic traditions; it was Marcus Aper who denied the decline of eloquence.[60]

The rise of *novi homines* into the ruling class, during the Republic as well as during the Principate, is something of which Velleius approves, and not only because it gives him an excuse to praise Sejanus.[61] The progressive assimilation of Italy into the Roman citizenship is a similar process; for Velleius this is what republican history is really about. But, parvenu as he is, he cannot help respecting the great men of the republican aristocracy, whether they were related to the imperial family and prepared to die for its cause or whether they were simply men who conveyed their support to the new regime in good time. There is nothing surprising in the fact that Velleius follows the Augustan view of the historical and political significance of the battle of Actium;[62] this view lies at the basis of his sense of history. Apart from remarks about the world-wide significance of the Empire, Velleius sees it as essentially the institution which ensures military victory for the Roman people.[63] Velleius had himself helped in some cases to win the victory. In the same way, in the two digressions in which Velleius characterizes republican history, Rome and Italy are seen as partners in a policy of expansion and conquest.[64] It is precisely because of Velleius' total loyalty to the dynasty, cemented in the shared perils of military service, that he is able to talk with military frankness of the scandals of the imperial family, obviously taking Tiberius' side.[65]

At the cost of contradicting Sir Ronald Syme[66] I believe that Velleius gives us a better idea than Tacitus of the atmosphere in Rome at the moment of the death of Augustus; it was a moment of fear and confusion.[67] Tacitus is far from events, which he takes for granted; in his secure knowledge of the outcome, Tacitus allows sarcasm to transform his account of the succession into a farce, in which hypocrisy, adulation, and servility all play their part. But Augustus' speculation on the *capaces imperii* allows us to see that the inevitability of despotism did not mean automatically the succession of another member of the family.[68] Hence the rumours of the real or presumed manoeuvres of Livia on behalf of Tiberius, who always remained, however, the son of Augustus' enemy. Suetonius has left a clear description of the insecurity of Rome and her government after the disaster of AD 9.[69] It is too easy to forget that divergent historical interpretations of Augustus' person and career derive from divergent political attitudes; the conspiracies against Augustus tell the same story. It was the *maiestas* of Tiberius, admitted even by Tacitus, which calmed men's fears and evaporated the dangers.[70]

XII

The dramatic vicissitudes in the private and public life of Augustus might easily have given rise to an interpretation of the Emperor based on the themes of *fortuna* and *felicitas*. It was an approach often applied where it was necessary to judge a great and controversial figure, since it gave an impression of impartiality and detachment, attributing everything to the force of ineluctable destiny. In fact, the well-known passage of Pliny, *Natural History* VII. 147–50, in a sense collects everything that there is in the way of anti-Augustan historiography based on the approach I have outlined.[71] The final element in the account, which is as a whole negative, is Augustus' failure to organize the succession as he wished, conferring it finally on the son of his political enemy. It is not clear how far the passage echoes attitudes current under the Flavian dynasty and judgements then current of Augustus and Tiberius. Certainly the tone is in no way pro-republican and Pliny seems implicitly to be contrasting Augustus with the present holders of imperial power. What is clear is that Pliny's negative view of Augustus covers the whole of his political life, beginning with his relationship with Caesar and including its later part, often seen in a positive light even by those who were not favourable overall.

Critical or hostile comments are always the expressions of opinion of traditionalist groups within the senatorial class.

Political and historical judgement are passed on Emperor and Empire in terms of the relationship established with old and new elements of the governing class and in terms of the attitude taken to its privileges. The bitter memory of the civil wars, of the origins of the Principate, is always present in interpretations along these lines. They are concerned almost exclusively with the exercise of power and the holder of power. Tacitus belongs at the end of this line of historians, whose activity covers over a century. He possesses a detailed knowledge of the divergent and indeed opposed interpretations of the career of Augustus. Carefully and painfully, he chose the overall evaluation which placed Augustus in a negative light and which was that of the traditionalist group of senators. The more one is obliged to admit the inevitability of a monarchic regime, the more essential it is to claim the right of the Senate to independent action. The difficult and unlikely reconciliation of two opposites may occur if lucky chance provides a good Emperor, or if a man possesses the rare ability to avoid abject servility and sterile opposition, while devoting his life to the service of the state. In other words, political attitudes and behaviour come down to questions of character and psychology. The paradigm of a servant of the state is of course Agricola; and it is worth remarking that in the value which Tacitus attaches to service of the state in describing his career he picks up some of the themes which I have described as characteristic of Greek historians of the Empire.

Tacitus' negative approach to Augustus in the *Annales* depended on the theoretical point that despotism meant an end of freedom, honesty, political participation, and the writing of history, as properly understood. Dio, on the other hand, had chosen a positive view of the imperial regime. In both cases, the choice was to a certain extent the result of the concerns of the ages in which the two men lived. On Tacitus, it would be hard to improve on what Syme has written. For Tacitus, the origin of the imperial regime and the subsequent development of political life are real problems of contemporary relevance. The result is a certain lack of interest in a precise historical location of the historical process, in the forces which originally shaped it. Everything is seen and judged in terms of the concerns which had arisen with hindsight, with resulting deformations and distortions. In *Annales* I. 9–10, the political concerns and historical interpretations of an entire epoch are condensed into a unified account of the merits and demerits of the reign of Augustus, as if in a pair of balancing speeches. The favourable version comes first and is shorter.

The *prudentes* spoke of his reverence for the memory of his father in the triumviral period, of the needs of the *res publica*, of the inevitability of the rule of one man if there was to be an end to civil strife. As far as the Empire was concerned, men recalled his conquests reaching to the ends of the earth, his work of political and administrative reorganization, the return of peace. It is these themes which are picked up and developed by the Greek historians of the Empire, in the context of an attempt to explain the benefits of the imperial system for the provinces.

The hostile version, in evident agreement with the remarks of Pliny, insisted on Octavian's hypocrisy, deceits, betrayals, and lust for power; it listed in minute detail all his machinations and all his crimes, against the Senate, the Pompeian party, Antonius. The achievement involved in bringing about the return of peace was recognized, but also the price paid in terms of defeats at the hands of the enemies of Rome and in terms of conspiracy and bloodshed at home. Family scandals and the conduct of Livia were recalled. It is obvious that Tacitus accepted this hostile version of the first *princeps*, and indeed applied its analytical approach to the reign of Tiberius and beyond. There does not, however, seem to be any political explanation for the attitude of Tacitus. It derives rather from an overall evaluation of the Empire, based largely on moral considerations. Already in *Annales* I. 2 Tacitus had touched on the notion that different political sympathies were the result of different interests and conditioning processes. Such factors, however, are not analysed or investigated in the course of Tacitus' historical narrative, for the simple reason that a different approach is taken for granted a priori. Tacitus' approach was quite different in the *Histories*, where in I. 4. 1 there is a detailed analysis of the forces at work and their origins.[72]

Although Tacitus gives a detailed account of how the succession to Augustus took place, there is hardly any reference to the gravity of a situation in which the capacity of the new regime to perpetuate itself was being tested for the first time.

There is merely a glimpse of the possibility of solutions other than that willed by the late *princeps*. The discussion dwells with unconcealed delight on the character and intentions of the new *princeps*, and carefully avoids any consideration of the uncertainties involved in the process of transition, because the significance of the episode has been reduced to vanishing-point in the course of the long unfolding of the regime. Augustus' discussion towards the end of his life of the *capaces imperii*, a discussion which was certainly neither academic nor empty, appears surreptitiously and incidentally as an excursus in the middle of the debate in the Senate of 17 September, AD 14, when we are presented with a bitter and sarcastic description of the hypocrisy of the Emperor and of the fear and servility of the Senate.

Tacitus is the last, almost impotent protagonist of an approach which applied to the historical interpretation of Augustus and the Empire the unattainable political ideal of a centre of power susceptible to influence from below. It is precisely from the failure of this ideal that Tacitus derives his dramatic capacity to provide a penetrating analysis of the ways in which the imperial power was actually exercised.

NOTES

I should like to thank Michael Crawford for translating this essay and for comment and discussion while it was being written.

1. For surveys of the historical sources, see E. Egger, *Examen critique des historiens anciens de la vie et du règne d'Auguste* (1844); *CAH* IX, 866 ff., Appendix: 'The literary authorities for Roman History, 44 BC–AD 70' (1934); A. Ferrabino, 'L'imperatore Cesare Augusto', in *Augustus. Studi in occasione del Bimillenario Augusteo* (1938), 1 ff.
2. Suet. *Tib*. 61. 3; Dio LVII. 24. 3; see R. Syme, *Roman Papers* I, 441.
3. Tac. *Ann*. I. 35. 3.
4. Joseph., *Vita*, 361–7.
5. Jacoby, *FGrH* 90 F 125, 126 (1–2); the general sense has clearly not been changed by the excerptor (Jacoby II C, 265). Cf. B. Z. Wacholder, *Nicolaus of Damascus* (1962); G. Dobesch, 'Nikolaos von Damaskus und die Selbstbiographie des Augustus', *Gräzer Beiträge* 7 (1978), 91 (fundamental); on the preface B. Scardigli, *Studi ital. filol. class.* 50 (1978), 245 ff. See also B. Scardigli, 'Asinius Pollio und Nikolaos von Damaskos', *Historia* 32 (1983), 12.
6. *FGrH* 90 F 135.
7. Texts of the inscriptions and full commentary by U. Laffi, *Studi Class. e. Orient.* 16 (1967), 5.

8. Vell. II. 89. 2; 92. 2; Suet. *Aug.* 98. 1–3.
9. F. Fabbrini, *L'impero di Augusto come ordinamento sovranazionale* (1974); cf. Gabba, *Clio* 11 (1975), 251–3.
10. *Legatio ad Gaium*, 143–7.
11. *Legatio*, 149; L. Troiani, *Athenaeum* 56 (1978), 304; idem, 'Gli Ebrei e lo stato pagano in Filone e Giuseppe', in *Ricerche di storiografia antica* II (1980), 195 ff.
12. *Legatio*, 153.
13. *On the Sublime*, 44; Pliny, *NH* XIV. 1–6: E. Gabba, 'Political and Cultural Aspects of the Classical Revival in the Augustan Age', *Classical Antiquity* 1 (1982), 55–6.
14. E. Gabba, 'L'impero romano nel discorso di Agrippa II (Ioseph., B.I. II, 345–401', *Rivista storica dell'Antichità* 6–7 (1976–7), 189.
15. Gabba, *Classical Antiquity* 1 (1982), 59–61; G. Mancinelli Santamaria, 'Strabone e l'ideologia augustea', *Annali Facoltà Lettere Perugia* 16. 1 (1978–9), 129 ff.
16. *de ant. orat.* I. 1–3; Gabba, *Classical Antiquity* 1 (1982), 43–50.
17. Even if it is an anachronism, the theory has a wider importance, since it reflects the fundamental role accorded to the upper classes and admits the possibility of assimilating worthy outsiders; cf. Lord Acton, *Essays on Freedom and Power* (1957), 71.
18. D. Ambaglio, 'Il trattato "Sul comandante" di Onasandro', *Athenaeum* 59 (1981), 353.
19. P. A. Stadter, *Arrian of Nicomedia* (1980). The position of Plutarch emerges from *de exilio* 605 b–c; *de tranq. animi* 470 c.
20. I accept virtually in its entirety the fundamental analysis of J. Bleicken, 'Der Preis des Aelius Aristides auf das Römische Weltreich', *Nachr. Akad. Wiss. Gött.*, Phil.-hist. Kl. 1966, no. 7, 225 ff.; J. H. Oliver, *The Ruling Power (Trans. Amer. Philos. Soc.* NS. 43, Part 4, 1953, 871–1003), remains important.
21. Dio was to pick the theme up and give it fuller treatment.
22. E. Gabba, *Appiano e la storia delle guerre civili* (1956), 3 ff.
23. *Praef.* 61; I should now put things differently in n. 1 on pp. 81–2 of the book just cited.
24. Suet. *Aug.* 28. 1; 101. 4; Dio LVI. 33. 1.
25. *Praef.* 24; BC I. 24; IV. 61 and 64; *Mithr.* 111.
26. *BC* I. 22: Gabba, *Appiano e la storia delle guerre civili*, 207 ff.
27. *BC* V. 538–49.
28. Tac. *Ann.* IV 33.
29. The most relevant recent work on Dio seems to me to be C. G. Starr, 'The Perfect Democracy of the Roman Empire', *Am. Hist. Rev.* 58 (1952–53), 13 ff.; E. Gabba, 'Sulla Storia Romana di Cassio Dione', *Riv. Stor. Ital.* 67 (1955), 289 ff.; F. Millar, *A Study of Cassius Dio* (1964); (rev. G. W. Bowersock, *Gnomon* 37 (1965), 469 ff.); D. Flach, 'Dio's Platz in der Kaiserzeitlichen Geschichtsschreibung', *Antike und Abendland* 18 (1973), 130 ff.; B. Manuwald, *Cassius Dio und Augustus, philologische Untersuchungen zu den Büchern 45–56 des dionischen Geschichtswerkes* (1979) (rev. M. A. Giua, *Athenaeum* 59 (1981), 254–5); M. A. Giua, 'Clemenza del sovrano e monarchia illuminata in Cassio Dione, 55, 14–22, *Athenaeum* 59 (1981), 317; 'Augusto nel libro 56 della Storia Romana di Cassio Dione', *Athenaeum* 61 (1983), 439; C. Letta, 'La composizione dell'opera di Cassio Dione: cronologia e sfondo storico-politico', in *Ricerche di storiografia greca di età romana* (1979), 117 ff. I have assumed knowledge of F. Millar, *The Emperor in the Roman World* (1977): cf. J. Bleicken, *Zum Regierungsstil des römischen Kaisers. Eine Antwort auf Fergus Millar* (1982).
30. In this context, unresolved dilemmas in the work of Dio are politically and historically valuable and important.

31. Dio LII. 15. 6–16. 4; LVI. 39, 5 and 40. 1; Tac. *Hist.* I. 16. 1: cf. Jos. *AJ* XIX. 162.
32. P. McKechnie, 'Cassius Dio's Speech of Agrippa: a Realistic Alternative to Imperial Government?', *Greece and Rome* 28 (1981), 150 ff.
33. Dio LVI. 44. 1–2.
34. LII. 41. 1–2.
35. LIII. 15. 2 and LII. 25. 6 ff.
36. LIII. 14. 1; 18. 4–5; 22. 3–5 (the passage includes some important reflections on the inextricable confusion which had arisen between outlay by the state and outlay from the private fortune of the Emperor).
37. LV. 25; the problem of expenditure on the army is very grave also in the age of Severus (LXXVII. 9–10), with the Emperor's favouring of the soldiers at the expense of the upper classes.
38. LIII. 17–19. 1. Dio describes well the loneliness of the Emperor, frightened and suspicious.
39. Dio adopts the same line in explaining the position of the Senate, whose meetings are described at LV. 1–6.
40. LII. 27. A. Smith, *An Inquiry into the Nature and Causes of the Wealth of Nations*, edited by E. Cannan (1976), II. 213–37.
41. LV. 16. 3.
42. LII. 28–30; E. Gabba, in *Studi in onore di A. Fanfani* I (1962), 41–68. Cf. LV. 25–6.
43. The common source of the two historians emerges clearly from a comparison of Tac. *Ann.* I. 9–10 with Dio LVI. 43–5; for the problem see Giua, *Athenaeum* 61 (1983), 439.
44. It must be admitted that the well-known phrase 'quisquis legisset eius historias ab initio bellorum civilium, unde primum veritas retro abiit', was used by the son in his *de vita patris* (*HRR* II. 98); and we cannot be absolutely certain that he reproduces the thought or wording of his father: J. Fairweather, *Seneca the Elder* (1981), 16.
45. Tac. *Hist.* I. 1. 1; Syme, *Tacitus* I, 145–6; G. E. F. Chilver, *A Historical Commentary on Tacitus' Historiae I and II* (1979), 35–6.
46. Sen. Rh. *Controv.* II. 4. 13 and IV, *praef.* 5; Sen. *de ben.* III. 27; *Cons. ad Marc.* I. 1–4; M. I. Finley, 'Censura nell'antichità classica', *Belfagor* 32 (1977), 605 ff: also, in English, in *TLS* 1977, 29 July.
47. A. B. Bosworth, 'Asinius Pollio and Augustus', *Historia* 21 (1972), 441; G. Zecchini, 'Asinio Pollione: dall'attività politica alla riflessione storiografica', *ANRW* II. 30, 2 (1982), 1265.
48. According to App. *BC* V. 539 Octavian had already written a similar work after 36 BC.
49. Seneca the Elder in Lactantius, *Div. inst.* VII. 15. 14 (*HRR* II. 91–2); A. Momigliano, 'The Origins of Universal History', *Annali Scuola Norm. Sup. Pisa*, ser. III, 12 (1982), 533 ff.; E. Noè, 'Gli excursus letterari nell'opera storica di Velleio Patercolo, *Clio* 18 (1982), 515.
50. P. Fraccaro, 'Livio e Roma' (1942), in *Opuscula* I (1956), 81 ff.; R. Syme, 'Livy and Augustus' (1959), in *Roman Papers* I (1979), 400 ff.
51. Livy III. 20. 5; IV. 6. 12; VII. 25. 9; VIII. 11. 1; X. 9. 6; XXVI. 22. 14; XLIII. 13. 1.
52. Livy III. 57. 7.
53. *Praef.* 4; VII. 29. 2.
54. Livy. VI. 12. 2.
55. Livy. XXI. 1. 2; IX. 16. 19.
56. G. V. Sumner, 'The Truth about Velleius Paterculus: Prolegomena', *Harv. Stud. Class. Phil.* 74 (1970), 257 ff.; E. Noè, op. cit. (n. 49).
57. II. 16. 2–3; 69. 5; 76. 1; 124. 4.

58. II. 15. 1–2: E. Gabba, 'Italia e Roma nella Storia di Velleio Patercolo', in *Esercito e società nella tarda repubblica romana* (1973), 347.
59. II. 66. 25; 71. 1–2.
60. P. Desideri, 'Lettura storica del Dialogus de oratoribus', *Miscellanea Treves* (forthcoming).
61. II. 127–8; Syme, *Tacitus* II. 570–1.
62. II. 86.
63. II. 89. 6: 'universa imago principatus'.
64. I. 14–15; II. 38–9.
65. II. 93. 2; 100. 2–5; 112. 7.
66. *Roman Revolution*, 410.
67. II. 123. 1; 124. 1–2.
68. Tac. *Ann*. I. 13. 2: R. Syme, *JRS* 45 (1955), 22 ff. = *Ten Studies in Tacitus* (1970), 30 ff.; R. Seager, *Tiberius* (1972), 48 ff.; B. Levick, *Tiberius the Politician* (1976), 68 ff.; M. Pani, *Tendenze politiche della successione al principato di Augusto* (1979).
69. Suet. *Aug*. 23. 1–3.
70. Vell. II. 124. 1; Tac. *Ann*. I. 46. 2; 47. 2.
71. E. Noè, 'Echi di polemica antiaugustea in Plinio, *NH* VII.147–150', *Rend. Istituto Lombardo* 113 (1979), 391 ff.
72. Syme, *Tacitus* I, 147.

IV. AUGUSTUS, GOVERNMENT, AND THE PROPERTIED CLASSES

CLAUDE NICOLET

PREFACE

One does not need to be as sceptical as Tacitus, to be inclined to believe that in most regimes it is the rich (the 'propertied classes') who are in a position to govern. Jean Béranger has recently shown that it was the wealth of the Emperors which, from Augustus onwards, represented the primary condition of power.[1] But this had surely been known since Crassus' famous remark about the need for a *princeps* to be able to support a legion from his own resources. Cicero's protestations were perhaps more genuine than those expressed in the next century by Seneca, concerning his brother Mela's decision to remain as *eques*.[2] During the Empire, as during the Republic before it, there was almost a plethora of choice amongst the speediest ways to fortune offered up by government to clever minds: from tax farming to the propaetorship of Sicily, the *princeps'* procuratorships or the *petitio honorum*. In short, the trappings of power consisted of both wealth and honour.

These generalizations are not enough. Expressions like 'wealth' and 'the propertied classes' can alter their meaning, even over a short period.[3] And in any case, every group or individual understands something different by them, according to circumstances.[4] Where the new regime inaugurated by Augustus is concerned, we must take things one at a time. I propose to treat them as follows: first, if possible, *who* can we call 'the propertied classes' in the new regime? (Who has what? Into what groups do they fall? Who defines them?) Next, how do these groups or individuals relate to the 'government' (another word which will need to be defined)? This question itself has two aspects: the direct part played, whether connected with their wealth or not, by these men in decision–making and administration, on the one hand. On the other, and it may well be the more important, the attitude or conscious policy of the new power with regard to wealth, to its various forms and to the activities which produced or maintained it (an attitude which might perhaps, in the absence of direct evidence, be divined *a contrario* from that towards poverty). This refers equally, for instance, to matters of finance as to legislation regarding goods, property, and contracts.

Civil wars and proscriptions, by the ruin (and death) of some, the good fortune or encroachment of others, had brought about a considerable social upheaval and, in so far as one plutocratic and oligarchic group came, at least in part, to take the place of another, a 'revolution'.[5]

Only very long and detailed study of a fundamentally prosopographical kind could indicate whether, in the forty years of Augustus' reign, the composition of the various levels of propertied persons, with the nature of their estates and the way in which these were acquired, suffered any profound modifications in relation to the preceding period. In any case, such research, being based on extremely fragmentary documentation, produces, at best, only approximations which, frequently, confirm the general impression. But there is another point: a purely economic, 'socio-professional' analysis of Roman society is no more possible for the age of Augustus than it is for the republican period.[6]

I. THE NEW CENSUS STRUCTURE OF THE *ORDINES*: THE SENATORIAL ORDER

The census structure of the Roman citizen body was reformed or restored several times during the reign of Augustus.[7] As it had always previously taken account, among a variety of other qualifications, of the size, and even in some respects, the composition, of its citizens' estates,[8] an analysis of the measures taken by Augustus and the reasons for them ought to provide us with an initial answer to our questions. But we should bear in mind some facts which are frequently forgotten. First, in the massive undertaking of classifying the citizen body (for essentially military, fiscal and political ends) which was called the *census* (as long as it functioned correctly, which is to say until the beginning of the first century BC), estimation of the *rationes pecuniae* was not exclusively determinant.[9] In fact the role of the censors consisted essentially of reviewing, in every case, the sum total of these qualifications including birth, physical ability, moral and professional behaviour – as well, of course, as property qualifications. Whence the emerging notion of *dignitas*.[10] But, for various reasons, these reviews became increasingly rare,[11] and almost certainly more and more difficult for the censors to carry out effectively in the first century BC.[12]

The importance which Augustus, once invested with the supreme power, attached to the institution of the *census* is sufficiently well attested, first by the *regimen morum legumque* (whatever it was called in law) attributed to him by Suetonius as early as 28 (*Aug. 27.* 10), then by the three great censuses he carried out in 28 BC, 8 BC, and AD 14 respectively, and which seem to have involved the entire civil population. But in addition to these general censuses, there were some partial ones, like that in 11 BC (Dio LIV. 35. 1), or in AD 4, this one confined to citizens domiciled in Italy and worth not less than 200,000 sesterces (Dio LV. 13. 4). In the end, as the table which Blumenthal drew up shows,[13] traditional five-year intervals between censuses were almost perfectly observed during Augustus' reign.

1. The Senatorial Census

What part were the strictly financial qualifications to play in his policies? To begin with, we must recall the fundamental rule of republican times which was, as I see it, the necessity (aside from all other conditions) to give proof of a minimal *census* in order to become either a senator or a knight. There was, during the Republic, a 'senatorial census'[14] which was, as far as we can see, no different from the equestrian census.[15]

This, I suggest, is why Dio states that at the moment when he was preparing his reorganization in 29 BC, Octavian realized that there were in the Senate 'contrary to its (required) dignity' 'numerous knights and even a great many foot soldiers',[16] which might certainly refer to centurions, but also to people lacking the equestrian census. Of the purging of the Senate in 28 (Dio LII. 42), we know only that it resulted in the more or less voluntary ejection of 190 persons, who were allowed to retain their *ornamenta*. But about the one in the year 18 we are, again thanks to Dio, much better informed. It is only to be understood, however, within the more general framework of the great moral and civil legislation initiated in 19 BC (*RG* 6). On this occasion, the number of senators was reduced to 600, after which, according to Dio, Augustus permitted all those with a census of 400,000 HS (and who fulfilled all the legal conditions), to be candidates for the magistracy. This was in fact the amount of the senatorial census he set at first. But later on he raised it to 1 million HS.[17] I have explained elsewhere that there may have been an intermediary stage fixed at 800,000 HS, if Suetonius is to be believed (*Aug*. 41. 3), but that on the other hand the figure of 1,200,000 put forward by him later ('ac pro octingintorum millium summa duodecies HS taxavit supplevitque non habentibus') results from a confusion: it was merely that in AD 4 Augustus made an exceptional grant to eighty young senators, bringing their *census* up above the required amount, to the precise figure mentioned by Suetonius.[18]

It is clear therefore that Augustus decided, by stages, to raise the census requirements for the magistracies and for the Senate. What is the significance of this decision, which was not a break with republican custom but nevertheless tended to underline a degree of differentiation between senators and knights? The answer is fairly straightforward and not very far to seek. It was quite simply a matter of strengthening a hierarchy. The Senate was again to become the most prestigious organ of the city; senators (and their *agnati*) would form the first of the *ordines*. They must be distinguished from the second by their wealth, as well as by their *dignitas*. Vespasian was to put this succinctly a century later: 'utrumque ordinem non tam libertate quam dignitate differe'.[19] Dio, in the speech, imaginary of course, but not necessarily untrue,[20] which he gives to Maecenas to serve as a blueprint for the Empire, takes care to state that henceforth the same criteria ought to hold good for recruitment to the Senate and to the equestrian order: birth, individual merit, and wealth.[21] This was not an empty slogan: behind each word there are precise conditions, usually legal ones, as we shall see. It is no accident that, in the everyday language, as well as in the poetry, of the period we find that dignity is founded on these three things: *locus, census, mores*, as the Latin has it.[22] Nor is this new: it was a commonplace of the ancient city; thus did the Athenian 'democracy' recruit its Areopagites (Philochoros, fr. 58), and thus do numerous texts, even dating from the very end of the Republic, when censorial control had disappeared, define membership of the *ordines*: 'qui eo ordine digni habentur' (for instance, Cicero, *Pro Q. Rosc. Com.* 42: 'si ex vita, homo clarissimus est'). But with Augustus, as Dio's Maecenas suggests, a more coherent system was taking shape.

2. *Heredity in the Senatorial Order*

The greatest novelty in his plans concerning the future recruitment to the Senate was not in fact the raising of the *census* required: it was in making an established norm of what under the Republic was only a tendency, the hereditary nature of the office.[23] For one thing, it was now expected that a senator's son would follow the same path – whence, the official recognition of what had been unofficially recognized since the time of the Triumvirate, the privilege for senators' sons of wearing the senatorial symbol of the broad purple stripe. For another, even more important point of view, Augustus made the *hereditary* insignia an additional condition for accession to these honours. As A. Chastagnol has demonstrated, we have excellent proof of this in Dio LIX. 9. 5, a passage showing that before Caligula 'the broad purple stripe conferred the hope of entering the Senate' and that 'only those born into the senatorial order had the right to it'. In this way there was constituted an *ordo senatorius* which from that time would include, beside the actual senators, their children and grandchildren and before long their near relations. A precise definition of this 'order' was all the more necessary in that henceforth it would concern private as well as public law (it had already, under the Republic, become involved with criminal law, through the device of the *leges repetundarum*). For the great social laws (*de adulteriis, de maritandis ordinibus*, the Lex Papia Poppaea, etc.) henceforth laid down precise disqualifications in matters matrimonial (*Dig.* XXIII. 2. 23. 44. with reference to freedmen and persons of ill repute) or testamentary. Whence the importance, even in jurisprudence, of a precise definition of the *condicio*.

3. Value of the Census Qualification

Certain plutocratic tendencies are obvious. But where the higher 'orders' of the civic hierarchy are concerned, the essential point is somewhat different. Firstly, even when raised to a million HS, the senatorial census was still modest in relation to the probable average of senatorial and even equestrian fortunes, to say nothing of the 'princely' wealth of the *piscinarii* of the Ciceronian period, their heirs and successors: we know, from the researches of T. P. Wiseman, I. Shatzman, R. Duncan-Jones, or E. Rawson,[25] that the estates of senators and knights at the end of the Republic were commonly counted in millions, or even tens of millions of HS. Nevertheless, and it is no paradox, convergent evidence extending as far as the time of Nero or even Hadrian, shows that in some cases senators, or likely candidates for magistracies, had either never had or had ceased to possess this minimum census: in such circumstances, it was the ruling powers themselves – first the Emperor from his private fortune, later perhaps the Senate from public funds – who decided whether (or not) to provide *those who seemed to deserve it* with the requisite capital.[26] Augustus himself, at the very end of his *Res Gestae*, refers to the 'incalculable' expenses he has been put to in giving money to his friends 'and to the senators whose *census* he has made up': 'quorum census explevit' (*App.* 4). Suetonius (*Aug.* 41) confirms it in the same general terms ('supplevitque non habentibus'). Dio, as always, is fuller and more precise: as early as 28 (LIII. 2. 1), Augustus 'gave money' to certain senators, so many of whom were impoverished that they shrank from the burden of the aedile-ship (LIII. 2. 1).[27] In 18 – or even later – when he had (again?) fixed a census, then increased it, he gave 'to certain men of good repute' what they were lacking (LIV. 17. 3). In AD 4, as we have seen, he again provided the necessary amount (for eighty of them actually going as high as 1,200,000 HS) for 'some young men' of the senatorial and equestrian orders – in order, we understand of course, to enable them to be candidates (LV. 13. 6). But a similar custom, it should be said, continued under his successors. Tiberius (LVII. 10. 1) and Claudius (LX. 11. 8) practised it likewise, although Claudius did accept the

resignations of impoverished senators. Finally, Nero introduced yearly renewable subsidies (Tac. *Ann.* XIII. 34. 2; Suet.
Nero 10), first on behalf of Valerius Messala and then of
various others.

But there is no better illustration of the exact nature of the
census obligation established by Augustus and the attitude of
the Emperors in these circumstances, than the affair, recorded
at length by Tacitus, of Hortensius Hortalus in AD 16. Hortalus,
the grandson of the great Hortensius, had received from
Augustus 1 million sesterces 'because he [the Emperor] desired
to keep up an illustrious family'. As a senator, Hortalus raised
four children, in accordance with Augustus' command, but
proved quite incapable of enlarging his fortune. He stood up in
the Senate and asked for a grant on behalf of his children (the
census provided by Augustus, divided into four, would not
have sufficed for them). Tiberius' initial response was negative:
gifts of that kind were at the Emperor's discretion, not an
obligation; the treasury would not be equal to all the demands;
'languescet alioque industria'; (such people would be) 'sibi
ignavi, nobis graves'.[28] But Tiberius again, in his funeral oration for Augustus, had clearly stated the reasons both for the
raising of the *census* by his adoptive father and for potential
generosity: 'Who could fail to mention his wishes for the
Senate? By purging it of the froth left by the civil wars, he
made it more worshipful. He elevated it by raising the *census*
and enriched it by his generosity.'[29] The aim was not personal.
It was not to reward wealth with the gift of political responsibilities, but, on the contrary, to restore a body politic to its
traditional greatness and prestige. Wealth was an advantage,
and law or custom ought (as it always had) to demand a
minimum level for the tenure of certain offices: Augustus was
not making any changes in the old census ideology which was
that of every ancient city. But other considerations had to
enter into the Emperor's choice and into the recruitment both
of magistrates and of the Senate: the continuity which the
heredity rule was now about to help to create, by forming an
ordo senatorius; also merit, moral rectitude, and *industria*. This,
again, is what emerges from Maecenas' 'speech', less anachronistic than it is said to be: 'Nevertheless, do not drive out any
respectable man on account of his poverty, but yourself pro-

vide the money which is needed' (LII. 19. 2). The advice to provide magistrates with an adequate salary (LII. 23. 1) derives from the same logic and Augustus effectively put it into practise (LIII. 15. 4). There can be no doubt that the object of this measure was to combat corruption and the previous extortion on the part of magistrates. So it is natural, therefore, that the fixing or even raising of the census qualification was not exclusively plutocratic in character but was clearly in line with the most distinctive traditions of the census-based city.[30]

II. THE EQUESTRIAN ORDER

The same may be said about the equestrian order. Census qualifications, although necessary, had never been sufficient to confer the *nomen* or *dignitas equestris*. From the unimpeachable evidence of the epigraphic law of 123 BC, for example, we can deduce that free birth (*ingenuitas*) was a condition strictly required, at least of those knights called upon to serve in the jury panels.[31] Moral conditions were also laid down. The Lex Roscia, for example, excluded from the fourteen rows reserved for the equestrian order those it called *decoctores*,[32] which is to say those who had failed to honour their bond, bankrupts, quite a different thing from merely having failed to meet the census requirement. It also excluded such people (whether originally knights or not) as hired themselves out as actors or gladiators, and other disreputable characters.

1. Controls on the Equestrian Order

In this field also, Augustus' acts, far from being revolutionary or even innovative, have all the appearance of a restoration. First, they involved reintroducing accurate and frequent checks on the composition of the equestrian order by means of the *cura morum*. This is why (assuming, as Maecenas suggests he should, the power which had belonged to the censors) he revived the traditional means by which the equestrian order was reviewed. On the one hand, there was the annual march past on 15 July of the Knights in military formation, the *transvectio* which was accompanied by an inspection (Suet. *Aug.* 38. 3; Dio LV. 31. 2 for AD 6, the year in which it was postponed). But on the other hand there was also a series of operations analogous to the *lectiones* of the Senate, by means of which he checked individual qualifications, assisted, on this occasion, by a senatorial commission (Suet. *Aug.* 39. 1), and which, in all probability, would have coincided roughly every five years with the taking of the census. This review inevitably concerned origins, respectability, and fortune all at once. The story told by Macrobius (*Sat.* II. 4) pinpoints two possible reasons for expulsion: wilfully dissipating one's patrimony and flouting the marriage laws.[33] Suetonius indicates another cause of *infamia*, an interesting one from our point of view because it shows the repression, by this means, of ordinary financial practices: 'quod pecunias levioribus usuris mutuati graviore faenore collocassent' (*Aug.* 39).

Thus, for the equestrian order as for the Senate, the census qualification, although certainly necessary, was not enough. What is more, as in the case of senators, Augustus, at least for some time, accepted the possibility of contravening it. 'Since many knights,' says Suetonius, 'ruined by the civil wars, no longer dared to seat themselves in the fourteen rows for fear of being penalized by the *lex theatralis*, he proclaimed [by means of an edict?] that this law should not apply to anyone who had possessed, or whose family had formerly possessed, equestrian status'.[34] On at least one occasion, in AD 4, if Dio is to be believed, he made up the census requirement for some young men of the equestrian order.[35] But, for the equestrian as for the senatorial order, the conditions also related to 'family' as much as to money and respectability. There is some argument as to whether free birth (attested, in my view, from 123 BC) had already been demanded by the Lex Roscia Theatralis: it seems to me more than likely, since – except for the granting of the *ius anuli*, a fictitious free birth – we know of no knight of freedman stock at the end of the Republic. Some sons of freedmen, on the other hand, like Horace, were able to become knights (presumably by way of the military tribunate),[36] but in the time of the civil wars. Restrictions of this kind were certainly strengthened by Augustus, at least towards the middle or the end of his reign, in connection with laws or provisions to limit the numbers of manumissions and the rights of freedmen. There is no serious reason to doubt, as some do, the existence under Augustus of a Lex Julia Theatralis,[37] which is mentioned by Pliny (XXXIII. 32) and glossed by Suetonius in a long chapter. But even if it consisted only of a succession of edicts, the result was very much the same: to render the civic hierarchy clearly visible and to place increased obstacles in the way of infringements of the rules.[38]

2. The Equestrian Census

Was the amount of the equestrian census modified, like that of the senatorial? All the evidence we have regarding the Lex Roscia which mentions a qualifying figure agrees on one of 400,000 HS. But, as I have pointed out, this positive evidence is all relatively late: the earliest comes from Horace and can be dated to the years 23–20 BC: 'Est animus tibi, sunt mores, est lingua fidesque, sed quadringintis sex septem milia desunt: plebs eris' (*Epist.* I. 1. 57). Was this the amount previously fixed by Roscius Otho? And, in 67, did it already represent the sum of the equestrian census? The argument, revived by U. Scamuzzi, is somewhat pointless, in the absence of reliable evidence. Whatever the facts as to the amount of the equestrian census, the figure of 400,000 HS is very well attested from countless sources after Augustus' time. And its justification is just the same, all things being equal, as for the senatorial census: as Asinius Gallus said to the Senate in AD 16, while speaking against a proposed sumptuary law, if the census distinguished a senator from a knight 'locis, ordinibus, dignitationibusque' (Tac., *Ann.* II. 33. 3), in the same way was a knight distinguished from a plebeian. Evidently, the aim was very far from plutocratic: social distinctions were not born of fortune; on the contrary it was fortune which ought to be one sign, among others, of the distinctions whose culmination was the *dignitatio* (which I would translate as 'fitness for office').

For if there was a need to purge the *ordines* morally and socially (as was to come about through the series of great social, demographic, and matrimonial laws) this was because they were intended for a purpose.[39] Once again, it was not a question of rewarding the rich, but of establishing an 'order'. In other words, in Charles Loyseau's admirable phrase, 'a rank expressly fitted for public office'.[40] Augustus himself was personally proud of his equestrian origin, (a fact attested to by a text of his quoted by Suetonius),[41] just as he was punctilious in matters of etiquette. The man who, in 41, had a soldier thrown out for sneaking into the equestrian rows at the theatre is very much the same one who, once Emperor, took such care over rank and persons when sending out his dinner invitations 'non sine magno hominum ordinumque dilectu'.[42] The only freedman he ever admitted to his table was the celebrated Pompeius Menas, whose treachery had served him so well that he was able to treat him as Louis XIV did Samuel Bernard.

3. The Functions of the Equestrian Order

To sum up: if we want to know the real range and significance of the census qualification required of knights, alongside those of 'family' and respectability, we have only to ask ourselves what was to be the purpose of this order once restored to its ancient prestige: a somewhat functional analysis which may enable us to evaluate the respective parts played by the economic and the civic. What emerges clearly is that the equestrian order, under Augustus, was intended to be essentially a group which would 'stand surety', a huge reservoir which would enable the *res publica* to recruit in sufficient numbers, suitable candidates for various essential offices.

(a) The militiae

First, I think, those offices which corresponded most nearly to the original meaning of the term 'equites': the *militiae*, which were beginning to be called, by the start of Tiberius' reign, the *militiae equestres* (Velleius, II. 111), or the *castrenses honores* (ILS 2682): the prefecture of a cohort, the military tribunate, the prefecture of an *ala*. This was undoubtedly one of the reasons why Augustus reinstated the military parades of 15 July, from which the sick, the disabled, and before long the *seniores*, withdrew of their own accord. In the *ordo* thus defined and passed under review, or rather among its young men, the sons of senators were also numbered, since they too were henceforth required to serve in the ranks of military tribunes.[43] But the senators' sons were certainly not sufficiently numerous to fill the 360 or so posts for senior officers that fell vacant annually:

the remainder fell to 'other' knights, subject, here again, to the Emperor's personal nomination. They had to be *honesti*, men at once rich and respectable: heirs to the old equestrian families like Ovid or Velleius Paterculus and his brother (but we note that these might receive an offer of the senatorial *latus clavus*; cf. *ILS* 2682); ultimately also the sons of freedmen, very respectable and highly recommended, like the M. Aurelius Zosimi f. Cottanus, who had the *commendatio* of his father's patron to thank for becoming a tribune (*ILS* 1949).[44] But Augustus dreaded the thought of a shortage of candidates who were 'respectable', *honesti* (which is proof enough that he was not satisfied with the census qualification), and a text of Suetonius, admirably illuminated by Syme, tells us that to this end ('ne honestorum deficeret copia'), he bestowed the equestrian *militia* (the rank of military tribune) on a number of municipal dignitaries who stood for office 'ex commendatione publica': it has been my pleasure to show that epigraphy, in the thirty or so examples it offers of these *tribuni militum a populo* (all datable to the reign of Augustus, and all Italians), entirely confirms both Suetonius and Syme.[45] Yet is it perhaps even more remarkable to note, with reference to the results obtained by Mme S. Demougin, that this kind of military tribune, many of whom pursued ordinary municipal careers, represents a considerable proportion of the prosopography of known knights of the Augustan period. Augustus evidently meant to restore to the equestrian order the military vocation which it had never, in fact, totally lost, even at the end of the Republic. Nothing illustrates this better than the anecdote recorded by Suetonius: when a Roman knight cut off the thumbs of his two young sons to keep them from military service, he had him sold at auction with all his belongings; but seeing that the publicans were about to buy him, he had him knocked down to one of his freedmen,[46] which proves, incidentally, that the man in question was probably a publican. We should compare this extract with the passage in which Velleius describes the panic in Rome and the exceptional measures taken by Augustus in AD 7, following the Pannonian rebellion. The expression he uses, 'senatorum equitumque Romanorum exactae ad id bellum operae' does not mean 'contributions' but personal enlistment, 'service' for which any potential *vacationes* which the publicans might traditionally have enjoyed had been suspended (Vell. II. 111. 1). In short, the equestrian order was a training school for young officers of good family. But it was also (and Dio states this clearly, LII. 25. 7) a body to which former centurions, upwards of the rank of *primipilus*, could be promoted in later life, just as Tiberius was to promote a famous jurisconsult, Masurius Sabinus, at the age of fifty (Pomp. *Dig.* I. 2. 49).

(b) The iudicia

The second vocation of the equestrian order under Augustus was to serve in the jury-panels. Here too, the continuity with the Republic is striking. Unfortunately, we know very little about the reform of the *decuriae* carried out by Augustus (here too we await the continuation of Mme Demougin's work).[47] The texts of Suetonius (*Aug.* 32) and Pliny (XXXIII. 30–4) are terribly elliptical, and the evidence of epigraphy too infrequent. There were from this time four *decuriae*, the fourth made up of *ducenarii*, that is of men with a census value of 200,000 HS. This means that the other three must have carried census requirements of more than that (300,000 HS possibly, 400,000 for certain). But other qualifications must have come into it, and Pliny, for example, in a vital piece of evidence, describes for us the inquiry (*inquisitio*) which presided over the recruitment of *iudices*.[48]

(c) The Public Contracts

The third traditional occupation, which one is always inclined to neglect where Augustus' time is concerned, was the farming of taxes.[49] It is a pure documentary accident that the publicans should, apparently, be almost entirely missing from the history of this period. Yet two positive pieces of evidence in Tacitus, one in the great picture of the Empire which he drew for the year AD 24, the other for 58 (at the time of the great plan for fiscal reform curiously projected among Nero's entourage), bear witness to the permanence and importance of corporations of tax-farmers.[50] Not only were the traditional taxes of the senatorial and imperial provinces always levied according to the procedure of the *locatio*, but we have positive evidence, thanks to epigraphy, that it was the same with the new indirect taxes introduced by Augustus (the 5 per cent on inheritances in AD 6 and the 2 per cent on the sale of slaves in AD 7). Tacitus explains, on the two occasions I have cited, that the publicans' companies in question were 'corporations of Roman knights'. And in 58, the senators opposed to the plan to abolish the indirect taxes invoked their 'official' nature, since they had been 'constituted' by tribunes or consuls in the time of the Republic. In my opinion, this expression refers to the great legally constituted 'limited' companies for which there had probably been laws to regulate their forms and organization since the time of the Gracchi, by obliging them to elect knights to key positions. Augustus, on the other hand, whatever may have been said, never manifested any hostility towards the publicans. On the contrary, in 36 BC, during the great pacification measures which marked the end of the war of Sextus Pompeius (and which so accurately foreshadowed those of the years 29/27) he abolished the *tributum* and all the exceptional taxes of the triumviral period in Italy (Appian. *BC* V. 540–1), but at the same time he remitted certain sums which the publicans owed to the treasury.[51] In 28 came another *beneficium*: he repaid the sureties given to the treasury before Actium and wrote off debts owed to the treasury.[52] Here again we are dealing, at least in part, with measures that could only benefit the publicans and *redemptores* (for I can see no other meaning for the word ἐγγύαι). It cannot therefore be seriously maintained that Augustus was deliberately aiming to deprive the knights of the immense sphere of activity represented by the farming of taxes. And on the contrary later epigraphy provides strong evidence that, until the second century AD, an equestrian procuratorial career might very well begin with some responsible position in one of the great tax-farming companies. At most, some hypothetical inference could be drawn from the action of Sentius Saturninus, the consul for 19 BC, who 'uncovered the malpractices of the publicans, punished their greed and returned the state's money to the treasury'.[53] Saturninus' real independence may be doubted. Consequently, I wonder today whether the precise rules of procedure of the *licitatio* which have been handed down to us in the *Sententiae* of Paulus, which I earlier suggested attributing to the Lex Julia de Publicanis of 59 BC, might not, in actual fact, date from the time of Augustus; and why not from 19 or 18 BC? In any event, these explicit texts do not permit of any talk of a weakening or disappearance of the *societates*. The Roman knights of Augustus' time were still providing publicans, no more nor less than under the Republic. They still constituted a formidable and consistently ostentatious financial aristocracy, a fact proved by Vitruvius' interesting observation (VI. 5. 2) about the houses that had to be built for them, which were veritable fortresses (since these houses had in all likelihood to double as the head offices of the companies).

(d) Adlection to the Senate

But, suppose we were to stop there, we should not comprehend the whole logic of the reorganization of the higher orders by Augustus. Once again, it was not in their own interests, individual or corporate, that he took pains, by a great many touches, to regulate the qualifications and functions of senators and knights: it was to encourage them to aim at a career of service to the state, which Suetonius expresses in the phrase: 'quo plures partem administrandae rei p. caperent' (*Aug.* 37. 1). This, too, is the convergent theme of the antithetical speeches which Dio gives to Agrippa, urging the re-establishment of the 'demokratia' – which is to say simply the *libera respublica* – and to Maecenas, supporting the Principate.[54] Both declare themselves in agreement that the new regime, whatever it might be, could only work by a (peaceful) collaboration among the 'better' class of people, the only problem being to avoid the fatal rivalries which had led to the civil wars. Augustus, in his majesty, re-established a 'purged' Senate composed of men who were at once 'noble', 'wise', and 'rich' (this last requirement carrying, as we have seen, civic or moral implications, as the guarantee of *industria*, rather than purely plutocratic ones). If the natural heirs of this new civic aristocracy were too few to ensure its continuity, the equestrian order would be there to provide it with the new but 'honourable' blood it needed.[55] Livy makes King Perseus say, in 169 BC, that the equestrian order was the *seminarium senatus*,[56] an expression which may have had an annalistic source: it was none the less wholly Augustan in inspiration (and this may be the reason why we meet it again in the *Vita Alexandri*). Here again, Maecenas can easily be made to speak prophetically: 'If any knight, having passed through the various career posts, distinguishes himself sufficiently to become a senator, his age should be no obstacle.'[57] What we have here is clearly an anachronistic description of the mechanism of the *adlectio* which did not appear until Claudius' reign. But in point of fact, all through the reign of Augustus and even of his successors, the *princeps* did not choose his new senators merely from among elderly knights with a career already behind them. By the granting of the *latus clavus*, as Chastagnol has shown, he could 'destine' young men of ordinary equestrian families for a senatorial career. Better still, in certain special circumstances, the *princeps* (or, in his absence, the Senate) could permit knights who had not even held the 'preparatory' offices of the vigintivirate to be appointed directly to certain magistracies; sometimes they could even be compelled to it.[58] In some cases, all the knights were authorized to stand for office. In others (Dio LIV. 30. 2. for 12 BC), knights were chosen who possessed the senatorial census. Reluctance to hold magistracies was thus a fairly constant phenomenon during the Principate (Ovid is a case in point). Some, as we see, even if they were willing to take on a magistracy now and then, preferred to revert afterwards to the status of knights. We may wonder about their motives. A generation or two earlier, at the end of the Republic, the theme of the *otium equestre*, which allowed them, sheltered from the 'storms' of public life, to devote themselves either to their private affairs (including, be it noted, the *publica* and the jury panels, which were not altogether private), or to the intellectual or even 'theoretical' life, cropped up with regularity.[59] And certain biographies on which I have laid stress before, illustrate it and enable us to comprehend its implications. Here too, we cannot observe any complete break at the time of Augustus. There were still knights who 'stood aside from public life' – whatever the activities they were engaged upon.

(e) Equestris nobilitas

Nevertheless what does emerge fairly clearly under Augustus is the opportunity for the knights to serve the *res publica* in a specific fashion. I am thinking of course of the procuratorships and the great prefectures. But on this point, the anticipatory outlook of Maecenas' speech, if we try to see it as the truth about the years from 27 BC to AD 14, would be particularly misleading: although the prefecture of Egypt had existed since 30 (this is, indeed, the clearest case and the key to it all), that of the Praetorian Guard was not created until 2 BC, of the Vigiles not until AD 6, and of the Annona not until about 8. Posts which were so few (and whose incumbents might remain in office, like the immortal C. Turranius, for thirty years)[60] would not have offered a great deal of scope for the ambitions of an entire order! There were, of course, also the financial procuratorships. But here too, and whatever the nature, public or private (or both at once), óf these posts, which were in any case acting 'in the name' of another authority, that of the *princeps*, their number was extremely small. For the reign of Augustus, as H. G. Pflaum showed, they did not exceed 23, which, whatever the duration of tenure, still only makes a very small number of incumbents, surely hardly greater than the number of knights enjoying promotion, either under normal or exceptional circumstances, to the senatorial order. What brought about the emergence of this equestrian career? The first thing to note is that it had, in fact, already begun to make its appearance under the Republic. The *principes* of the city had private procurators who were also knights in many cases. This is perfectly understandable: the same social background, the same friends, often the same education united the two orders as we have seen. What was more, the juridical nature of the equestrian status, that is to say the absence of magistracies, left such men with time to occupy their leisure with a particular sort of business – which was often, but not exclusively, financial: whence their acknowledged competence. Then, on the other hand, their membership of an officially constituted *ordo*, subject to review by the authorities, with a high level of moral and property qualifications, conferred on them (as several texts demonstrate) a kind of *dignitas* and even *auctoritas*, both individually and collectively, which made their services especially valuable, for example in legal matters.[61] It was during Augustus' reign and in deference to his wishes that things began to settle down. But very slowly and cautiously. For to confer on knights who, in the eyes of traditional civic law, remained private men the responsibility of military command, to say nothing of jurisdiction, presented considerable difficulties to the Roman mind. Nothing could be more significant in this respect than Octavian's fears in 32, when he appointed Maecenas *praefectus urbi*, of finding him treated with contempt and his orders not obeyed by the troops 'because he was only a knight' (Dio LI. 3. 5). The point here is not one of social origins, but of professional competence. But it was this very reason which, a year later, made Augustus take the step of entrusting Egypt, although *redacta in provinciam*, to a knight and not to a senator.[62] Augustus was quite naturally torn between his desire to restore the Senate to its traditional pride of place in the state and his fear of seeing the emergence of rivals, which caused him to fall back on the 'friendship' of men he could rely on, honourable men, but who, in a sense, remained private ones and therefore both more dependent on himself and more independent of the Senate. Whence, the cohort of the *princeps*' 'knightly friends': Sallustius Crispus, Maecenas, and plenty more. But are we to imagine that this was from social choice, from a 'modesty' which would be very surprising in the great-nephew of Julius, the husband of Livia, the adoptive father of Claudius? No, the reason was political, it was one of the 'imperial secrets'. And nothing shows this more clearly than the fact of Julia's marriage after the death of Agrippa: Augustus was thinking of many candidates, one of them 'etiam ex equestri ordine', as Suetonius says (*Aug.* 63. 3). Tacitus gives us, at some length, the last word on that affair: the man was none other than the *princeps*' old officer and confidant, C. Proculeius. Many years later, in a similar case Tiberius, refusing the hand of Livia, the widow of Drusus, to Sejanus, nevertheless states categorically that Augustus had only contemplated it because Proculeius was 'insigni tranquillitate vitae, nullis reipublicae negotiis permixtus' (*Ann.* IV. 40). But let us read carefully what follows: the husband of an imperial princess could not long remain in obscurity – this brilliant marriage would have made him either an heir or a rival. So it was a matter of cold political calculation. It was not because they were rich or because they were 'modest' that the knights were the procurators or friends of the *princeps*. It was because, for some tasks on which, in the new regime, it was better not to shed too much light, there was no shadow of republican legitimacy between them and the *princeps*.

III. WEALTH, POWER, AND PROPERTY: THE NEW ORDER OF THINGS

A study of the two orders (*uterque ordo*), their recruitment and the way in which they were employed, has enabled us to see the ambiguous relations between wealth, birth, and power in the new regime. But the propertied classes were not confined to the *ordines*. There were plenty of rich men in Rome, in Italy, and in the provinces, outside the *ordines*, and plenty of ways of being or becoming wealthy.[63] In establishing, not without thought, the new order of things, Augustus, as heir to a rich private family, as Caesar's heir, and as one burdened with the cares of state, undoubtedly had ideas, aims, perhaps a policy on this subject. Can we discover them? Economic literature is rare, not to say nonexistent in Rome.[64] Yet statesmen did express themselves, at least indirectly, on these matters: Cicero, on a practical and theoretical level (for example in *de lege Manilia* and *de officiis*), Sallust or the well-informed author of the *Letters* attributed to him.[65] Caesar himself, with his *brevitas imperatoria*, gives his point of view on such questions as the moratorium on debts or the actions of the law on behalf of debtors.[66] But these questions are precisely those which touched the *res publica* closely, and were concerned with the maintenance of order.

Yet the moneyed men, the landowners and tradesmen who thought of nothing but the ways to make money, did exist, in great numbers. They undoubtedly knew a great deal about the subject, but they were very reluctant to disclose what they knew, although not their grievances. These 'philosophers of the Janus' as Cicero comes close to calling them, liked results better than theories: 'but on problems of this kind, concerning the acquisition, investment, and proper use of money, certain worthy persons whose seat is in the midst of the Janus discourse better than any philosopher in any school' (*de off.* II. 87). The civil wars might have interrupted these musings to some extent, but we meet the characters and their pithy philosophy again, in the years 30–23, castigated in the first *Epistle* of Horace: 'O cives, cives, quaerenda pecunia primum est;/ virtus post nummos': haec Janus summus ab imo/prodocet' (*Epist.* I. 1. 53 ff.). Is it by accident that these lines appear just before the famous ones: 'Est animus tibi, sunt mores, est lingua fidesque,/sed quadringinti sex septem desunt: plebs eris'? The new regime had claimed to restore the morality and dignity of the old orders; the results were somewhat slow in coming. Money seemed still to be king. Was this really the aim of the new order of things?

1. The Tax System

A good test of a government's real intentions in these matters is often to be found in its fiscal policy.[67] Not enough importance is generally attached to these questions, which seem to be pushed into the background by the grander ones of legitimacy and power and by the ostentatiousness of the *princeps'* private generosity as displayed in the *Res Gestae*. The importance these considerations assume, on the other hand, in book LII of Dio has long been noted, not only in chapters 28–30 of Maecenas' speech but also (which has occasioned less discussion) in Agrippa's defence of the traditional *res publica*.[68] The anachronistic or anticipatory aspects of these reflections is obvious. Even so, as we shall see, the problem did not present itself in such very different terms to Augustus himself. In order to understand it properly, we must start from the impossible situation in which the whole of the Empire, but principally Italy (as the only region populated entirely by citizens), found itself between 49 and 36 BC, during the civil wars.[69] The fiscal immunity, which by 60 BC had become almost total, enjoyed by citizens in Italy, had given way to its opposite, an accumulated financial burden. Dio sums it up in a celebrated passage:[70]

In fact, the reintroduction of taxes which had previously been abolished, the creation of new, the institution of levies on slaves and land, affected most people only slightly. But that those who were at all well off, not only senators and knights but also freedmen, men or women, might be put on the roll [for a kind of exceptional tithe, cf. XLVII. 16. 1. in 42], this annoyed everyone excessively.

The proscriptions only added to this extraordinary drain of

people's fortunes: 'thus private individuals were able to save nothing or almost nothing because, in addition to the other exactions, they were obliged to find slaves for the navy, buying them if they had none, and senators had to mend the roads at their own expense. Only those who bore arms got rich.'[71]

Now it has long been recognized that Augustus' final victory owed much to the abolition of most of these measures by 36 BC, at the time of his victory over Sextus Pompeius. The remission of tax arrears, of arrears of money owed by publicans and others in debt to the treasury, the abolition of a number of duties, were impressively presented by Octavian under the slogan *pax et securitas*, about which I shall have more to say, although his opponents claimed that he was making a virtue of necessity.[72] These measures of fiscal indulgence are certainly likely to have affected a fairly broad social spectrum, but they must have interested the rich, the senators and knights, and also publicans, most of all. Augustus undoubtedly remembered the lesson learned by Octavian. And from then on his fiscal policy was one of immense caution. Things as a whole were to return to the situation at the end of the Republic, when citizens (which from that time onwards meant Italy) became the fiscally privileged, exempt from all direct levies on their wealth and nearly all indirect contributions, for instance from internal customs dues at any rate. (Dues at the Italian frontiers, initiated or increased by Caesar,[73] would remain.) This was one condition of the popularity so necessary to the regime. The first to benefit were, of course, the rich. And so the new regime, seen from this angle, looks like one which avoided taxing wealth (in Italy, although not, of course, in the provinces).

But in spite of the enormous sums accounted for by Augustus in his *Res Gestae* as the total of his 'personal contribution' (2,400 million HS), the financial difficulties only increased, and especially towards the end of the reign, when the army 'pension fund' (*aerarium militare*) needed replenishing. For this was the key to the regime: it was the only way to reconcile the existence of a permanent volunteer army, as necessary to the individual ruler as to peace abroad, with the abolition of land grants to veterans and the ending of soldiers' resettlement, decided in 13 BC.[74] Once the *princeps*' initial capital of 170 million HS was exhausted (and offers from private individuals declined), a permanent solution had to be found. The history of the introduction of the inheritance tax (the *vicesima hereditatium*) in AD 6 and its ratification in 13, is sufficiently familiar.[75] On the one hand, Augustus only got the Senate to agree by first, in 6, invoking the posthumous authority of Caesar and, in 13 (the tax had not been abolished but was rousing some opposition), by threatening to replace it with a direct tax on landed property, public and private, whether built on or not,[76] and by commencing census operations. This threat was enough to get the 5 per cent tax on inheritances accepted as the lesser evil. This tax, which only applied to citizens, was in practice an extremely conservative one, since, first, it spared inheritances in the direct line and, secondly, it only affected inheritances and legacies above a certain figure (Dio LV. 25). It was therefore a proportional and not a graduated tax and one which, while sparing the poor, in Dio's rather vague phrase, favoured the family at the expense of the particular social institution of leaving money to friends, freedmen, or the *princeps*.[77] In addition one must mention the 1 per cent tax on sales at auction contemporary with the *vicesima*, and the long-established 5 per cent tax on the manumission of slaves.[78]

Analysed in economic and social terms, the inheritance tax has some striking characteristics. It breaks with the brutal simplicity of the traditional system of taxation in cities: the direct but intermittent taxation of wealth which was closely bound up with civic and economic privilege and patriotic sacrifice. It was also a change from the severe, but arbitrary, blows which the civil wars had dealt to property and wealth. It took care to avoid any suggestion of *tributum ex censu* (although there were to be some desperate exceptions at the time of the Pannonian rebellion in AD 7.) It struck at wealth, very moderately, only in its movable forms: its real effect was probably to discourage the breaking up and too rapid decay of private estates. So that it was perhaps less a tax on property than a tax which encouraged the handing down of property within families. On the other hand, the fairly general exemption accorded to modest inheritances, confirmed by the limitation of the *census* of AD 4 to those whose possessions came to more than 200,000 HS, is further evidence of an anxiety not to burden the poor. In short, the fiscal system was empirical, and its sole aim was to cope with military expenditure, but more for fear of the troops than in their interests; and it spared the wealth of the citizens as far as possible. The revenues of the state came principally from the *patrimonium* and the provincial *vectigalia*, which were not affected; they continued to be raised by publicans, under the ultimate responsibility of the magistrates, but with the same risks of corruption and abuse as before, except for more effective controls.[79] But the provinces also gained fresh and very adequate advantages from the restoration of peace and an end to the abominable practices of the civil wars. In the last resort, the fiscal system was bearable because it was quite simply the guarantee of the security of property. This is certainly the inference of the fiscal proposals which Dio puts into the mouth of Maecenas, many of which were actually anachronistic: 'But I know also that if (the inhabitants of the Empire) are no longer subject to any abuse, and are convinced in fact that it is for their own good and so that they may enjoy the remainder of their possessions without fear (that they are taxed), they will be very grateful to you'.[80]

2. Protection of Property

The protection of property, the safety of the individual, the rejection of the abominable abuses of the time of the civil wars, recourse to taxes as near as possible to the civic fiscal system so well outlined by Agrippa (LII. 6. 4–5): this was, in the long run, the watchword of the new regime and, it appears, the enduring source both of its popularity and its legitimacy. The almost formulary precision of this part of 'Maecenas' speech' is vouched for by the precise echoes which are to be found in such authentic texts as Tiberius' funeral oration for Augustus: 'Who would not choose to live in safety, without troubles, to be rich without risk, to enjoy the advantages of city life without fear, and without the constant anxiety of maintaining it?'[81] And Dio himself adds: 'combining the old freedom with the monarchy, he established at one and the same time freedom for the citizens, security, and order.'[82] It is worth noting that the same formula, undoubtedly government-inspired, recurs in Velleius; after Actium: 'finita bella civilia, revocata pax . . . restituta vis legibus, iudiciis auctoritas, senatui majestas, . . . prisca illa et antiqua rei publica forma revocata rediit cultus agris, sacris honos, securitas hominibus, certa cuique rerum suarum possessio . . .' (II. 89. 3–4). This new order, the re-establishment of law and order, reaches its peak with the adoption of Tiberius: 'tum refulsit spes liberorum parentibus, viris matrimonium, dominis patrimonii, omnibus hominibus salutis, quietis, pacis, tranquillitatis.'[83] But this safety for a man's patrimony, this guarantee for possessions was not, of course, intended solely for the propertied classes; in the new regime, it was essential that everyone should have his place. Augustus was already proclaiming this in his famous 'foundation edict' of 27 January, with regard to which Suetonius, having quoted its crucial passages, makes this point: 'fecitque ipse se compotem voti nisus omni modo, ne quem novi status paeniteret' (Aug. 28. 4). Tiberius echoed this in 14 when he observed that the late princeps had also thought of the people, assuring them 'an abundance of the necessities of life, and security of property'.[86] Suetonius, in his Life of Augustus, makes many observations to this effect: the example he gives of Augustus' attitude to the frumentationes is typical. He would have liked to abolish them, he himself wrote in his Memoirs, in order to encourage a return to agriculture. He abandoned the idea, for fear of ambitio, but he did regulate them 'ut non minorem aratorum ac negotiantum quam populi rationem deducerent' (42. 5). And what we know of the Lex Julia de annona, which set a firm limit to the freedom of contracts, though so dear to Roman law, in matters concerning the corn merchants' companies, in order to combat speculation, is a striking illustration of this policy.[85] The new regime attached considerable importance to wealth and property, but it in no way went in for woolly economic liberalism. The order implied an equal solicitude for all on the part of the state. The humblest properties must be safeguarded, just like the greatest estates, against all threats of attack, whether from private or public sources. Men must be able to sail in peace, and the sailors of Alexandria who saluted the dying Augustus in AD 14 knew that well.[86] Was this the end of the Roman Revolution?

3. *Landed Property and Movable Property*

Such at least were the ideological or, one might say, political intentions of the new regime. How did they work out in practice? In other words, do we really notice any effort towards, or an actual improvement of, the means which society placed at the disposal of private individuals of all classes to protect their rights, including their property rights? And can we also discern more subtle intentions of favouring this or that type of property – in land or movables for instance?[87] The new and formal character of Augustan legislation is, in fact, something we have long been aware of. It intervened, through the series of great demographic, matrimonial, and judicial laws, in a much more noticeable fashion than at the time of the Republic in the sphere of private law, which until then had been more readily left to the responsibility of the *ius honorarium* (the edicts of the praetors and aediles) and to jurisprudence. Here, too, there can be no unequivocal answer. Regarding the *princeps'* attitude towards property, we cannot risk the same generalizations as those who, for example, would see it simply as a policy of 'favouring the slave-owners'. (The prohibitions of the laws Fufia Caninia in 2 and Aelia Sentia in 4 concerning manumissions were directed against slave-owners at least as much as against the slaves.) It is another commonplace, due to the importance of the 'back to the land' theme in the great literature of the Augustan period, to talk likewise about measures 'favouring rural property'. In fact, detailed evidence is rather rare. Setting aside the undeniably impressive work of colonization, in Italy and in the provinces, in the literature of the *Gromatici*, the Augustan phase (one might easily call it a stratum), has left substantial terminological and geographical traces. And Augustus himself, in his new incarnation which was to supersede the triumvir and the proscriber, took great care to carry out his policy for the future by avoiding expropriations, which is to say by granting land, often a long way away, or awarding compensation to dispossessed cities or individuals. But if we overlook the abolition of land taxes in Italy, I can see nothing, either in the legislation or even in the 'official' jurisprudence of Augustus' time, which would seem to be particularly favourable to rural property. The regulation of the distributions of free corn (that is the reduction to a *numerus clausus* of the urban recipients) took as much account of the interests of the farmers, Suetonius tells us, as of the people or the merchants. The only contribution of any importance to the benefit of property in fact concerns security, the safeguards of public order. The laws relating to *vis publica* and *privata* of 17 BC tend to put an end to all forms of 'private justice' and some of their crucial chapters clearly concern what was not merely pure and simple violence, but actually ancient rural custom, witnessed for instance at the time of the *Pro Caecina*, for the eviction of a debtor or of one whose title to a property was in dispute.[88] But it should be noted also that these same laws prohibit the violence that creditors could use on debtors (that is to say, execution on the person),[89] a fact which cannot precisely be described as favourable to money-lenders. Similarly, the Lex Julia de cessione bonorum, possibly a revival of a Caesarian law, also released the debtor's person by deduction on his estate.[90]

4. The Problem of Debt

As to the problem of debt, Augustus' attitude may have been less traditional.[91] In 7 BC there had been trouble in the forum and debtors had been suspected of starting fires in order to obtain *tabulae novae* (Dio LV. 8. 6): the authorities' initial response was to put down the riot, to restore order in the streets. But soon afterwards, taking advantage of some 'income' to the treasury (unclaimed assets? confiscations?), Augustus lent interest-free, for three years, sums amounting to a total of 60 million HS.[92] This was undoubtedly a break with the past. During the Republic, the 'problem of debt' (in reality quite a different one in every case) was traditionally dealt with either by violence or by fixing a maximum interest level which was more or less observed. The treasury did not 'lend' money to citizens (at least we have no evidence of it for a reliable historical period). But what sort of debtors are we talking about? τοῖς δεομένοις, says the text of Zonaras, which does not necessarily mean ὀφείλοντες. What is more to the point, Suetonius, evidently alluding to the same incident, which he classes among the examples of Augustus' open-handedness (*Aug.* 41. 2), states that these loans were made exclusively to those who could produce goods in surety to twice the value of the loan. The indices of the crisis, the remedies employed, recall too closely what we know of the famous 'liquidity crisis' of AD 33[93] for us not to see it as a phenomenon of the same kind. But clearly, if the remedy was seen as putting funds at the disposal of those debtors who possessed sufficient collateral, then the matter was not a case of conflict between the haves and the have-nots, but a problem of the settlement of debts within the property-owning class. At the most we can picture two competing forms of investment, investment in land and investment in movable property. But the imperial treasury's intervention in no way compromised the property principle.

5. *Restrictions in the Laws of Property*

The truth is that, although we may note some interventions which modified its practice somewhat, these would always be in particular spheres or circumstances and for obvious reasons. The Lex Julia de modo aedificiorum, if such a thing ever existed, (but there were at all events some such measures under Augustus, possibly in the form of edicts: Suet. *Aug.* 89; Strabo V. 3. 7), imposed on property law with regard to buildings the restrictions necessary to an increasing urbanization, but invoking republican precedents (Suetonius). The Lex de annona, as we have seen, interfered in the constitution of the *societates*, but in the name of the needs of the *annona*. The sumptuary laws (Gel. II. 24. 14) likewise were only perpetuating an old republican tradition. Nevertheless, bearing in mind these general considerations, it must be stated once again that other branches of Augustus' legislation do reveal a highly systematic intervention in spheres and activities of immediate concern to the propertied classes. The Lex Julia de maritandis ordinibus, for instance, prohibited bachelors or married men without children from accepting inheritances or legacies. (It also, as we have seen, prohibited the inclusion in wills of clauses binding the heir not to marry, on the lines of 'si uxorem non duxeris' etc. Paulus, *Sent.* III. 46. 2). This was undoubtedly a restriction on the freedom to dispose of one's own property. To be sure, we know it was possible to circumvent the legal prohibitions by the device of *fideicommissum*: 'for their part,' says Gaius (II. 286), 'those bachelors who were prohibited by the Lex Julia from inheriting or accepting legacies were formerly considered entitled to receive *fideicommissa*' (meaning: the products of a *fideicommissum*). Moreover, it is also known (*Inst*. II. 23. 1) that *fideicommissa*, which had no legal standing under the Republic, began to acquire one at the personal intervention of Augustus, 'determined by consideration of the persons involved' (*gratia personarum motus*). But P. A. Brunt has made the point (*Italian Manpower*, p. 561) that it was not easy for Augustus to favour those who were trying to circumvent his own law. So it was probably in order to *avoid* this loophole that 'in some cases' (but in those cases only) he provided a way out for the *fideicommissa* through the consuls. So that it was not a matter of extending a liberty but, on the contrary, of supervising its exercise on behalf of the higher interests of the state. If the motive of that was indeed the safeguarding of property, the safeguards were not unconditional.

6. The Traditional Civic Ideal

Was such an ideal and such an application of it either new or original? Need we recall that in 44 Cicero, in his *de officiis*, made security of ownership, the safeguarding of the 'natural' law of property, the principal reason for the creation of political ties: 'Hanc enim ob causam maxime, ut sua tenerentur, res publicae civitatesque constitutae sunt' (II. 73); 'in primis autem videndum erit ei, qui rem publicam administrabit, ut suum quisque teneat neque de bonis privatorum publice deminutio fiat.' He further strongly rejected the prospect of a *tributum*, but he adds that should it prove unavoidable, 'care must be taken that everyone understands that, if they want indemnity, they must bow to necessity' (II. 74). But upholding property did not mean governing on behalf of the rich alone: government must be established – Plato had said so – on behalf of all,[94] and especially by procedures of conciliation and arbitration. The Ciceronian echoes in Augustus' policies are not merely a constitutional disguise: they are the affirmation of an old civic ideal. The *res publica* was established in the interests of property in general, but it ought to act in such a way that all might peacefully enjoy the 'necessities of life'. Wealth was respectable and even required of those who must, in one way or another, administer the affairs of the community; but on condition that it was honourably come by, by *industria* and without injustice.[95] Neither was it the principal condition for the necessary hierarchy of orders and dignities.[96] There was a small difference between Cicero and Augustus, however, the difference between freedom and servitude. Under the new ruler, Roman citizens could at least enjoy 'law and order.' But the price paid for it was very dear: 'omnes ruere in servitium'.

NOTES

1. J. Béranger, 'Fortune privée impériale et état', *Mélanges Georges Bonnard* (1966), 151 = *Principatus* (1973), 353 ff. Sec Tac. *Ann.* I. 8. 6: 'provisis etiam heredum in rem publicam opibus'; recently H. Bellen, 'Die "Verstaatlichung" des Privatvermögens des röm. Kaiser im I. Jahrhundert n.C.', *ANRW* II. 1 (1974), 91 ff.

2. Cicero, *Par. Stoic.* VI. 45 (the celebrated phrase concerning 'exercitum alere', but which is correctly interpreted in *de off.* I. 25: 'qui in republica princeps vellet esse'); Tac. *Ann.* XVI. 17. 3: the famous 'ambitio praepostera' of Annaeus Mela: 'simul adquirandae pecuniae brevius iter credebat 'per procurationes . . .'; cf. H.-G. Pflaum, *Les Procurateurs équestres* I (1950), 165. But it should be noted that Mela's father and brother, Seneca the Rhetorician and Seneca the Philosopher, give a completely different interpretation of his 'vocation': that he wanted to devote himself to philosophy (Sen. Rh. *Contr.* II, *Praef.* 3; Sen. *Cons. ad Helviam*, 18. 2).

3. Cf. e.g. M. Raskolnikoff, 'La richesse et les riches chez Cicéron', *Ktema* 2 (1977), 357 ff.; R. Syme, 'La richesse des aristrocraties de Bétique et de Narbonnaise', ibid. 373 ff.

4. Who, for example, were the *inopes* against whom the *quaestor aerarii* Obultronius Sabinus acted with such severity in AD 56 (Tac. *Ann.* XIII. 28. 5)? Were they 'poor' penniless taxpayers or rather, as seems likely (Tac. *Ann.* III. 31. 7; Livy IV. 15. 8), public-works contractors, which alters the picture entirely? On this role of the *quaestores*, Mommsen, *DP* IV. 251; Tac. *Ann.* XIII. 28. 5: 'tanquam ius hastae adversus inopes inclementer augeret.' In AD 21, Corbulo held an 'execution' on certain contractors (*mancipes*) found guilty of fraud, selling them up to the benefit of the state (Tac. *Ann.* III. 31. 7).

5. The whole of Augustus' reign carried the marks of these upheavals and of the 'remedies' which had to be found for them: Livy, *praef.* 9: 'haec tempora, quibus nec vitia nostra nec remedia pati possumus perventum est.'
   It may not be altogether an accident, due to his dependence on a so-called Augustan 'Hauptquelle', that Pliny the Elder selected as an example of the most extreme and shocking concentration of wealth the fabulous C. Caecilius C.l. Isidorus who, in 8 BC, left several hundred million sesterces in his will, *NH* XXXIII. 135; cf. also L. Tarius Rufus, *NH* XVIII. 36 (100 million HS due to the generosity of Augustus); under Augustus also Cn. Cornelius Lentulus the Augur,

118   AUGUSTUS, GOVERNMENT,

(*cos.* 14 BC): Sen. *Benef.* II. 27. 1–2; cf. R. Syme, *RR* 382; 400; P. Brunt; 'Two Great Roman Landowners', *Latomus* 34 (1975), 619; as regards the supposed Augustan main source, M. Rabenhorst's theory, *Der ältere Plinius als Epitomator des Verrius Flaccus* (1907), is largely discredited. Isidorus claimed to have lost money in the civil wars: but this freedman of the Metelli had not grown rich by his own *industria* alone. Pliny rightly places him in line with the legendary Crassus and, incidentally, with Sulla, which is doubtless a commonplace. But suppose we reread the *Parad. Stoic.* VI: Crassus' fortune is cited there as an example not only for its size but for its origins, being almost entirely accumulated by felonious means and, above all, by the use of political power (*Parad.* VI. 46), in a period when it was to say the least unusual.

6. Cf. C. Nicolet, 'Les classes dirigeantes romaines sous la République', *Annales* (1977), 726, esp. 744. And recently, J. H. D'Arms, *Commerce and Social Standing in Ancient Rome* (1981), 66 ff.; 149 ff.

7. Exposition and references in V. Gardthausen, *Augustus und Seine Zeit* I. 2 (1896), 913 ff.; II. 531 ff.; but chiefly F. Blumenthal, 'Zur zensorischen Tätigkeit des Augustus', *Klio* 9 (1909), 493; D. Th. Schulz, 'Die Zensus der ersten Prinzeps', *Mnemosyne* 5 (1937), 161.

8. Mommsen, *DP* IV. 35–108; J. Suolahti, *The Roman Censors* (1963), 32–56; G. Piéri, *Histoire du cens à Rome* (1963); C. Nicolet, *Le Métier de citoyen dans la Rome républicaine²* (1979), 71–121; idem, *Les Structures de l'Italie romaine²* (1979), 185–203; *L'Ordre équestre* I. 69–102.

9. Evidence for the inclusion of the *rationes pecuniae* in the declaration to the censors comes, for the years 75–45, from the *Tab. Her.* (*CIL* I². 593 = *FIRA²* I. 13), line 147: 'et rationes pecuniae ex formula census'; but that it goes back further is shown by, among other things, the *pugilaria* held by the citizens in the relief of Domitius Ahenobarbus: cf. henceforward M. Torelli, *Typology and Structure of the Roman Historical Relief* (1982), esp. pp. 9–10. For the literary evidence, C. Nicolet, *Le Métier de citoyen*, 97–103 (Livy VI. 27. 6; Cic. *Pro Flacco*, 79–80; *II Verr.* 1. 107; *Schol. Bobb.* 169 St.; Livy XXXIX. 44. 3 etc.).

10. In the words of the *Lex Cornelia de XX quaestoribus* (*CIL* I². 587; *FIRA* I². 10), line 33: 'quos eo ordine dignos arbitrabuntur'. Compare Cic. *II Verr.* 3. 184; cf. C. Nicolet, 'Les finitores ex equestri loco', *Latomus* 29 (1970), 72, on pp. 102–3; on the *ordines* of *scribae, apparitores*, etc., Mommsen, *DP* I. 392 (with the inscriptions *Bull. Comm.* 1884, 11; *CIL* VI. 435; 1944; 1810; *Cod. Theod.* VIII. 9. 1); B. Cohen, 'La notion d'ordo dans la Rome Antique', *Bull. Ass. G. Budé*, 1975, 259; idem, 'The Roman Administrative Ordines' in *Des ordres à Rome* (forthcoming, Presses de la Sorbonne, 1984).

11. I am grateful to the kindness of T. P. Wiseman for the information that he has modified the opinion on this point which he expressed in his otherwise admirable article, 'The Census in the First Century BC', *JRS* 59 (1969), 59. Cf. P. Brunt, *Italian Manpower*, 104–6.

12. For the limitation of the powers of the censors, Dio XXXVIII. 13; XL. 57; *Schol. Bobb.* 132 St.; for the fire in the Temple of the Nymphs, C. Nicolet, *CRAI* 1976, 29.

13. Op. cit. (n. 7).

14. C. Nicolet, 'Le cens sénatorial sous la République et sous Auguste', *JRS* 66 (1976), 20. This was not the opinion held by Mommsen (*DP* II. 147; VII. 50), but was, on the other hand, regarded as self-evident by J. J. Madvig, *L'État romain* I (1882), 135–50, and by M. Gelzer, *Die Nobilität der röm. Republik* (1912) (= *The Roman Nobility*, 1968), 4 ff. My own opinion, which was by no means new (cf. art. cit. n. 4), was nevertheless contested most courteously (although I was not convinced) by A. Guarino, 'Il mestiere del senatore', *Labeo* 24 (1974), 20 (= *Inezie*

di giureconsulti (1978), esp. 42). I was, however, supported by a sheaf of convergent texts: Polybius VI. 19. 1–5; Varro *ap.* Aulus Gellius III. 18; Livy, *Per.* 23. 60; etc.

15. The question is discussed in a manner both repetitious and superficial, in a very long work by U. Scamuzzi, 'Studio sulla lex Roscia theatralis', *Riv. stud. class.* 17 (1979), 133–65; 259–319; 18 (1970), 5–57; 374–447. All the texts (including the least relevant, such as for example every literary reference to sums like 400,000 HS and so forth) are brought together. The conclusions are precarious: that there existed under the Republic an equestrian census of 250,000 HS; that it was only after the Lex Roscia of 67 that this figure was raised to 400,000 HS. But that at the same time, the senatorial census was 800,000 HS (the only text to provide a basis for this conviction is Suetonius' remark, *Aug.* 41. 3: 'senatorum censum ampliavit ac pro octingentorum milium summa duodecies sestertium taxavit supplevitque non habentibus.' But I think that the successive details provided by Dio LV. 13. 6 are to be preferred to the too elliptical version of Suetonius). On this view Augustus – contrary to Dio's explicit statement – speedily raised the senatorial census to 1,200,000 HS. Scamuzzi (1970, 33 ff.) is unable to produce convincing evidence for this last figure, which is explicitly contradicted by Tacitus (e.g. *Ann.* I. 75. 5: II. 37. 2, etc.).

16. Dio LII. 42. 1: πολλοὶ μὲν γὰρ ἱππῆς πολλοὶ δὲ καὶ πεζοὶ παρὰ τὴν ἀξίαν ἐκ τῶν ἐμφυλίων πολέμων ἐβούλευον. It is true that the phrase is a *topos* which recalls what Sallust said of Sulla's Senate (*gregarii milites*).

17. LV. 17. 3: τάς τε ἀρχὰς ἅπασι τοῖς δέκα μυριάδων οὐσίαν ἔχουσι καὶ ἄρχειν ἐκ τῶν νόμων δυναμένοις ἐπαγγέλλειν ἐπέτρεψε. τοσοῦτον γὰρ τὸ βουλευτικὸν τίμημα τὴν πρώτην εἶναι ἔταξεν, ἔπειτα καὶ ἐς πέντε καὶ εἴκοσι μυριάδας αὐτὸ προήγαγε. The figures are expressed, as usual, in the ratio of 1 drachma = 1 denarius = 4 sesterces. There is, it must be confessed, a difficulty. In LIV. 26. 3 (for 13 BC) Dio Cassius repeats what he said for 18 BC: τὸ μὲν πρῶτον δέκα μυριάδων τὸ τίμημα αὐτοῖς ὥριστο; but he adds: 'because a great many estates had been ruined in the civil wars'. So that he seems to be meaning to say that the figure of 400,000 HS 'fixed' in 18 was in some sort a 'reduction'. This is how U. Scamuzzi understands it. In fact, Dio's words can be taken in quite another way. Augustus wanted to fix (τάττειν) a census for senators, and naturally one distinct from the traditionally adequate equestrian census. But he gave up the idea in 18, and only carried it out in 13. One pointer is that, about 20 BC, there seems to have been a 'restoration' of the census requirement relating to the equestrian census of 400,000 HS. The first direct evidence on this point dates from precisely this period: Horace, *Epist.* I. 1. 58: '. . . sed quadringentis sex septem milia desunt:/plebs eris'. Indeed Suetonius' famous story concerning the illusory belief of Caesar's soldiers, in 50 BC, that he was promising them 'ius anulorum cum milibus quadragenis' would be very much to the point, if only the text were contemporary and did not date from the time of Hadrian; we should be wary of Suetonius' supposed accuracy.

18. *JRS* 66 (1976), 32 (see Dio LV. 13. 6). The criticism is not arbitrary. Suetonius assembles – with no chronological exactitude – features which are typical but which he frequently interprets wrongly or inadequately. A comparison with the annalistic narratives of Dio Cassius or Velleius often makes it possible to limit the scope of Suetonius' *exemplum*. Cf. in general *Suétone historien* by J. Gascou, in course of publication, and some typical examples in T. Reekmans, 'La politique économique et financière des autorités dans les *Douze Césars* de Suétone', in *Historiographia antiqua*, . . . *in honorem W. Peremans* (1977), 265.

19. Suet. *Vesp.* 9 (cf. Nicolet, *Ordre équestre* I, 239); note that as early as Cicero's time, the equestrian order was 'second in dignity' after the Senate: 'proximus huic dignitate' (*de domo*, 74).

20. To reject the arguments contained in book LII out of hand, as an intrusion from the Severan age, is, in my view, a methodological error (cf. what Dio himself says LII. 41. 1–2 essential). In addition to the classic studies by P. Meyer (1891) and M. Hammond, *TAPA* 63 (1932), 88. cf. recent work on the subject by F. Millar, *A Study of Cassius Dio* (1964), 102–18, and B. Manuwald, *Cassius Dio und Augustus* (*Palingenesia* 14, 1979), 20 ff., and esp. C. Letta, 'La composizione dell'opera di Cassio Dione: cronologia e sfondo storico-politico', in E. Gabba (ed.) *Ricerche di storiografia greca di età romana* (1979), 117 ff. esp. 167–70 (which deals chiefly with the chronology of the redaction, subsequent to the beginning of the reign of Severus Alexander).

21. LII. 19. 2: ἀντὶ δὲ δὴ τῶν ἄλλων τούς τε γενναιοτάτους καὶ τοὺς ἀρίστους τούς τε πλουσιωτάτους ἀντεσάγαγε (= the knights).

22. Texts conveniently collected, unfortunately without regard to chronology, by U. Scamuzzi, op. cit (n. 15), 1969, 262–3 (Horace, *Ars Poet.* 383 ff.; a good comparison with the Senate in Cicero, *de leg.* III. 10; 28–9; Martial V. 27. 1, etc.). On *locus*, see my observations in *Latomus* 29 (1970), 72–103.

23. I summarize the convergent conclusions of my own article, previously cited, and of A. Chastagnol, 'La naissance de l'*ordo senatorius*', *MEFRA* 1973, 583; and ' "Latus clavus" et "adlectio": l'accès des hommes nouveaux au Sénat romain sous le Haut-Empire', *RHD* 53 (1975), 375 ff.

24. In particular, it was necessary, at a time when the Senate had been purged several times, to know whether the rank of those excluded could be passed on: Ulpian (*Dig.* I. 9. 7) refers to opinions held by Labeo and Proculus on this matter: 'sed eum, qui posteaquam pater eius de senatu motus est concipitur et nascitur, Proculus et Pegasus opinantur non esse quasi senatoris filium'. Cf., finally, L. Raditsa, 'Augustus' legislation concerning marriage . . .', *ANRW* II. 13 (1980), 278.

25. T. P. Wiseman, *New Men in the Roman Senate, 139 BC–AD 14*, (1971), esp. 191–202; I. Shatzman, *Senatorial Wealth and Roman Politics* (1975); R. Duncan-Jones, *The Economy of the Roman Empire*² (1982); E. Rawson, 'The Ciceronian Aristocracy and its Property', in M. Finley (ed.), *Studies in Roman Property* (1976), 85; cf. also the series of articles 'Sources et formes de la richesse dans le monde romain', in *Ktema* 2 (1977), 157–380.

26. Tacitus, *Ann.* I. 75. 5; II. 37. 2; 48. 1; XIII. 34. 2; (XI. 25. 5); Dio LIV. 17. 3; LVI. 41. 2; LVII. 10. 3; LX. 11. 8 (Claudius authorizes those unable to meet the *census* to withdraw): etc; cf. SHA, *Hadr.* 7.

27. On the problems of the refusal, on the part of sons of some families, to undertake senatorial responsibilities, see my observations in *JRS* 66 (1976), 31, 35, and 55 (difficulties for the tribunate, the aedileship etc.). Claudius, during his censorship, punished such refusals by the loss of the *equus publicus* (Suet. *Claud.* 24. 2). Impoverishment, sometimes, was merely an excuse, or was untrue. This 'refusal of honours', which has nothing much in common with the 'refusals of power' proper to Emperors (J. Béranger, 'Le Refus du pouvoir', *MH* 5 (1948), 178 = *Principatus*, 196), has some precedents and numerous causes: but the great moral laws (*de adulteriis, de maritandis ordinibus*, etc.) which, in the field of private law as well as in matters of inheritance, created so many obligations and disabilities for senators, certainly had a good deal to do with it. Cf. Mommsen, *DP* VI. 2. 57–63.

28. *Ann.* II. 37. 2: 'Nepos erat oratoris Hortensii, inlectus a divo Augusto liberalitate deciens sestertii ducere uxorem, suscipere liberos, ne clarissima familia extingueretur . . .'; 38. 1: 'si quantum pauperum est venire huc et liberis suis petere pecunias coeperint, singuli numquam exsatiabuntur, respublica deficiet.' In the end, Tiberius gave 200,000 HS to each of the children.

29. Dio LVI. 41. 3: ὧν τὸ φαῦλον τὸ ἐκ τῶν στάσεων ἐπιπολάσαν ἀλύπως ἀφελὼν τὸ λοιπὸν

αὐτῷ τε τούτῳ ἐσέμνυνε καὶ τῇ αὐξήσει τοῦ τιμήματος ἐμεγάλυνε τῇ τε δόσει τῶν χρημάτων ἐπλούτισεν·, etc. The word ἐμεγάλυνε must convey the idea of *maiestas* (cf. Velleius II. 89. 3: 'restituta vis legibus, iudiciis auctoritas, senatui maiestas . . .')

30. Another argument, of very different origin, might have played a part: the intuitive sense of a kind of 'inflation', what we might call a change in the scale of values, in particular of money of account. For the ancients, this sense was linked to several others: the increase in the power, and in the size of the Roman Empire; the 'growth of luxury', at once a sign of greatness and bringing the risk of decadence. Consequently, it was necessary for the census qualifications to adapt, in every way, to these changes. Aristotle had already stated it very clearly (*Pol.* V. 8. 1308^b; cf. my observations on 'L'idéologie du système centuriate' in *La filosofia greca e il diritto romano* (Rome, Acc. Naz. dei Lincei. Quad. 221, 1976), 137. This sense finds expression in the great speeches on the sumptuary laws by Asinius Gallus, in AD 16 (Tac. *Ann.* II. 33. 3–5), and in 22 by Tiberius himself (III. 53–5). Notice, in III. 55, Tacitus' personal excursus on the 'luxury' which marked the Julio-Claudian era. But, as Syme justly remarks in *Tacitus* I. 325, the theme of Gallus' speech in 16 had already appeared in a speech by Hortensius in 55 BC (Dio XXXIX. 37. 3).

31. *Lex repetund.* (*CIL* I². 583 = *FIRA²* I. 7, line 14 (and 17): 'quos legerit, eos patrem tribum cognomenque indicet' (instead of the complete phrase: 'patrem aut patronum'. cf. *Tab. Her.*, line 146).

32. U. Scamuzzi, op. cit. (n. 15). 1969, 269; 1970, 47–53 (*Schol. Gronov.* p. 281 St.).

33. The penalties were naturally graduated: *nota* with or without *infamia*, expulsion from the order, etc. Still very useful is A. H. J. Greenridge's little book, *Infamia* (1894), esp. 88 ff.

34. Suet. *Aug.* 40. 1: 'Cum autem plerique equitum, attrito bellis civilibus patrimonio, spectare ludos e quattuordecim non auderent metu poenae theatralis, pronuntiavit non teneri ea, quibus ipsis parentibusve equester census unquam fuisset.'

35. Dio LV. 13. 6: ἐπειδή τε συχνοὶ τῶν νεανίσκων ἔκ τε τοῦ βουλευτικοῦ γένους κἀκ τῶν ἄλλων ἱππέων ἐπένοντο μηδὲν ἐπαίτιον ἔχοντες, τοῖς μὲν πλείοσι τὸ τεταγμένον τίμημα ἀνεπλήρωσεν, ὀγδοήκοντα δέ τισι καὶ ἐς τριάκοντα αὐτὸ μυριάδας ἐπηύξησε. (This is what Suetonius refers to, *Aug.* 41. 3. cf. above). In fact, the words Dio uses may show that, among the *iuniores* of the equestrian order, only those who were the sons of senators were concerned, or at least, among the rest, (κἀκ τῶν ἄλλων ἱππέων), those who, by the granting of the *latus clavus* and the senatorial census, Augustus wished to encourage to solicit honours. Cf. my interpretation, *JRS* 66 (1976), 32, 36.

36. Cf. S. Demougin, 'Notables municipaux et ordre équestre à l'époque de la deuxième guerre civile', to appear in *Les Bourgeoisies municipales* (proceedings of Naples Conference, 1981).

37. U. Scamuzzi, op. cit. (n. 15) 1969, 311; G. Rotondi, *Leges Publicae Populi Romani* (1912), 462; contra, B. Biondi, in *Acta Divi Augusti* (1945), 201; Pliny, *NH* XXXIII. 32: 'et lege Julia theatrali . . . sedisset.'

38. The Senate could also intervene in this domain if necessary: cf. the proposal put forward by L. Junius Gallio in AD 32, Tac. *Ann.* VI. 3. 1, and very badly received by Tiberius, to give the *ius in XIV sedendi* to soldiers (or former soldiers) of the praetorium.

39. Nothing illustrates better this vocation and function of the *ordines* than the two formulae which appeared recently in the *S.C. de matronarum lenocinio coercendo*, found at Larino and published in 1978, which refer (line 5) to the 'dignitas ordinis (eorum)' and (line 12) to those 'qui eludendae auctoritatis eius ordinis gratia' etc.:

(V. Giuffrè translates 'il prestigio oneroso', which is scarcely overdoing it); the two words illustrate very well the two sides of the idea of *ordo*: privilege and obligation, a collective vocation which can override individual choice. On this text, see V. Giuffrè, 'Un senato-consulto ritrovato', *Atti Acc. Sc. Mor. Pol. Napoli*, XCI (1980), 5.

40. I am here quoting from a sixteenth-century French jurist who used his admirable understanding and exposition of the Roman orders to elucidate, in his own way, the feudal and regalian law of his own time: C. Loyseau, *Traité des ordres et des seigneuries* I. 6 (1610), 4.

41. Suet. *Aug.* 2. 5: 'ipse Augustus nihil amplius quam equestri familia ortum se scribit vetere ac locuplete'. A trait common to a whole 'class' of Roman or municipal knights, at the end of the Republic, who, locally, were not in the least 'plebeian' but, on the contrary, displayed a genuine dynastic pride: 'Maecenas atavis edite regibus'. There is nothing contradictory between this and their admiration for the Roman 'dynasties', to which they were often allied by marriage (as in the case of the young Octavian himself, who was to move easily from the dynastic pride of Velletri to the dynastic pride of Rome). Some inadequate observations on the subject in M. Reinhold, 'Augustus' conception of himself', *Thought* 55 (1980), 36. This does not mean that there are not some grounds of truth in the gossip put about by Antony and others about the *argentarii* or *divisores* that Augustus numbered among his forbears on both the maternal and the paternal sides (Syme, *RR*, 112 ff.); these activities were not so much frowned upon as is claimed (for the *divisores, Ordre équestre* I. 603–5; II. 911; 997; 1068–9).

42. Suet. *Aug.* 74. 1: 'convivabatur assidue nec unquam nisi recta, non sine magno hominum ordinumque dilectu. (2) Valerius Messala tradit, neminem umquam libertinorum adhibitum ab eo cenae acepto Mena, sed asserto in ingenuitutem post proditam Sex. Pompei classem.' On the other hand, Augustus dined at his freedmen's houses, especially in order to watch the games (Suet. *Aug.* 45. 1), likewise Tiberius, Dio LVII. 11. 4–5.

43. Cf. my observations, *JRS* 66 (1976), 36–7. The distinction between the *iuniores equestris ordinis* and the *seniores* is attested to by Dio LIII. 13. 6; of these *iuniores*, the sons of senators wore the broad stripe. This therefore is how I propose to reconstruct lines 55–6 of the *Tabula Hebana*: 'et qui ordini[s equestris iuniores erunt, ii qui latum cla]vom habebunt, qui eor. officio fungi volent . . .' On the distinction between the tribunes who were *laticlavii* and those who were *angusticlavii*, see Dio LIII. 15. 2 and Suet. *Aug.* 38. 2. In theory, the selection was the Emperor's, but in fact it was made by the *ab epistulis*: cf. T. Flavius Abascantus, whose functions are described by Statius, *Silvae* V. 1. 80 ff.; 95–8 (Mommsen *DP* V. 124, n. 1).

44. Velleius II. 101: 'tribuno militum mihi visere contigit'; 111: 'finita equestri militia designatus quaestor, etc'.; anon. *ILS* 2682 (near Corfinium): 'reliquid libero[s], unum maximis municipi honorib. iudiciis August. Caesaris usum, alterum castresibus eiusdem Caesaris August. summis [eq]u[es]tris ordinis honoribus et iam superiori destinatum ordini . . .'; M. Aurelius Cottanus (*ILS* 1949): 'Cottanum meum produxit honore tribuni, quem fortis castris Caesaris emeruit'.

45. Suet. *Aug.* 46. 2: 'ac necubi aut honestorum deficeret copia . . . . equestrem militiam petentis etiam ex commendatione publica cuiusque oppidi ordinabat . . . .'; cf. Syme, *RR*, 364, n. 1, for the parallel with the *tribuni militum a populo* ('perhaps'). The corpus of the latter which I made in '*Tribuni militum a populo*', *MEFR* 79 (1967), 29, entirely substantiates this hypothesis. On the other hand, I was probably wrong in seeing the same thing in the 'tres eq. Rom. a plebe' of the Narbonne Altar (*CIL* XII. 4333 = *ILS* 112 = *FIRA* III². 73; C. Nicolet,

'L'inscription de l'autel de Narbonne et la commendatio des chevaliers', *Latomus* 22 (1963), 721; this relates rather to the *Augustalitas* ; Caligula, too, is known to have recruited knights (Dio LIX. 9. 5): I should be inclined to relate this fact to the creation of the fifth *decuria* (Pliny, XXXIII. 33); Cf. P. Kneissl, *Chiron* 10 (1980), 291. We know that in the same chapter, Suetonius claims that Augustus, in order to 'equalize the status and dignity' of the colonial *decuriones* with those 'of the City', envisaged a local, postal vote in the Roman elections. The proceeding would not be absurd: this was how the local *census* was supposed to work according to the *Tab. Her.* But this is a completely isolated piece of evidence. I wonder if Suetonius was not confusing it with the preliminary vote, which was also *obsignatum*, of the *equites decuriarum* revealed by the *Tabula Hebana*.

46. Suet. *Aug.* 24: 'Equitem Romanum, quod duobus filiis adulescentibus causa detrectandi sacramenti pollices amputasset, ipsum bonaque subiecit hastae . . .'. Velleius, II. 111: 'habiti itaque delectus, revocati undique et omnes veterani, viri feminaeque ex censu libertinum coactae dare militem (cf. Dio LV. 31. 1–3) . . . senatorum equitumque romanorum exactae ad id bellum operae'. *Operae* indicates personal service, the fact of being 'employed', *operas dare*. P. Brunt has shed the essential light on the maintenance of conscription during the Empire: 'C. Fabricius Tuscus and an Augustan Dilectus', *ZPE* (1974), 161, and 'Conscription and Volunteering in the Roman Imperial Army', *Scripta classica Israelica* 1 (1974), 90. On the penalties, cf. *Dig.* XLVI. 16. 4. *pr.* 9. On the *vacatio militiae* of the publicans, Livy XXIII. 49. 2 (unusual?).

47. But cf. her exhaustive article, 'Les juges des cinq décuries originaires de l'Italie', *Ancient Society* 6 (1975), 143 ff., to which I have referred for the previous bibliography. For an interpretation of some passages of Pliny's text, J. L. Ferrary, 'Pline . . . . et les chev. Rom. sous la République', *REL* 58 (1980), 313 ff.

48. Pliny, *NH* XXIX. 18: 'inquisitio per parietes agitur.'

49. From Hirschfeld until L. Neesen and M. R. Cimma quite recently, the suppression of a great many publicans' companies, whether in the imperial or even the senatorial provinces, has been regarded as a certainty. Some, e.g. M. R. Cimma, *Ricerche sulle società di publicani* (1981), 102, even credit Caesar (with his so-called suppression of all the companies in Asia) with the idea of this systematic policy. Others incline to Augustus or Tiberius. I do not think that this is so, at least for the reign of Augustus, but I shall return to the subject elsewhere.

50. Tacitus, *Ann.* IV. 6. 4, is categorical, although elliptical: 'at frumenta et pecuniae vectigales, cetera publicorum fructuum societatibus equitum Romanorum agitabantur.' In AD 23, even if we read *frumentum vectigale*, this can only refer to the traditional *decumae* of the corn-producing provinces; then to the indirect taxes and finally to all the other state revenues. For AD 58, *Ann.* XIII, 50–1. There is some question of the abolition of the *cuncta vectigalia* (and 50. 2 seems in fact to contrast the *tributa* with them). Yet I do not think that *vectigalia* means only 'indirect taxes' (an irrelevant distinction); in any case, grain was included in the partial reforms already carried (51. 3). For this episode, cf. lastly (with caution) C. Gatti, 'Nerone e il progetto di riforma tributaria', *Par. Pass.* 30 (1975), 41; and 'Studi Neroniani I', in *Atti del centro di ricerche e docum. sull'antichità classica* VIII (1976–7), 83; M. R. Cimma, op. cit. (n. 49), 128–9. On the meaning of Tacitus' expressions 'societates equitum Rom.' (IV. 6. 4) and 'vectigalium societates a consulibus et tribunis plebii constitutae acri etiam tum populi Romani libertate' (XIII. 50. 3). cf. C. Nicolet, 'Deux remarques sur l'organisation des soc. de publicains', in H. van Effenterre (ed.), *Points de vue sur la fiscalité antique* (1979), 69 ff., esp. 78–9.

51. Appian *BC* V. 540: καὶ τῶν εἰσφορῶν τοὺς ἔτι ὀφείλοντας ἀπέλυε καὶ φόρων τελώνας τε καὶ τοὺς τὰ μισθώματα ἔχοντας ὧν ἔτι ὀφείλοιεν; Dio Cass. XLIX. 15. 3: τὸν τε φόρον τόν ἐκ τῶν ἀπογραφῶν καὶ εἰ δή τι ἄλλο ἔτι τῷ δημοσίῳ ἐς τὸν πρὸ τοῦ ἐμφυλίου πολέμου

χρόνον ἐπωφείλετο ἀφῆκε. Cf. E. Gabba, *Appiano Lib. V*, 217, on the two interpretations current in Rome regarding these concessions; and the useful observations by R. Scuderi, 'Problemi fiscali a Roma in età triumvirale'. *Clio* (1979), 341.

52. Suet. *Aug.* 32. 4: 'tabulas veterum aerarii debitorum, vel praecipium calumniandi materiam excissit'; Dio LIII. 2. 3: καὶ τὰς ἐγγύας τὰς πρὸς τὸ δημόσιον πρὸ τῆς πρὸς τῷ Ἀκτίῳ μάχης γενομένας, πλὴν τῶν περὶ τὰ οἰκοδομήματα, ἀπήλλαξε, τά τε παλαιὰ συμβόλαια τῶν τῷ κοινῷ τι ὀφειλόντων ἔκαυσε. There is a clear distinction between genuine sureties (ἐγγύαι = *praedes obsignatae*), and simple arrears. 'Securities' could concern only publicans.

53. Vell. II. 92. 2: 'cum . . . . protraxisset publicanorum fraudes, punisset avaritiam, regessisset in aerarium publicas.' In the article cited in note 50, I suggested that the strict rules of the *licitatio* as laid down by Paulus, *Sententiae* V. 1ᴬ (= *Dig.* XXXIX. 4. 9) might go back to the Lex de Publicanis of Caesar, in 59 BC. We are also reminded of some Augustan legislation: cf. a *caput* from the Lex Julia de Vi Publica, 'de iis qui nova vectigalia exercent' (*Dig.* XLVIII. 6. 12; cf. B. Biondi, *Acta Divi Aug.* 132); cf. also the 'Lex Julia Peculatus' (if, indeed, that really belongs to Augustus), where the *caput* 'de residuis' (*Dig.* XLVIII. 13. 5, *pr.* 1–2) may refer to the publicans (Biondi; op. cit. 165).

54. Dio LII. 8. 4 (Agrippa): νῦν δὲ πᾶσά σε ἀνάγκη συναγωνιστὰς πολλοὺς, ἅτε τοσαύτης οἰκουμένης ἄρχοντα, ἔχειν, καὶ προσήκει που πάντας αὐτοὺς καὶ ἀνδρείους καὶ φρονίμους εἶναι. LII. 15. 1 (Maecenas): αὐτόν σε μετὰ τῶν ἀρίστων ἀνδρῶν νομοθετεῖν. Note also 19. 1 (on the selection of senators and magistrates, cf. above); 4 (for the equestrian order).

55. Dio LII. 25. 6 (Maecenas): Ὅστις δ᾽ ἵ ἄν τῶν ἱππέων διὰ πολλῶν διεξελθὼν ἐλλόγιμος ὥστε καὶ βουλεῦσαι γένηται.

56. Livy XLII. 61. 5: 'equites enim illis principes iuventutis, equites seminarium senatus' (cf. XXIII. 23. 6); SHA *Alex*. 18: 'Idem libertinos nunquam in equestrem locum redegit, afferens seminarium senatorum equestrem locum esse.'

57. Cf. n. 55 above.

58. Cf. S. Demougin, 'Ordre sénatorial et ordre équestre sous les Julio-Claudiens', in *Epigrafia e ordine senatorio, 1981*, (forthcoming).

59. Nicolet, *L'Ordre équestre* I. 699–722; cf. J. H. D'Arms, *Commerce and Social Standing in Ancient Rome* (1981), 62, in which I am justly criticized for underestimating the leaning towards commercial or financial 'affairs'; altogether overdone and inadequate at the same time, on the other hand, is the article by C. and O. Wikander, 'Republican prosopography: some reconsiderations', *Opuscula Romana* 12. 1 (1979), 1; on a case such as Atticus' (by no means an isolated one, as I have shown) cf. recently M. Labate and E. Narducci, 'Mobilità nei modelli etici e relativismo dei valori: il 'personnage di Attico', in A. Giardina and A. Schiavone (eds.), *Società Romana e produzione schiavistica* III (1981), 125. In order to clear up a slight misunderstanding on p. 129: I did not reject 'any typological element' in the life of Atticus, seeing everything in terms of 'individual choice', in contradiction of R. Syme's theory, in which one of the chief bases of the *consensus* to the *princeps*' power is seen as the desire of the Italian 'bourgeoisie' to create an area of independence and autonomy for its own economic activities with regard to the service of the state. It is more complex than that. The 'urban bourgeoisie' as a whole is one thing; the 'equestrian order' (of which Atticus was a *princeps*), restored by Augustus, quite another. Cicero in 49, actually complained of the lack of interest shown by the Italian middle class in the politics of the state: 'nihil prorsus aliud curant nisi agros, nisi villulas, nisi nummulos suos' (*Att.* VIII. 13. 2; cf. VIII. 7. 5; VIII. 16. 1). But was Atticus 'uninterested' in politics? Cicero calls him in so many words, *natura*

πολιτικός (*Att.* IV. 6. 1, 55 BC; cf. *Fam.* II. 8. 1, to Caelius, where he uses the same word); but Atticus actually *chose* to shun the 'servitude' of honours. Which did not prevent him offering advice to first Pompey, then Cicero and others (and before long to Antonius and Octavian himself: the result of which was a dynastic marriage of his daughter to Agrippa!). So that this 'choice' was not made by him with regard solely to 'chrematistics' but, given his epicureanism, it was another way of approaching public life. It was in contrasting it with the opposite 'choice' of a knight's son soliciting honours (like Cicero) that I talked of individual motivations. But such motivations come in series: before Atticus, C. Flavius Pusio, Cn. Titinius, C. Maecenas, *iudices* in 91 BC (*Pro Cluentio* 153–4); contemporary with him, C. Rabirius Postumus, C. Matius, C. Oppius, Q. Sextius Niger, who preferred the 'cabinet' of the new leader; after him, Maecenas or Gn. Sallustius Crispus (Tac. *Ann.* III. 30). This social stratum, these 'princes' of the equestrian order, had nothing in common with the 'philosophers of the Janus', occupied exclusively with their *nummi*, mocked both by Cicero (*de Off.* II. 87) and, twenty years after, by Horace (*Epist.* I. 1. 52).

60. C. Turranius Gracilis, Prefect of the Annona, and before that Prefect of Egypt, from AD 14 to 48. See H. Pavis d'Escurac, *La Préfecture de l'annone* (1976), 317–19; H.-G. Pflaum, *Les Procurateurs équestres* (1951), 29–33.

61. *L'Ordre équestre* I. 423–34.

62. Tac. *Ann.* XII. 60. 3; Dio LI. 3. 4; 17. 1; LIII. 13. 1. 62. He certainly put a prefect of equestrian rank in charge of Egypt. But he refused permission to go there not only to senators but also to *equites Romani inlustres*: Tac. *Ann.* II. 59. 4; the expression Tacitus uses shows that it was not a matter of this or that legal classification (e.g. knights entitled to the *latus clavus*, or some other assumption) but simply of knights who were 'eminent' or 'important' (in the eyes of the *princeps*); these were in contrast to the *equites modici* (I. 73. 1). Cf. my observations in *L'Ordre équestre*, 225–30.

63. For Augustus' social and economic policies, I have selected a number of titles from a superabundant list of publications: F. de Martino, *Storia della costituzione Romana* IV (1974), 21 ff., 310 ff., 521 ff.; L. Polverini, 'L'aspetto sociale del passagio dalla republica al principato', *Aevum* 38 (1964), 241 ff.; 439 ff.; 39 (1965), 1 ff., is well informed and intelligent (although I cannot agree with his definition of the equestrian order). This is more than may be said for V. A. Sirago, *Principato di Augusto, concentrazione di proprietà e di poteri nelle mani dell'imperatore* (1978), ill informed occasionally to the point of caricature (see p. 97, which speaks of 'ever-increasing monetary devaluation'; p. 133; etc.); neither is there anything new in S. I. Kovaliov, 'Le cause delle guerre civili', in L. Canali (ed.) *Potere e consenso nella Roma di Augusto* (1975), 3 (text dating from 1953). Still worth consulting are the great syntheses of the years 1937–8 in Italy, at the time of the bi-millenary, even though they bear the impression of the 'ideologies' and of the political problems of the time: *Augustus: Studi in occasione del bimillenario Augusteo* (1938), esp. V. Arangio-Ruiz, 'La legislazione', 101–46, with bibliography; A. Momigliano, 'I problemi delle istituzione militari di Augusto,' 195–216; G. Cardinali, 'Amministrazione territoriale e finanziaria', 161–94; and the *Conferenze Augustee* published in 1939 by the Univ. Cattolica del S. Cuore, esp. A. Calderini, 'Le riforme sociali di Augusto', 119–38; and even more, B. Biondi, 'La legislazione di Augusto', 139–262. The normative texts are collected in AA.VV. (S. Riccobono, N. Festa, H. Gabrici, V. Arangio-Ruiz, and B. Biondi), *Acta Divi Augusti* I (1945) (only number published). Finally, for many aspects, Z. Yavetz, *Plebs and Princeps* (1969).

64. I have made an inventory and taken stock in 'Il pensiero economico dei Romani',

in L. Firpo (ed.), *Storia delle idee politiche economiche e sociali* I: *Antichità classica* (1982), 877–960 (with bibliography); essential is G. Tozzi, *Economisti greci e romani* (1961).

65. These *Letters* are the place to study attitudes towards property and wealth: cf. provisionally C. Virlouvet, 'Le Sénat dans la seconde *Lettre* de [Salluste] à César', soon to be published in *Des ordres à Rome*.

66. Caesar, *BC* III. 21–4; cf. M. Frederiksen, 'Caesar, Cicero and the Problem of Debt', *JRS* 56 (1966), 128.

67. Add to the works cited in my *Tributum* (1976), 1 and 95–6, more recently M. Corbier, *L'aerarium Saturni et l'aerarium militare* (1974); and L. Neesen, *Untersuchungen zu den direkten Staatsabgaben der röm Kaiserzeit (27 v. chr.–284 n. Chr.)* (1980).

68. Dio LII. 6. 1–5. (this text is historically more relevant to the Hellenistic period and to the Roman Republic than to the imperial age, as I shall show elsewhere); for the financial aspects of Maecenas' speech, E. Gabba, 'Progetti di riforme economiche e fiscali in uno storico dell'età dei Severi', *Studi . . . A. Fanfani* (1962), 1–32 (referring to Dio LII. 28); the title is self-explanatory. On some precise aspects, contemporary meaning is clear. On the publication of the accounts of the Empire by Augustus, abandoned by Tiberius and reintroduced by Caligula, Dio LIX. 9. 4 (cf. also LIII. 19. 1, on secrecy; Aelius Aristides makes a similar observation).

69. Nicolet, *Tributum*, 87–98; R. Scuderi, art. cit. (n. 51) (table on pp. 367–8).

70. Dio XLVII. 16. 3–4; 17. 3; cf. Nicolet, *Le Métier de citoyen²* (1979), 242–9.

71. Dio XLVII. 17. 3. We must, however, abandon a purely 'fiscalist' interpretation of the second proscriptions. Cf. henceforth the thesis by F. Hinard, 'Les Proscriptions à Rome'; to appear in *Coll. de l'École francaise de Rome*.

72. Dio XLIX. 15. 3–4; Appian, *BC* V. 540. See K. Scott, 'The political propaganda of 43–30 BC', *Mem. Amer. Acad. Rome*, 11 (1933), 7, on pp. 33–4.

73. Suet. *Div. Jul.* 43. 1. perhaps in relation to the sumptuary laws (Suet. ibid.; Dio XLIII. 25. 2).

74. The decision to replace grants of land by sums of money, the essential step, dates from 13 BC. Dio LIV. 25. 5–6: καὶ τὰ χρήματα ὅσα παυσάμενοι τῆς στρατείας, ἀντὶ τῆς χώρας ἥν ἀεί ποτε ἤτουν, λήψοιντο. It was vital to reassure landowners. The resources of the *princeps*'s treasury were adequate to cope with this expense for almost twenty years, until AD 6. Unless the decision taken in 13 was not to take effect until twenty years later.

75. Bibliography in *Tributum*, 96. Nothing has yet superseded R. Cagnat's excellent chapter in *Étude historique sur les impôts indirects chez les Romains* (1882), 175–226.

76. Dio LVI. 28. 6: ἐπί τε τοὺς ἀγροὺς καὶ ἐπὶ τὰς οἰκίας τὴν συντέλειαν ἤγαγε, καὶ παραχρῆμα μηδὲν εἰπών, μήθ' ὅσον μήθ' ὅπως αὐτὸ δώσουσιν, ἔπεμψεν ἄλλους ἄλλη τά τε τῶν ἰδιωτῶν καὶ τὰ τῶν πόλεων κτήματα ἀπογραφομένους. For the limitation to citizens, see Pliny, *Paneg.* 37; the tax affected legacies as well as inheritances: Dio LV. 25. 5 (τῶν τε κλήρων καὶ τῶν δωρεῶν) the tax does not affect 'close relatives or the poor' (discussed in Cagnat, op. cit. 184–5; the exact level of exemption may not have been fixed until Trajan, Pliny, *Pan.* 40).

77. Some excellent observations in Cagnat, op. cit. 224; cf. H. Pavis d'Escurac, 'Pline le Jeune et la transmission des patrimoines', *Ktema* 3 (1978), 275. One would like to be able to estimate in absolute and in relative terms the 'fiscal burden' represented by the *vicesima*, but that hope is vain. We know that the *praemium militare* of a praetorian was 20,000 HS, and of a legionary 12,000. But we can only make a very approximate calculation of the annual fluctuations of payments, in any case irregular, under Augustus. Cf. hereafter the cautious estimates of M. Corbier, 'L'Aerarium militare' in *Armées et fiscalités* (1977), 97–234. The *vicesima* would bring in 35 million HS a year, which would amount to a gross tax on property

transfers to the value of 700 million HS (for a citizen body numbering some 4 to 5 million); this represents – in order of magnitude – barely 700 estates equal to the senatorial census. In short, it is clear that this tax really affected only a very few, very rich people.

78. Tacitus, *Ann.* I. 78; Suet. *Calig.* 16. Dio LV. 31; LIX. 9.
79. Cf. naturally the *S.C. Calvisianum de repetundis* (4 BC) in the fifth Edict, lines 73–144. Noteworthy is the formula in the fifth edict by which Augustus proclaims the *senatus consultum*: ἐξ οὗ δῆλον ἔσται . . . ὅσην φροντίδα ποιούμεθα ἐγώ τε καὶ ἡ σύγκλητος τοῦ μηδένα τῶν ἡμῖν ὑποτασσομένων παρὰ τὸ προσῆκον τι πάσχιν ἤ εἰσηπράττεσθαι. Cf. the commentary by F. de Visscher, *Les Édits d'Auguste* (1940), 139 ff.
80. Dio LII. 29. 1–2: ἄν μήτε προσεπηρεάζωνται καὶ τῷ ἔργῳ πεισθῶσιν ὅτι πάντα ταῦτα καὶ ὑπὲρ τῆς σωτηρίας σφῶν καὶ ὑπὲρ τοῦ τὰ λοιπὰ ἀδεῶς καρποῦσθαι συνεσοίσουσι.
81. Dio LVI. 40. 1: τίς μὲν γὰρ οὐκ ἄν ἕλοιτο ἀπραγμόνως σώζεσθαι καὶ ἀκινδύνως εὐδαιμονεῖν, καὶ τῶν μὲν ἀγαθῶν τῶν τῆς πολιτείας ἀφθόνως ἀπολαύειν, ταῖς δὲ δὴ φροντίσι ταῖς ὑπὲρ αὐτῆς μὴ συνεῖναι.
82. Dio LVI. 43. 4: καὶ ὅτι τὴν μοναρχίαν τῇ δημοκρατίᾳ μίξας τό τε ἐλεύθερόν σφισιν ἐτήρησε καὶ τὸ κόσμιον τό τε ἀσφαλὲς προσπαρεσκεύασεν.
83. Velleius II. 103. 5. Such a formula was no novelty: it was the ideal of all good governments. J. Hellegouarc'h, in his Budé edition of Velleius Book II (1982), 246, indeed notes this parallel with Cicero, *de domo* 17: 'reditu meo . . . . spes oti, tranquillitas animorum, iudicia, leges, concordia populi, senatus auctoritas' etc. But much more interesting is the parallel with proclamations by Octavian in 36: κατήγγελλέ τε εἰρήνην καὶ εὐθυμίαν (Appian, *BC* V 540), with the commentary of E. Gabba, ad. loc. who keeps εὐθυμία (*securitas*) instead of the correction εὐθυνία (*abundantia*) proposed by Mendelssohn.
84. LVI. 41. 4: τῶν λοιπῶν 'Ρωμαίων, οἷς ἔργα, χρήματα, ἀγῶνας, πανηγύρεις, ἄδειαν, ἀφθονίαν τῶν ἐπιτηδείων, ἀσφάλειαν οὐκ ἀπὸ τῶν πολεμίων οὐδ' ἀπὸ τῶν κακούργων μόνον, ἀλλὰ καὶ ἀπὸ τῶν ἐκ τοῦ δαιμονίου οὐχ ὅτι μεθ' ἡμέραν ἀλλὰ καὶ νύκτωρ συμπιπτόντων, παρεσκεύασε. The *erga*, of course, works carried out for the people, not work on behalf of the people. Augustus' policy with regard to the *plebs* is not my subject; cf. the wholly contradictory judgements of Sirago, op. cit. (n. 63), 132, and Yavetz, op. cit. (n. 63), 95–101. One small point: [Aurelius Victor], *De Caes., Aug.* 29, asserts that Augustus 'cives sic amavit ut tridui frumento in horreis quondam viso statuisset veneno mori, si e provinciis classes interim non venirent'. This is probably the result of a mistranslation of a *topos* on the life of Augustus of which we have a summary in Pliny, *NH* VII. 149: 'cuncta deinde tot mala, inopia stipendi, rebellio Illyrici, servitiorum delectus, iuventutis penuria, pestilentia urbis, fames Italiae, destinatio expirandi et quadridui media maior pars mortis in corpus recepta, iuxta haec Variana clades.' All these misfortunes, in fact, concern the end of the reign. But an attempt at suicide by fasting 'for four days' is not necessarily connected with famine, and we have no mention of the 'four days' grain' which remained in the granaries. Augustus was undoubtedly greatly concerned with the *annona*, but he had, on the other hand, considered abolishing the free *frumentationes* (Suet. *Aug.* 42. 4–5). On this subject, we await the thesis of C. Virlouvet, *Tessera frumentaria*, to be published in 1984.
85. Date unknown, if indeed it is Augustan at all (B. Biondi, *Acta Div. Aug.*, 200); *Dig.* XLVIII. 12. 2. *pr.*:'Lege Julia de annona poena statuitur adversus eum, qui contra annonam fecerit societatemve coierit, qua annona carior fiat'; 1–2: 'ne quis navem nautamve retineat . . .'.
86. Suet. *Aug.* 98. 2: 'per illum se vivere, per illum navigare, libertate atque fortunis per illum frui'.
87. Cf. B. Biondi, 'La legislazione di Augusto', *Conferenze Augustee* (1939), 139, esp.

248–60; cf. A. Guarino, 'Gli aspetti giuridici del Principato', *ANRW* II. 13 (1980), 3; L. F. Raditza, op. cit. (n. 24), 278.

88. See B. Biondi, op. cit. 252. Paulus, *Sent*. V. 26. 3 (*Acta Divi Aug*. 134): 'tenetur qui quem armatis hominibus possessione domo villa agrove deiecerit expugnaverit, obsiderit clauserit.'

89. Paulus, *Sent*. V. 26. 4 (*Acta Div. Aug*. 136): 'creditor chirographarius si sine iussu praesidis per vim debitoris sui pignora, cum non haberet obligata, ceperit . . .'; *Dig*. IV. 2. 12. 2: 'qui vim adhibuit debitori suo ut solveret'.

90. Gaius III. 78 (Rotondi, *Leges Publicae*, 451). But V. Giuffrè has rightly shown that the law concerned is Caesar's: 'Profili politici ed economici della "cessio bonorum" ', *Riv. studi Salernitani*, 1971, 3.

91. I refer briefly to M. Frederiksen, *JRS* 56 (1966), 127; and to the synthesis by V. Giuffrè, s.v. 'Mutuo', *Enciclopedia del diritto* XXVII (1977), 414–44.

92. Dio LV. 12. 3ᵃ: Χιλίας τε καὶ πεντακοσίας μυριάδας δραχμῶν ἀτόκους τοῖς δεομένοις δανείσας ἐπ' ἔτη τρία, ἐπῃνεῖτο παρὰ πάντων καὶ ἐσεμνύνετο. Suet. *Aug*. 41. 2: 'et postea, quotiens ex damnatorum bonis superflueret, usum eius gratuitum eis, qui cavere in duplum possent, ad certum tempus indulsit.' Suetonius is generalizing, as always, and is less accurate than Dio. Describing the fire and the riots of 7 BC, Dio (LV. 8. 6) writes: καὶ τὸ μὲν τοῦ πυρὸς αἴτιον ἐς τοὺς χρεωφείλας ἀνεφέρετο.

93. Tac. *Ann*. VI. 16–17 (17. 4: 'donec tulit opem Caesar disposito per mensas miliens sestertio factaque mutandi copia sine usuris per triennium, si debitor populo in duplum praediis cavisset'.); Suet. *Tib*. 48; Dio LVIII. 21. 5.

94. Cicero, *de off*. I. 85: 'duo Platonis praecepta . . . unum, ut utilitatem civium sic tueantur ut, quaecumque agunt, ad eam referant, obliti commodorum suorum; alterum, ut totum corpus rei publicae curent, ne, dum partem aliquam tuentur, reliquas deserant . . . . qui autem parti civium consulent, partem neglegunt, rem perniciosissimam in civitatem inducunt, seditionen atque discordiam . . .'; I. 86: 'gravis et fortis civis et in republica dignus principatu . . . totamque eam sic tuebitur ut omnibus consulat . . .'; II. 83 (Aratus of Sicyon): 'At ille Graecus . . . omnibus omnibus consulendum putavit.'

95. Cicero quotes the opinion of Hecaton of Rhodes, according to whom 'neque enim solum nobis divites esse volumus, sed liberis, propinquis, amicis, maximeque reipublicae' (*de Off*. III. 63). Cf. G. Tozzi, op. cit. (n. 64), 294.

96. Cf. P. Brunt, 'Augustus e la respublica', in *La rivoluzione romana* (1981), 236. For the awareness of the civil-war generation of passing through a period of revolutions (*civiles commutationes*), cf. the famous letter from Cicero to Lucceius, *Fam*. V. 12. 4 (cf. in the same volume, A. Michel, 'Cicerone e l'idea di Rivoluzione', 186–202). Augustus himself (like Bonaparte later on), was so anxious to 'close' or 'finish' these revolutions that he pardoned retrospectively those who had fought in them, or whose fathers had fought in them (cf. his retort on the subject of Cato, Macrobius, *Sat*. II. 4. 18: 'Quisque praesentem statum civitatis commutari non volet et civis et vir bonus est').

I should like to thank Erich Segal for preparing the English text of this essay.

V. SENATORIAL SELF-REPRESENTATION: DEVELOPMENTS IN THE AUGUSTAN PERIOD

WERNER ECK

In one of his letters to Atticus Cicero stresses how grateful the provincials were that as governor he had reduced the burdens of billeting. For this they promised to honour him with statues, temples, and four-horse chariots; but he accepted only the decrees and prevented their being carried to fulfilment.[1] To be sure, a few days later, in another letter to Atticus, he writes that he has heard that Appius is having a gateway built at Eleusis and this gives him the idea of having something comparable built in the Academy; for he wants to leave some memorial of himself at Athens, which he loves.[2]

What Cicero in 50 BC merely contemplated in his letter to Atticus was undertaken, in actual reality, or carried out in practice, by many others, not only by Appius Claudius Pulcher at Eleusis. Monuments of the kind referred to by Cicero were part of the means by which senators could be given publicity, their self-esteem gratified, and the public influenced.

Very varied forms of aristocratic display were developed during the Republic.[3] The place was generally Rome, as the centre of politics: here there was noticeable competition from other senatorial families, here too the *populus Romanus*, as voters and as clients, could be influenced. The honouring of senators was aimed to a far lesser degree at the towns of Italy and (initially to a restricted extent only) at provincial cities.[4] A certain shift of emphasis in this respect appears to have set in during the last decades of the Republic. The purpose of all such measures was to display the individual and his entire family as well. None the less, in their self-advertisement senators' financial capacities and political or artistic fancies were not allowed a completely free rein. Rather, these were controlled to a not inconsiderable extent by the Senate; so, for example, the holding of triumphs or the erection of many buildings were only permitted in the first place by *senatus consulta*.[5] Thereby, at least for the inner circle of ruling noble families, the principle of aristocratic equality was preserved. Competitiveness only became the prevailing ethos with the full-scale breakdown of the underlying consensus from the late second century BC.[6] Ruthless pushing forward of the individual was to become a decisive element. Pompey in 79 BC wanted to offer the people the spectacle of four elephants, instead of horses, drawing his triumphal car. It was only the narrowness of the *porta triumphalis* that caused the project to founder.[7] In the holding of his games as aedile in 58 BC Aemilius Scaurus went beyond anything hitherto seen; in particular, the luxury with which his theatre was endowed outdid all previous performances.[8] C. Verres could admire himself in a forest of statues erected by various communities.[9] Other forms of display, especially having one's portrait on coins, first became possible through Caesar; and even his republican-minded assassins did not shrink from adopting this new brand of self-advertisement.[10]

With Octavian's final victory in the Civil War, relative political equality was destroyed. Neither by the propagating of the *res publica restituta* nor by the description of the ruler as *princeps* could this fact be conjured away.[11] Tacitus in the *Annales* speaks of Augustus, after winning over the soldiers by gifts, the people by provision for the food supply, and everyone by the delights of political peace, gradually increasing in power, while he took to himself the 'munia senatus magistratum legum'.[12] Allied with this, however, was the outward portrayal and emphasis of his person before the public, through honours of a kind both old and new.[13] Nor did Augustus forget to include these, in all their details, in his *Res Gestae*: chapters 9–14 in particular present, almost in the manner of a catalogue, the broad spectrum of possibilities. Ever detectable therein, if not always explicitly spelt out, is the sense of a competition that has been won, of special quality, compared with others who had likewise obtained, or were able to obtain, honours.[14] Yet at the same time the avowal is also given that under him no general monopolization of such public forms of display had been wished for by the holder of power.[15] That would also have been ruled out. For, however empty a disguise for the real conditions in which power was exercised the concept of the *res publica restituta* might be, yet it retained considerable significance for some time in the outward forms of public life. Hence, with the official recognition of Augustus' powers in 27 BC, immediate and radical alteration in the possibilities for self-advertisement by the senatorial aristocracy is not to be expected; not even at Rome, the centre of power, where aristocratic aspirations and the ruler's power existed side by side and could thus come into conflict.

The changes in the political structure were bound, however, to have their effects in this sphere as well, in spite of great discretion on Augustus' part.[16] The assumption of the *praenomen imperatoris* was already an advance signal: thereby the monopolization of *imperator* as a title was adumbrated.[17] A clearer sign was Octavian's refusal, in 28 BC, to let Licinius Crassus dedicate the *spolia opima* in the temple of Jupiter Feretrius. It was only possible to block the public documentation of martial excellence, in comparison with which Octavian would by no means have come off favourably, by the deployment of an underhand dodge.[18] Already in 27 BC a new conflict over possible modes of self-advertisement was witnessed. Objection was taken to Cornelius Gallus, first prefect of Egypt, because, according to Cassius Dio, he had had statues of himself set up practically all over Egypt, and had his deeds inscribed on the pyramids.[19] It is immaterial whether this was the sole, or the central, political point of the charge which finally led to his downfall.[20] This reproach could only have carried weight if a specific conception existed of the modes in which even so powerful a friend of the victor in the civil war was able – or was not permitted – to have himself portrayed before a provincial public.

Portraits and inscriptions were, however, a fundamental means by which individuals could be honoured in their lifetime and their memory preserved after death. To be sure, Horace mocks the people, standing wonderingly before *tituli* and *imagines*.[21] Yet this wonderment was matched by the value set on inscriptions by the leading members of Roman society. In 46 BC the Senate decreed that Caesar's name should be carved on the Capitoline temple in place of that of Catulus;[22] in 44 BC, according to Cassius Dio, Caesar was praised for handing over to Antonius the construction of the Rostra and the building inscription associated with it.[23] Augustus, too, stresses in *Res Gestae* 20 his rebuilding of the Capitol and of Pompeius' theatre at his own expense 'sine ulla inscriptione nominis mei'.[24] So great, evidently, was the significance of having one's name on public buildings such as the Capitol that credit could still be gained even from abstinence.

Thus inscriptions, in the estimation of the Augustan age as well, could be not only a means of documentation but at the same time a way to influence public opinion, to present an individual to a public. This was so, in particular, because inscriptions were not conceived in a vacuum, but were associated with some kind of monument, set up to an individual to preserve his *memoria*.[25] Since some inscriptions therefore possessed the characteristics of a social and political demonstration, they could also be affected by the more or less open struggle over self-advertisement between the *princeps* and the senatorial aristocracy, above all at Rome itself.[26] Monument and inscription formed, for a Roman, a self-evident unity, to be sure; an inscription without the object to which it belonged was scarcely conceivable. The inscription was normally secondary, what mattered was the object. In consequence, reference will frequently be made, in the observations that follow, first to monuments and only later to inscriptions. In what follows only selected aspects of senatorial self-advertisement can be discussed; but in view of the complexity of the problem and the volume of material, this is unavoidable.

In principle, inscriptions ought to document something. They demand, in most cases, a public that can read them. Nonetheless, one cannot start from the premiss that inscriptions were all composed for the same specific purpose. Hence with senatorial self-advertisement too one must assume a variety of function and with this a differing importance of epigraphic texts: 'a provincial dedication is not the same thing as an epitaph or an elogium.'[27] Of course, difficulties not infrequently arise in determining what function an inscription actually had. Findspot, circumstances of discovery, and the precise description of the stone or architectural context are often unknown or at least inadequately transmitted.[28] Hence in not a few cases it is impossible to determine the purpose of an inscription;[29] scholarly evaluation is then reduced to the text itself, which in normal prosopographical studies is generally sufficient in any case. Yet to restrict attention to the text alone, for example to the *cursus honorum*, is to overlook the fact that the text was only presented to the contemporary public and immediate posterity in association with the monument to which it belonged; this was how it was able to make its impact, how indeed it was supposed to do so. Yet it is precisely this aspect that must stand at the forefront of the complex of questions under discussion here. For it is naturally not immaterial when assessing purpose, whether an inscription belongs directly to a funerary context, i.e. was erected for someone already dead, or whether a living person was being honoured either before the general public, or within a senatorial house. Details cannot be gone into here; one can give no more than a few indications of the direction in which the material points. Inscriptions in which senators appear in their capacity as office-holders, as for example on *terminatio* stones, are omitted from consideration here. Even if the nature of the activity cannot be determined with exact precision in such texts, there can be no doubt that the context is administrative.

The overwhelming majority of all epigraphic texts from the city of Rome that were set up by senators or members of their families, or were inscribed for them, may be either actual funerary inscriptions or at any rate have been erected after their death. Out of some 260 published in *CIL* VI and about which closer precision is possible,[30] some 180 may be assigned to this category. As well as texts that were placed on tombs as dedicatory inscriptions, there are not a few that were carved on sarcophagi or urns.[31] Others are found on funerary altars[32] or bases which in most cases probably supported a statue of the deceased.[33] It is however precisely in such cases that the place where they were set up is of considerable importance, so that the exact purpose can be determined. A statue could be erected on the occasion of a person's death inside a tomb or an enclosed funerary garden. Here the sole spectators would be the family[34] – quite otherwise, for instance, than with the funerary monument of the Plautii near Tivoli.[35] There the wall with inscriptions built in front of the tomb was intended, for once quite irrespective of the monumental tomb itself, to impress upon the passer-by the importance of the dead members of the family. This was doubtless the usual requirement. By contrast, the arrangement which either P. Paquius Scaeva or his descendants hit upon, understandably found no imitators: his massive sarcophagus, in which he and his wife were laid at Histonium, has no reference to the deceased on the outside; but on the inside wall of the sarcophagus the entire *cursus honorum* is engraved.[36]

But other inscriptions may have preserved the memory of the deceased in his house, either in the *lararium*, as we know for two of the Volusii in their villa near Lucus Feroniae,[37] or among statues of him in the *atrium* as well.[38] These were no doubt the forms which had in time somewhat changed in comparison with the *stemmata* of republican families. That statues of the dead could also be erected in *loca publica* can be seen for example with Titinius Capito. This person requested from Nerva permission to honour L. Iunius Silanus, a victim of the Pisonian conspiracy, with a statue in the Forum Romanum.[39] Examples of this kind can scarcely be recognized in the surviving epigraphic material;[40] and no doubt they will not have been all that frequent, since at least from the time of Claudius, if not indeed already from the Augustan period, the Senate – or, of course, the Emperor – had to give approval in principle.[41]

This applies, however, in the same way to monuments in honour of the living. Hence one must work on the assumption that many honorific inscriptions were in all probability set up on private land, often inside the house. In *CIL* VI there are about eighty examples of such inscriptions from Rome. Private individuals and cities alike paid their respects in this way.[42] Three texts found on the Caelian, all honouring L. Marius Maximus, *cos.* II 223, may serve as illustration. The concentration of the texts on the same spot permits the inference that the senator's house was there. While one inscription was set up by a person who cannot be closely identified, the second was put there by a *primipilus* who had served under Marius Maximus in Germania Inferior, the third probably by a centurion of III Cyrenaica. Two of the inscriptions were composed many years before the death of the honorand.[43] P. Numicius Pica Caesianus, who was quaestor in the province of Asia, probably in the Augustan period, was honoured, by this province as well as by a set of clients, with two *trapezophora*; this too was probably inside his own house rather than anywhere else.[44]

By contrast, all inscriptions prompted by *princeps* or Senate, or, in most cases, by the two of them jointly, were aimed at the general public. The location of such texts was public places and buildings, and in temples too. The Forum Romanum, Forum Augusti, and Forum Traiani are mentioned, likewise, for example, the Saepta Iulia, the Basilica Iulia, the theatre of Pompeius, and the 'area Apollinis in conspectu c[uriae] in Palatio', as well as various shrines.[45] However, texts that may be securely located are astonishingly small in number.[46] Restraint in granting such honours cannot be regarded as the reason, although, for example, it has been supposed on the basis of Cassius Dio LXVIII. 15. 3^2 and 16^2 that Trajan awarded this distinction to no more than four persons all told.[47] Far more likely an explanation is limited survival, as a result of the particularly sweeping destruction of such monuments.[48]

If one takes these findings seriously, considerable differentiation must be made between the various categories of inscriptions from the point of view of self-advertisement. In many cases the intended onlookers were not the general public but a smaller, circumscribed group of persons.[49] But if so, all these texts have a markedly reduced significance, since they could have influenced the general public either not at all or only in a limited degree.[50] Above all, one must stick to the point that a considerable portion of all monuments whose existence we may infer from the inscriptions were erected not for the living but for persons already dead.[51] This being so, such texts could not serve to advertise the persons named in them, but, at the most, their family. The fact that it is precisely in Rome that senatorial inscriptions of a funerary nature appear to a far greater extent than in the Italian regions,[52] not to mention the provinces, is the natural result of the legal and practical links that bound the members of the *ordo amplissimus* to the capital of the Empire.

In the *Res Gestae*, as already mentioned, Augustus prides himself on having restored the Capitol and the theatre of Pompeius 'sine ulla inscriptione nominis mei'. Tacitus stresses similar behaviour by Tiberius.[53] The difference from later times will be clear when one recalls, for example, the building inscription of the Pantheon. Certainly the Severan restoration of the temple retains the original lapidary text: 'M. Agrippa L.f. cos. tertium fecit'.But Septimius Severus and Caracalla are named at length as the rebuilders.[54] The epigraphic material of the city of Rome largely matches this latter pattern, as far as public buildings or administrative measures are concerned. The arrangements to carry out a building programme or a restoration derive from the ruler,[55] no differently from the way that Q. Lutatius Catulus, during his consulate in 78 BC, had the *tabularium* built.[56] The Emperor replaced the republican magistrate. Yet this general impression does not hold good for the Augustan period – or for that of Tiberius. The urban magistrates such as the consuls and praetors, as far as this was publicly documented at Rome by inscriptions, operate on the instructions of the senate, *ex senatus consulto*; Augustus does not make an appearance. L. Calpurnius Piso and M. Sall(u)vius, as *praetores aerarii*, in accordance with a senatorial decree had *terminatio* stones set up for a piece of land that was purchased from public funds.[57] Various pairs of consuls built aqueduct arches *ex s.c.*[58] Likewise Naevius Surdinus carried out the paving of the Forum Romanum, doubtless by decree of the senate. The bronze letters, almost 40 centimetres high, are today visible once again in the paving of the Forum.[59]

When Augustus himself appears in an epigraphic text engaged in similar activity, the formula is no different from that of the regular magistrates. In 8 BC the consuls C. Asinius Gallus and C. Marcius Censorinus had *terminatio* stones set up on the Tiber. The formula runs: 'C.Asinius Gallus C. Marcius Censorinus consules ex senatus consulto terminaverunt'.[60] An exactly identical formula had been used under the censors of 54 BC.[61] A year later, in 7 BC, the transaction was repeated by Augustus; the only difference in formula is that Augustus alone is named, and with the *tribunicia potestas*.[62] To judge from the outward form no difference existed between regular magistrates and *princeps*. Both here portray themselves to the public in the same manner. This was certainly not the whole reality. Yet the visual impression did form a part of this reality. Indeed, one can trace, in an impressive way, precisely in the *terminatio* stones of the Tiber bank the manner in which outward appearances shifted with the changes in substance. The second and third colleges of *curatores alvei Tiberis*, in office under Tiberius, still appear in the manner already quoted.[63] But at the beginning of Claudius' reign Paullus Fabius Persicus and his fellow-curators, in spite of still being named in the nominative, were already erecting 'cippi ex auctoritate Ti. Claudi Caesaris' and no longer 'ex s.c'.[64] While this formula was retained under Vespasian, Trajan and Hadrian,[65] it finally altered completely under Antoninus Pius. The Emperor, named at the head of the text in the nominative, is the person who arranged the *terminatio*; the *curator* A. Platorius Nepos Calpurnianus, in the ablative, is the functionary who carried out the task.[66] The relative positions in which Emperor and senatorial office-holders were placed on public record match the actual conditions of power.[67]

By contrast it would be difficult to decide whether to define the inscription on the Pantheon pediment marking the restoration by Septimius Severus and Caracalla as the record of a piece of public building or as an imperial *liberalitas*. The reason is not least the entire manner in which Rome was furnished with representative public buildings and constructions in republican times.[68] Alongside the buildings erected by the Senate and magistrates stood others that were owed to the munificence – by no means selfless – of individual families. It was still so in AD 22, as Tacitus remarks: 'erat etiam tum in more publica munificentia'.[69] The examples that he is able to adduce by way of illustration are all indeed early Augustan. For he notes that Augustus did not restrain Taurus, Philippus, and Balbus from using booty or any financial resources 'ornamentum ad urbis et posterum gloriam'. Nor would the modern scholar be in a position to produce other examples, whether from the literary sources or from epigraphic texts. To be sure, one knows positively of large buildings erected by senators at Rome in the post-Augustan period as well – such as the baths of Cn. Domitius Ahenobarbus in AD 32, on the via Sacra, the 'horrea Lolliana, Galbiana, Volusiana', or the 'insula Volusiana'.[70] But all these structures were intended for personal use or had a commercial purpose; they were not, however, buildings for the inhabitants of Rome. Decisive evidence for the discrepancy between the Republic and the period from Augustus onwards is supplied by Suetonius and Tacitus. Every case of an individual mentioned as the builder of large buildings under Augustus concerns senators who had held a triumph.[71]

This is precisely where, very early on, a major element in senatorial public display was eliminated by Augustus. For it is undisputed that it was from the triumph that members of the Roman ruling stratum derived the highest kind of boost to their image and gained specific social prestige.[72] Of course, the title *imperator* was, for a short time only, a distinguishing factor; but victory over enemies of the Roman people and the act of ceremonial entry into the city remained bound up with the individual and his family, as demonstrated not only by the *Fasti triumphales* but also by numerous *elogia* in the Forum of Augustus.[73] Political pretensions within the commonwealth depended to a considerable extent on the recognition of such deeds by the community. Thus here is the sphere in which a change was most to be expected; the army was too unambiguously the basis of Augustus' power to permit free competition for influence on the army and for prestige to continue in existence. On 27 March 19 BC L. Cornelius Balbus triumphed over the Garamantes, the last *triumphator* who did not belong to the imperial family.[74] The honorific arch which was erected for Augustus in the Roman forum to commemorate his victory over Cleopatra and the winning back of the standards from the Parthians, probably in 19 BC, also carried the *Fasti triumphales*.[75] With the entry for Cornelius Balbus' triumph the fourth and last tablet was full.[76] No more space was left to record any further triumph – a conjunction perhaps adventitious but certainly symbolic.

How the change was carried through in detail is obscure. Victories from which the right to a triumph might have derived continued to be won in the decades following – and not merely by the legates of Augustus, who possessed no independent *imperium*. For the proconsuls of Africa, at least, still had an army at their disposal in the last years of Augustus. Thus L. Passienus Rufus appears as *imperator* on an African inscription,[77] and Cossus Cornelius Lentulus, *cos. ord.* 1 BC, by his victory over the Gaetuli won the name Gaetulicus for his son.[78] Neither held a triumph, which indeed in the case of Lentulus was excluded, for, according to Dio LV. 28. 2, he was not appointed by lot but nominated by Augustus. This meant apparently, in spite of the title proconsul, no independent *imperium*. At any rate, on a dedication to Mars the inhabitants of Lepcis Magna stress that the province of Africa was liberated from the threat of the Gaetuli 'auspiciis imp. Caesaris Aug. . . . ductu Cossi Lentuli . . . procos'.[79] The late descendant of the man to whose case Augustus had made appeal in 28 BC, in opposition to Licinius Crassus, would in fact have been unable to dedicate *spolia opima*. Still, it was Africa that saw in AD 22 the last proconsul who, although not a member of the *princeps*' family, gained the title *imperator*.[80] While if Claudius granted the conqueror of Britain, A. Plautius, an *ovatio*, as substitute for a triumph, that is to be regarded as an indication of that Emperor's well-known eccentricity, not as a reversal of the conditions created by Augustus from 19 BC onwards.[81]

It is certainly difficult to conceive that these conditions were created in legal fashion by the direct statutory removal of the proconsuls' rights. This would have too seriously undermined the political foundations of the *res publica restituta* when the internal situation was still unstable. Far likelier is the possibility that Agrippa's conduct set the tone. He declined a triumph in 19 BC and 14 BC, although possessed of independent *imperium*.[82] Furthermore, the triumph decreed for Tiberius in 12 BC was not accepted by Augustus,[83] for all that Tiberius, as stepson of Augustus, had been pushed into a special position after Agrippa's death. Was anyone in the Senate able or willing, when such *exempla* existed, to risk proposing, against the ruler's explicit political wishes, the grant of a triumph to, say, a proconsul of Africa? He had no greater rights than the son-in-law, or the stepson, of the *princeps*.

Thus it was very early on that Augustus deprived potential rivals of a critical means of self-enhancement. But at the same time he struck at the other means by which many *triumphatores* had sought to prolong the recollection of their victory beyond its immediate celebration and thereby to bestow permanence on their own person: by the display of booty or the erection of buildings.[84] Even if the origin of this public transaction is to be seen in the fulfilment of vows to the gods, yet the decisive motive had become the display of the victor's person. Pompeius had set a high standard with his theatre on the Campus Martius and the games at its opening.[85] And during the triumviral period it was, precisely, the *triumphatores* who had not held back from these opportunities to influence the *populus Romanus*. Thus Munatius Plancus, for example, had the Temple of Saturn restored 'de manib(iis)', as is stated on an inscription in the Forum Romanum;[86] likewise Asinius Pollio the *atrium libertatis*, with the first public library in Rome.[87] It was probably not until after Octavian's defeat of Antonius and his political agreement with the victor that C. Sosius, resolute opponent of Octavian in 32 BC, restored the Temple of Apollo at the southern end of the Campus Martius. As the elder Pliny records, the temple was actually named after its builder, Apollo Sosianus.[88] Similarly the Temple of Diana on the Aventine, restored by L. Cornificius after his triumph in 33 BC, still bore the appellation Cornificia on the Severan plan of the city.[89] After his threefold triumph Octavian placed himself in this tradition, in that he had the Via Flaminia as far as Ariminum renewed, including all its bridges.[90] He invited other *triumphatores* to follow his example; but only C. Calvisius Sabinus and M. Valerius Messala Corvinus seem to have taken up his suggestion;[91] both renewed a portion of the Via Latina, to which milestones of Calvisius Sabinus still testify; they are the last milestones in Italy which do not name the *princeps*.[92] The road already had a name, of course, which made it less enticing as an investment. L. Cornelius Balbus, the last to celebrate a triumph without belonging to the ruling house, is also the last to have erected a public building at Rome bearing his own name: the Theatrum Balbi.[93] For the Balnea Surae appear to have been built by Trajan himself to honour his closest collaborator, Licinius Sura.[94] This finding is not contradicted by Suetonius, *Aug.* 29. 4. f., according to which Augustus often encouraged the *principes viri* to erect new buildings or to restore or decorate old ones, in accordance with their financial resources. All the examples that he gives concern senators who had achieved a triumph in the period up to 19 BC. This is confirmed by Tacitus in the passage already cited.[95] To be sure, it is clear from Tacitus that under Tiberius an obligation still positively existed, and was felt, for public buildings to be maintained by the family of the original builders. Aemilius Lepidus had put to the Senate the proposal that he should be allowed to restore and decorate the 'basilica Pauli, Aemilia monimenta', at his own expense. But at the same time it is also noted that after a fire in the theatre of Pompeius, Tiberius provided the funds for its restoration, 'eo quod nemo e familia restaurando sufficeret'.[96]

This on its own in no way explains, of course, why neither under Augustus nor under succeeding *principes* are there any further references to senatorially financed building activity in Rome, as had after all been normal up till the early years of the Augustan principate. Naturally, the specific category of triumphal buildings was no longer possible, with the monopolization of the triumph by the *princeps* or his family;[97] but many senatorial families would have been perfectly capable, financially, to undertake this, as is documented by not a few epigraphic examples from Italy and, from the late first century AD, from the provinces too.[98] In the Augustan period large permanent theatre buildings were erected by senators at, for example, Volaterrae and Herculaneum.[99] M. Herennius Picens, *suff.* AD 1, furnished the town of Veii with the funds for a large building;[100] at Corinth a stoa, the building of which he had paid for, was actually named after P. Memmius Regulus.[101] Nothing comparable is known for Rome, in spite of the voluminous epigraphic and literary source-material. It cannot, certainly, be attributed to lack of demand. For apart from the not infrequent need for restoration, numerous fires alone constantly created space for new buildings. Yet new buildings, so far as we know, were virtually without exception initiated by the Emperors, partly in collaboration with the senate.

One must therefore see the break with republican practice, still operative in the early Augustan period, in the fact that public building activity in Rome was regarded, not in a legal sense, but, doubtless, in terms of practical politics, as a prerogative of the *princeps*, after Augustus, with his building

programme, for buildings both sacred and profane, proclaimed far and wide in the *Res Gestae*, had set the decisive
precedent.[102] In so far as senators were disposed to pursue
these ancient forms of public self-enhancement, the towns
outside Rome were their possible field of activity; direct
rivalry with the *princeps* was thereby avoided.[103] The effect of
the monarchical position of the *princeps* was to produce in this
area an equality of non-representation.[104]

The triumph, triumphal buildings, and the festivities linked
with their completion thus already disappear at the start of
the Augustan period from the repertoire of senatorial self-
advertisement.[105] Since, however, victories were still won by
senators, even if, from now on, in most cases under the
emperor's auspices, a replacement had to be created for the
actual victor in battle: this was the *ornamenta triumphalia*.[106]
They were actually a substitute, but evidently soon lost this
character. The frequent mentions in senatorial inscriptions
testify to their high prestige value.[107] This prestige was of
course derivative, for the grant of the *ornamenta* by the Senate
in the post-Augustan period doubtless always derived from
the proposal of the ruler,[108] even if the proposer's name were
deliberately omitted, as was the case with the future Emperor
Nerva, who omitted the name of the proposer of AD 65 in a
building inscription from Sentinum.[109]

Together with the *ornamenta* there was linked, as a permanent element of public display, the *statua triumphalis*.
Augustus made room in his Forum not only for past members
of the *gens Iulia* as far back as Venus, Mars, Aeneas, and
Romulus, but also for the *summi viri* of republican times, not
exclusively, although predominantly, senators who had
gained victories over enemies of the *populus Romanus*.[110] But
along with the past so too the present and the future were to be
on hand; Augustus directed, as at any rate Dio LV. 10. 3
records, that all those who had celebrated a triumph or had
gained the *ornamenta triumphalia* should be honoured with a
statua aenea in his Forum. A *titulus* on the base informed the
observer of the reason for the distinction. Thus Velleius notes
that the insignia were decreed for M. Vinicius on account of
his deeds in Germany:'cum speciosissima inscriptione
operum'.[111] Augustus alone must have proposed the grant of

the *ornamenta* by the Senate well over thirty times, while at least forty further cases are attested up to the end of the Hadrianic period.[112]

Under Augustus the link with an actual success in war seems always to have been preserved; but later the *ornamenta* and the *statua triumphalis* associated with them, too, could be awarded as a general distinction, divorced from any military transaction. When such statues were decreed for Petronius Turpilianus, Nerva, and Tigellinus on the occasion of the unmasking of the Pisonian conspiracy in AD 65, that was no more than an extreme variant.[113] The particular type of the *statua triumphalis* also achieved independent existence by being used quite separately from the *ornamenta*. L. Volusius Saturninus, *suff.* AD 3 and *praefectus urbi* for more than sixteen years on end, died in AD 56. Among the nine statues decreed on this occasion were included three *statuae triumphales*, which assuredly were not derived from earlier successes of Saturninus, for example as governor of Dalmatia.[114] The Augustan pattern was of course retained to the extent that those statues that were made of bronze got a place in the Forum of Augustus: yet two further statues were fashioned from marble and set up in the 'templum novum divi Augusti'.[115]

Thereby the type of statue created under Augustus, which belonged to the repertoire of substitutes for the triumph that was no longer granted, became a means for senators, above all, to distinguish themselves. *De facto*, the power of disposal lay exclusively with the Emperor, even if formally a senatorial decree was framed on each occasion. This conclusion probably applies, moreover, not only for *statuae triumphales*, but for all forms of statuary in so far as they were erected in Rome in public places, in shrines or in their entrance halls. Whereas Metellus Scipio displayed on the Capitol an entire 'turma inauratarum equestrium' of his forbears, about which Cicero waxes sarcastic because the inscriptions were muddled up,[116] from Augustus onwards this would only be possible through a senatorial decree, which meant, with the sanction of the *princeps*.[117] The Emperor's sanction thus became the norm, or rather functioned as a special mark of honour.[118] This meant a state of dependence, even for the great families, a restriction of the means of personal display.

Of course, it did not go so far as to strike out from the senatorial repertoire an entire genre of statuary. It has indeed been supposed that the equestrian statue was the preserve of the *princeps*, as being a particularly monumental variety.[119] Yet it is hard to see why this type of statue in particular should have been removed from senators, whereas, for example, Emperors as well as senators and knights alike could be portrayed in the *statua loricata*.[120] The numerous pieces of evidence in which *statuae equestres* for knights are mentioned would necessarily render such an assertion impossible.[121] Yet for senators as well not a few definite examples of equestrian statues are attested, although only one is preserved as direct evidence, namely the one of M. Nonius Balbus at Herculaneum.[122] But several inscriptions mention such honours, and other cases may be deduced from the size of the bases;[123] as for Celsus Polemaeanus in front of his grandiose library and tomb at Ephesus,[124] for T. Trebellenus Rufus at Concordia in the late Augustan period,[125] or for P. Memmius Regulus, governor jointly of Macedonia and Achaia, at Athens.[126] That it is often impossible to reach a decision whether or not an equestrian statue originally stood on a particular base is a reflex above all of the widespread absence of measurements or of the inadequate descriptions in many *corpora* of inscriptions. A systematic investigation would doubtless produce quite a large number of such monuments from the imperial period as a whole.[127]

But in Rome too equestrian statues were evidently not regarded by the rulers as being in competition with their own need for self-display. Nero in AD 56 had such a monument erected near the Rostra by decree of the Senate for the deceased city prefect Volusius Saturninus;[128] and a text from Trajan's Forum even seems to attest (for an unknown person), as well as statues 'in aede divi Iuli' and 'in saeptis Iuliis', an equestrian statue 'in rostris'.[129] All the same, one should not entirely disregard the limited quantity of the evidence for this type of honour at Rome itself. It could indicate a certain reserve by the rulers as far as the area of the city itself is concerned.[130]

In general statues of senators were very numerous and very varied in type; the senatorial decree for Volusius Saturninus alone names five different kinds.[131] These types are, to be sure, distinguishable only with great difficulty, in so far as the statues have survived at all. In few cases can they be attributed to a specific individual.[132] For the historian, therefore, all that can be used is what can be concluded from the epigraphic evidence for statues.[133] It is hardly necessary to underline what has been lost in this sphere too. This applies particularly to Rome, the central stage for senatorial self-display and competition. Of the nine statues that were erected for L. Volusius Saturninus, each of which naturally had an inscribed base, there has at last, very recently, been published a single small fragment of one base.[134] And of the more than eighty cases in which *ornamenta triumphália*, which means a corresponding *statua triumphalis* as well, or the honorific statue alone, were granted at Rome, to our knowledge, up to the time of Hadrian, not a single inscription is securely attested.[135] In the course of the excavations in the Forum Romanum, the Forum of Augustus, and the Forum of Trajan, a series of honorific inscriptions was indeed found: but the overwhelming majority of these belong to the fourth and fifth centuries.[136] In so far as they refer to persons from the first three centuries AD, they seem for the most part to have been erected for senators who were already dead, as not only the example of Volusius but many references in Tacitus and other authors would suggest.[137] All the same, such honours from Emperor and Senate may in total have been numerous. The abundance of these honours would tend to diminish the probative value of any individual monument.[138]

In spite of the variety in types of statuary the monuments will have been somewhat monotonous. As far as we can tell in Rome on the basis of the surviving material, almost all permanent honours of living or dead senators consisted in the erection of a *statua pedestris* with attached base and inscription irrespective of whether the honour derived from Emperor and Senate or from private persons;[139] once one leaves out the rare *statuae equestres*, the monuments were thus fashioned in a substantially uniform way;[140] to give personal prominence to an individual was not possible in this manner, except by the agglomeration of a particularly large number of statues for a single individual.[141] For Rome of the imperial period there is no documentary evidence for a monument that by its proportions or even by the originality of its form, would have been

lifted above the tedium of the average public honorific monument.[142] All the greater alertness must therefore be provoked
by two monuments that in no way conform to this general
impression. The first was probably made about 20 BC, the
other is undated.

In the excavations at Largo Argentina fragments of nine
inscriptions came to light, which had been set up by the
communities of the Carietes and Vennenses to L. Aelius
Lamia.[143] Lamia was governor of Hispania Ulterior from about
24 to 22 BC. To these nine texts is to be added a further
fragmentary inscription which has long been known.[144] What
is out of the ordinary is not merely the number of inscriptions;
rather, the editor, Marchetti Longhi, suggested that the texts
were probably all inscribed on slabs that abutted against one
another,[145] thereby producing an inscribed wall about 9 to 10
metres in length. Possibly the marble tablets were fixed to a
bathron on which statues of the honorand, perhaps in the form
of small equestrian portraits, were arranged.[146] The monument certainly did not resemble what we know from Rome in
the later period.

Still more remarkable, however, was another monument
that was once erected at Rome for a member of the senatorial
ruling stratum. Transcriptions of the texts on five marble slabs
– apparently lost – have been known since the second half of
the sixteenth century.[147] The fragments, which fit together,
derive from a monument to a former proconsul of Pontus-
Bithynia. Of the name of this governor only the filiation, L.f.,
and the *cognomen* Rufus survive. Mommsen, in a comprehensive treatment of the manuscript versions of this text,
thought of identifying the proconsul Rufus with a certain C.
Cadius Rufus, attested as governor of Pontus-Bithynia by
coins of the Julio-Claudian period.[148] More recent studies have
properly cast doubt on the identification.[149]

The text of the inscription has no particularly telling characteristics, apart, perhaps, from the number of Bithynian towns
which participated in erecting the monument to their former
proconsul: according to the manuscript versions there were
six, including Nicomedia, Apamea, Prusias ab Mare, Prusias
ab Hypio, and Prusias ab Olympo. There is no specific reason
for the Bithynian communities to honour the proconsul; Rufus

appears as the towns' *patronus* and *euergetes*. Hence one could include this text in a series of many other inscriptions, erected in Rome and in numerous other cities of the Empire, especially of Italy, for governors by individual communities or by the entire province. Such texts are normally inscribed on statue bases.

Yet the proconsul Rufus was not honoured in such a run-of-the-mill fashion. A few years ago a fragment of the inscription was found in the church of the Collegio Romano di Camposanto Teutonico, making it possible to calculate the size of the monument.[150] A measured reconstruction-drawing of the whole text produces a line of at least seven, but with great probability eight metres; and, instead of six towns, as hitherto supposed, most probably there were eight named as dedicators.[151] An approximately comparable length of line on an inscription may be found on the attic of the two honorific arches erected under Tiberius for Drusus and Germanicus in the Forum of Augustus, near the Temple of Mars.[152] The height of the letters in the present inscription is also extraordinary: the first line, which contained the name of the honorand, was about 25 centimetres high; a comparable letter-size is met with at Rome on an inscription erected by the Senate for Lucius Caesar and found in the ruins of the Basilica Aemilia in the Forum Romanum.[153] Both these dimensions permit the conclusion that we are dealing with an impressive monument, well above average size. Eight Bithynian cities had it erected, and dispatched at least nine ambassadors for the purpose.

No clear decision can be reached over the monument's type. All the same, some indications can be given. In spite of the size of the letters in the first line, it can hardly have involved an inscription from the attic of an honorific arch. For, apart from the fact that neither from the republican period nor from the principate do we have any evidence for the erection of such a monument at Rome by provincial cities,[154] the letters which form the names of the Bithynian ambassadors in the last lines are too small to have been legible at any height above the ground.[155] One must, rather, postulate an architectural structure in which the inscription could be viewed from more or less the eye-level of the beholder. This probably requires one

to infer that statuary was erected on the monument; at the least
one would expect the proconsul's statue. But since a single
statue, even if it were to have been over life size, would in no
way have matched the proportions of the substructure, one
has to reckon with a group of statues, including perhaps the
individual cities in the guise of their city-goddesses. Such a
monument was, in any case, erected for Tiberius in AD 20 by
fourteen cities of Asia. The colossal statue of the Emperor was
surrounded by fourteen smaller statues representing the
cities.[156]

But however the monument may have been designed in
detail, its grandiose character and the intention to honour the
proconsul Rufus and bring him into prominence before the
Roman public, are indisputable. If one compares this monument with everything that is known at Rome itself of
monuments in honour of persons outside the *princeps'* family
from the Augustan period onwards, its virtually unique
character is manifest. Only for L. Aelius Lamia, from about
the end of the 20s BC, can anything similar, if not fully comparable, be identified. Must one therefore conclude that the
monument to the proconsul Rufus is only conceivable at latest
in the early phases of the Augustan period? Subsequently,
indeed, would it have been in disconcerting competition with
the aspirations of Augustus or his successors?[157] The question
cannot be answered conclusively at present, since we cannot
date the proconsul. Still, our other information makes an
answer in this sense rather probable.[158] Under the changed
conditions in Rome itself, monumental forms of expression
were doubtless suitable only for the *princeps* in person; this is
paralleled by the observation made about public buildings.[159]
Similarly, as regards monumental tombs, Augustus had soon
established a limitation, even though imposing funerary
monuments, such as the tomb of the Plautii near Tibur, the
pyramid of Cestius in Rome, and the tomb of Munatius
Plancus near Caieta, were entirely possible.[160] However we
lack the comprehensive study of such funerary monuments
which would permit general conclusions in this area.

The two senatorial honorific monuments just discussed
exhibit comparable features in their inscriptions. Apart from
the name, in each case the position of patron is given promi-

nence, further the office through which, with great probability, that role came to be undertaken in the first place, that of proconsul in the case of Rufus, of *legatus pro praetore* in that of Lamia. The latter's praetorship and membership of the college of *XVviri sacris faciundis* are also registered. If one compares inscriptions for patrons of provincial communities from the later period, it is striking that these generally mention not merely a single office, but the entire career.[161] Indeed the bulk of the other monuments, such as most funerary and many building inscriptions, record, in an almost stereotyped fashion, all the offices of the particular senators in question. The *cursus honorum* is the typical form in which senators displayed themselves before the public in the imperial period. This had not always been so.

The earliest examples of a complete, or at least largely complete, listing of offices are the *elogia* from the tombs of the Scipios.[162] It may be that the *tituli* below the wax masks of dead ancestors were the prototype. Likewise, the offices and achievements were brought before the public once more, after a senator's death, in the *laudatio funebris*.[163] A life that had run its course was thus summed up in its entirety. And even if no noteworthy *res gestae* were linked to the individual magistracies, the stages in the *cursus honorum* provided evidence that the *populus Romanus* had recognized the dead man by distinguishing him through election to office. The *cursus honorum*, which appeared in the funerary inscription, was, so to speak, the political life history of the dead man reduced to its essentials.[164]

There is a whole series of inscriptions of senators from the republican period in which the entire career of offices is set forth. In so far as their original function can be determined, we are dealing almost exclusively with funerary inscriptions.[165] By contrast, no unambiguously honorific inscription, in which this phenomenon may be observed, can be cited for a person who was still alive. Inscriptions on monuments in honour of the living name the office which was significant for the dedicators, that is to say, no doubt, the official position which provided the occasion for the honour.[166] There does not follow a recapitulation of all more or less recently held offices. This was not necessary, not least because the latest office was generally also the highest in rank and thereby unmistakably characterized the political status of the honorand. Sulla, for example, was honoured in Rome, and at Suessa, Sutrium and Alba Fucens, only as dictator. Likewise, numerous senators were honoured at Rome and, especially, in the eastern provinces, as governors or patrons.[167] In the early Augustan period, too, certain cities and the *koinon* of Crete still honoured M. Nonius Balbus at Herculaneum only as proconsul.[168] Quite different was the case with, for instance, Q. Glitius Atilius Agricola, *cos. suff.* 97. On eleven inscriptions at Augusta Taurinorum, it was quite natural, even for a series of provincial cities, to set out his entire *cursus honorum*, not merely one office or his highest magistracy;[169] and the same thing occurs with the *cos.* II of the year 105, C. Antius A. Iulius Quadratus, at Pergamum, even though Greek epigraphic tradition was quite unfamiliar with this type of honour.[170] The *cursus honorum*, spelled out and listed in all its individual stages, became a significant means of describing to the public the rank and significance of a living person as well.

It is – almost inevitably – impossible to establish precisely when this method of putting a leading personality on display in his own lifetime first became fashionable.[171] The earliest absolutely certain example is L. Aquillius Florus Turcianus Gallus, to whom inscriptions were set up at Corinth and Athens as proconsul of Achaia, perhaps around 3 BC, with his full *cursus honorum*, beginning with the vigintivirate and going up to his latest magistracy, the proconsulship.[172] The honorand may well have participated in the composition of the texts himself. Likewise Augustan are, no doubt, inscriptions for Cn. Pullius Pollio from Forum Clodii, P. Tettius Rufus Tontianus from Atina, T. Trebellenus Rufus from Concordia, and P. Numicius Pica Caesianus from Rome itself.[173] However it remains uncertain whether all the instances just listed concern an honorific inscription for a living person. All other texts from the Augustan period in which the entire *cursus honorum* appears – and there are, after all, thirty cases – derive from tombs or were put up after the honorand's death. In the post-Augustan period, however, this type became even more customary for the living as well.

There is a possible explanation for this. Augustus had a

gallery of leading Romans set up, alongside the ancestors of the Julian family, in his Forum. Below their statues in each case, besides their noteworthy deeds, all their individual offices were set forth, as for example the texts demonstrate for Q. Fabius Maximus, C. Marius, and L. Licinius Lucullus.[174] Of course, it is scarcely possible to regard these as the direct prototype, since all these Romans were long since dead.[175] Yet Augustus also ordained that statues should be set up in his Forum to those who had the distinction of the *ornamenta triumphalia*. That this actually happened is not of course directly attested for the Augustan period, but it is at least under Claudius at the latest, if the 'statua triumphalis Cn. Senti Saturnini' recorded on wax tablets from Pompeii refers to the consul of 41.[176] Since it was Augustus' wish that Rome's past should be directly associated with the present through the depiction of great senators,[177] one may well postulate a formulation of the new inscription according to the pattern of the texts beneath the statues of the *viri antiqui*. And in so far as tangible specimens from later periods survive, they always adduce the entire *cursus honorum*, as well as a reference to the senatorial decree.[178] Beneath the statue which was decreed for L. Volusius Saturninus in the Forum of Augustus one can hardly assume that there would have been a less extensive text than in the *lararium* of his villa at Lucus Feroniae; in other words, at least his complete consular career.[179]

If this assumption is valid, it is clear that at Rome during the Augustan period not a few inscriptions will already have been on view on which, as was earlier the case only after death, all offices and duties were mentioned which had been undertaken in the service of the *res publica*, or, now, that of the *princeps* too. Thereby a new means had been invented by which members of the senatorial ruling stratum could display themselves to the world around them. Is it not probable that this model was speedily imitated and taken over in other places and situations as well?

Curiously enough, the individuals for whom this type of honour is already on record, in all probability, under Augustus,[180] were not members of great republican families or the leading collaborators of Augustus. For those people, if our epigraphic material as a whole is in some degree representative, the old style, in many cases in the funerary sphere, but in particular with honours from communities or individuals, remained the norm: it sufficed to mention consulate and priesthood, or simply the name alone. M. Claudius Marcellus, son-in-law of Augustus, was just called *patronus* on an honorific inscription in the Forum at Pompeii.[181] And for Q. Volusius Saturninus, *suff.* 12 BC, it was sufficient to characterise him on an honorific inscription in the Forum of Lucus Feroniae as consul and *VIIvir epulonum*.[182] The future, however, belonged to the new style, with listing of the *cursus honorum*.[183]

NOTES

For comments and criticism I am grateful to various participants in the Colloquium, but above all to Friedrich Vittinghoff and Edgar Pack who also both read a previous draft. H. Krummrey and G. Lahusen also very kindly placed at my disposal proofs of as yet unpublished works. Anthony Birley (text) and Fergus Millar (notes) took on the not inconsiderable task of the translation into English. I am grateful to them also, as to Glen Bowersock for his support.

The following abbreviations are used in this paper:

L. Friedländer, *Darstellungen aus der Sittengeschichte Roms in der Zeit von Augustus bis zum Ausgang der Antonine*⁹, ed. G. Wissowa (1920) = Friedländer, *Sittengeschichte*.

A. E. Gordon, *Quintus Veranius consul A.D. 49, Univ. Calif. Publ. in Class. Arch.* 2, 5 (1952), 231 ff. = Gordon, *Veranius*.

D. Kienast, *Augustus. Prinzeps und Monarch* (1982) = Kienast, *Augustus*.

G. Lahusen, *Untersuchungen zur Ehrenstatue in Rom. Literarische und epigraphische Zeugnisse* (1983) = Lahusen, *Ehrenstatue*.

H. Löhken, *Ordines dignitatum. Untersuchungen zur formalen Konstituierung der spätantiken Führungsschicht* (1982) = Löhken, *Ordines dignitatum*.

M. Pape, *Griechische Kunstwerke aus Kriegsbeute und ihre öffentliche Aufstellung in Rom. Von der Eroberung von Syrakus bis in augusteische Zeit* (Diss. Hamburg, 1975) = Pape, *Kunstwerke aus Kriegsbeute*.

I *Volusii Saturnini. Una famiglia romana della prima età imperiale (Archeologia – Materiali e problemi* 6, 1982) = *Volusii*.

K. Tuchelt, *Frühe Denkmäler Roms in Kleinasien. I: Roma und Promagistrate* (1979) = Tuchelt, *Denkmäler*.

O. Vessberg, *Studien zur Kunstgeschichte der römischen Republik* (1941) = Vessberg, *Kunstgeschichte*.

1. Cic. *Att.* V. 21. 7: 'nullos honores mihi nisi verborum decerni sino, statuas, fana, τέθριππα prohibeo.' The fact that Cicero did none the less receive honorific statues is proved by a monument on Samos, Tuchelt, *Denkmäler*, 48.

2. Cic. *Att.* VI. 1. 26: 'volo esse aliquod monumentum'; he continues, significantly: 'odi falsas inscriptiones statuarum alienarum'. On the monument as the vehicle of *memoria* cf. Cic. *Verr.* II. 4. 69; 79; 82; cf. also Dio LIV. 23. 6. Cf. n. 25 below.

3. I know of no treatment of the phenomenon as a whole. There are however treatments of various aspects by different authors, see e.g. Tuchelt, *Denkmäler*,

45 ff. for statues, shrines, and buildings in the Greek East; Vessberg, *Kunstgeschichte*, 26 ff.; Pape, *Kunstwerke aus Kriegsbeute*, 53 ff.; on the use of coin see A. Alföldi, 'The Main Aspects of Political Propaganda in the Coinage of the Roman Republic', in *Essays in Roman Coinage presented to H. Mattingly* (1956), 63 ff.; T. P. Wiseman, 'Legendary Genealogies in Late-Republican Rome', *Greece and Rome* 21 (1974), 153 ff.; T. Hölscher, 'Die Geschichtsauffassung in der römischen Repräsentationskunst der späten römischen Republik', in *Actes du 9ème congr. int. numismat. Berne Septembre 1979* I (1982), 269 ff.; M.-L. Vollenweider, 'Verwendung und Bedeutung der Porträtgemmen für das politische Leben der römischen Republik', *Mus. Helv.* 12 (1955), 96 ff.; E. Welin, *Studien zur Topographie des Forum Romanum* (1953), 130 ff. In general on the question of representation in the Principate, and particularly in Late Antiquity, see Löhken, *Ordines dignitatum*.

4. Cf., e.g., the setting up of military trophies by L. Mummius in various Italian towns: Trebula Mutuesca (*ILLRP* 327); Cures Sabini (328); Nursia (329); Parma (330); Fabrateria Nova (*AE* 1973, 134); also in Italica in Spain (*ILLRP* 331) and in Rome itself (*ILLRP* 122). Scipio Africanus after the conquest of Carthage had items of booty restored to various cities in Sicily and re-erected there in his name (Cic. *Verr.* II. 2. 3; 4. 73 ff.).

5. e.g. *Verr.* II. 4. 69: 'Tuus enim honos illo templo senatus populique Romani beneficio, tui nominis aeterna memoria simul cum templo illo consecratur.' For the honouring of Claudius Marcellus through the construction of a library and the Theatre of Marcellus see *RG* 21; Livy, *Per.* 140; Plut. *Marc.* 30; Suet. *Aug.* 29. 4. On the triumph, Mommsen, *Staatsrecht* I³. 134 ff. On senatorial permission for the erection of monuments, Pape, *Kunstwerke aus Kriegsbeute*.

6. Ch. Meier, *Res Publica amissa*² (1980), 50 ff.; 116 ff.; 162 ff.

7. M. Gelzer, *Pompeius* (1949), 43; on the significance of the *porta triumphalis*, H. S. Versnel, *Triumphus* (1970), 132 ff. Cf. also the right granted to L. Cornificius, *cos.* 35 BC, to ride home from banquets on an elephant, and the remark on this point by Syme, *RR*, 238: 'a token of changed times and offensive parody of Duillius.'

8. Cic. *de off.* II. 57; Pliny, *NH* VIII. 64; 96; XXXIV. 36; XXXV. 127; XXXVI. 50; 113 ff. Even Ammianus has occasion (XXII. 15. 24) to speak of the games.

9. Cic. *Verr.* II. 2. 150. For literary references to honorific statues and monuments during the Republic in Rome see esp. Vessberg, *Kunstgeschichte, passim.*

10. Vessberg, *Kunstgeschichte*, 148 ff.; M. Bieber, 'The Development of Portraiture on Roman Republican Coins', *ANRW* I. 4 (1973), 871 ff., esp. 879 ff.; J. M. C. Toynbee, *Roman Historical Portraits* (1978), 50 ff.

11. Syme, *RR*, 313 ff.; P. Sattler, *Augustus und der Senat* (1960), 58 ff. Most recently, Kienast, *Augustus*, 67 ff. with comprehensive bibliography.

12. Tac. *Ann.* I. 2. 1.

13. See e.g. A. Alföldi, *Die zwei Lorbeerbäume des Augustus* (1973); idem, *Die monarchische Repräsentation im römischen Kaiserreiche* (1970); idem, *Der Vater des Vaterlandes im römischen Denken* (1971); as regards the exceptional honours voted to Gaius and Lucius Caesar and Germanicus cf. also the new texts from near Seville, which greatly expand our knowledge of the details, hitherto based on the Tabula Hebana: see J. González and F. Fernández, 'Tabulae Siarenses', *Iura* 31 (1980), 1. For monumental self-representation in Rome itself cf. e.g. P. Zanker, *Forum Romanum. Die Neugestaltung durch Augustus* (1972); idem, *Forum Augustum* (1968); E. Buchner, *Die Sonnenuhr des Augustus* (1982) = *Röm. Mitt.* 83 (1976), 319 ff. and 87 (1980), 355 ff.

14. See e.g., *RG* 12: 'qui honos [ad ho]c tempus nemini praeter [m]e e[st decretus].' On the significance of 'primus' within the social structure see also G. Alföldy, *Die Rolle des Einzelnen in der Gesellschaft des Römischen Kaiserreiches* (1980), 22 ff.

15. The patronage of cities was by no means concentrated on the Emperor, although, or because, the institution had been emptied of political content, cf. F. Engesser, *Der Stadtpatronat in Italien und den Westprovinzen des römischen Reiches bis auf Diokletian* (Diss. Freiburg, 1957); L. Harmand, *Le Patronat sur les collectivités publiques des origines au Bas-empire* (1957) (incomplete). The Emperor was therefore never directly involved in the appointment of city patrons, *pace* J. Nichols, 'The Emperor and the Selection of the *patronus civitatis*', *Chiron* 8 (1978), 429 ff.; see W. Eck, 'Wahl von Stadtpatronen mit kaiserlicher Beteiligung?', *Chiron* 9 (1979), 489 ff.

16. Thus it is significant that, in the crucial sphere of the Roman corn-supply, from 22 BC onwards senators progressively lost all opportunities for personal publicity; see Sattler, op. cit. (n. 11), 77; G. Rickman, *The Corn Supply of Ancient Rome* (1980), 62 ff., although the equestrian Praefectus Annonae seems to have been appointed for the first time between AD 8 and 14, see H. Pavis d'Escurac, *La Préfecture de l'annone* (1976), 29. Augustus also took steps to provide fire precautions after Egnatius Rufus, by his measures in this area, had made a great impression on the population of the City, see Dio LIII. 24. 4–6; Vell. Pat. II. 91. 3; 92. 4. Similarly, the names of the *triumviri monetales*, which had reappeared on coins minted in Rome in about 20 BC, disappear again before the end of Augustus' reign; cf. e.g. K. Kraft, *Gesammelte Aufsätze zur antiken Geldgeschichte und Numismatik* I (1978), 42 ff.; for a different view A. M. Burnett, *Num. Chron.* 17 (1977), 45 ff.; Kienast, *Augustus*, 324 ff. Particular problems are created by the appearance of portraits of some governors on coin-issues of provincial cities: In Asia: M. Tullius Cicero (*BMC Lydia*, 139, 13 ff.), M. Valerius Messala Potitus (*Syll. Aulock*, 3342; Jenkins, *Br. Mus. Qu.* 22 (1960), 72), C. Asinius Gallus (*BMC Troas*, 24; *Ashmol. Mus. Coins Emp.* I, 1261 ff.), P. Cornelius Scipio (Babelon, *Inventaire Waddington*, 991), Q. Fabius Maximus (*BMC Phrygia*, 95; *Ashmol. Mus. Coins Emp.* I. 1385 ff.); in Africa: P. Quinctilius Varus, L. Volusius Saturninus, Africanus Fabius Maximus; evidence in B. Thomasson, *Die Statthalter der römischen Provinzen Nordafrikas von Augustus bis Diokletianus* II (1960), 13 ff.; see M. Grant, *From Imperium to Auctoritas* (1946), 229; 379 ff.; idem, *Roman Imperial Money* (1954), 90 ff.; *Aspects of the Principate of Tiberius* (1950), 162 ff.; see further G. Stumpf, 'Eine Porträtmünze des A. Vibius C.f. C.n. Habitus Proconsul von Africa unter Tiberius', *Schweiz. Münzbl.* (1983) (printing); Syme, *Roman Papers* I, 293;U. Vogel-Weidemann, *Die Statthalter von Africa und Asia in den Jahren 14–68 n. Chr.* (1982), 45 ff. Cultic honours also largely disappeared from the provinces before the end of Augustus' reign, see e.g. Chr. Habicht, in *Le Culte des souverains dans l'Empire romain* (1972), 47 ff.; according to him the latest attested case is C. Marcius Censorinus, *SEG* II. 549; see G. W. Bowersock, *HSCPh* 68 (1964), 207; C. P. Jones, *Phoenix* 31 (1977), 80; Tuchelt, *Denkmäler*, 105 ff. (in his view there was also a cult for C. Vibius Postumus, *procos. Asiae* probably between AD 12 and 15; cf. U. Vogel-Weidemann, op. cit. 220 ff.). For a probable cult of T. Statilius Taurus in Thespiae cf. L. Moretti, *Athenaeum* 59 (1981), 74 ff. This gradual fading away certainly proves that it was in no way a matter of direct intervention on the part of Augustus. It is rather that a degree of caution will have developed on the part of both the honorand and those who voted honours which will have led steadily to an awareness of how inappropriate such things now were. Moreover there will have evolved on the part of the provincial communities a growing consciousness of how dependent apparently all-powerful governors were.

17. R. Syme, 'Imperator Caesar: A Study in Nomenclature', *Roman Papers* I, 361 ff.

18. Dio LI. 24. 4; *PIR²* L 186; on the problem of imperatorial acclamations see most recently R. Syme, *Phoenix* 33 (1979), 309 and E. Badian, in *Romanitas-Christianitas. Festschrift J. Straub* (1982), 38.

19. Dio LIII. 23. 5; cf. *CIL* III. 14147. 5 = *ILS* 89895 with the proud record of his *res gestae*.

20. Syme, *RR*, 309 ff.; J.-P. Boucher, *Caius Cornelius Gallus* (1966), 38 ff.; 50 ff. (rejecting the view that the erection of statues had anything to do with his fall, which is too radical). Recently, in the same sense the comprehensive discussion of L. J. Daly (with W. L. Reiter) 'The Gallus Affair and Augustus' lex Julia maiestatis: a Study in Historical Chronology and Causality', in C. Deroux (ed.), *Studies in Latin Literature and Roman history* I (1979), 289; further S. Mazzarino, 'Un nuovo epigramma di Gallus e l'antica "lettura epigrafica" ', *Quad. Catanesi* 2 (1980), 7 (with references to the preceding Literature).

21. Horace, *Sat.* I. 6. 15 ff. For the relevance of honorific inscriptions for the *gloria* of the honorand cf. I. Kajanto, 'Un'analisi filologico-letteraria delle iscrizioni onorarie', *Epigraphica* 33 (1971), 3. Cf. also *AE* 1976, 677–8, in which, as late as the reign of Trajan, reference is still made to the bronze tablets on the Capitol on which the treaty with the ancestors of Iulius Agrippa was inscribed. By contrast the overturning of statues was equivalent to the abolition of a man's *memoria*, see Cic. *Pis.* 93; Tac. *Ann.* III. 14. 4.

22. Dio XLIII. 14. 6.

23. Dio XLIII. 49. 1 ff.

24. Cf. also *RG* 19: 'porticum ad circum Flaminium, quam sum appellari passus ex nomine eius, qui priorem eodem in solo fecerat Octaviam'; cf. Suet. *Aug.* 31. 5. But compare Dio LIV. 23. 6 attesting the opposite procedure on the part of Augustus. See A. Stein, *Römische Inschriften in der antiken Literatur* (1931), 35 ff. On the Theatre of Pompey, compare however *CIL* VI. 9404: 'theatrum Aug(ustum) Pompeianum'.

25. Cf. n. 2 above; and *RG* 35: '[appell]av[it me pat]re[m p]atriae idque in vestibu[lo a]edium mearum inscribendum et in c[u]ria [Iulia e]t in foro Aug. sub quadrig[i]s, quae mihi ex s.c. pos[it]ae [sunt, censuit]'; on the Clipeus Virtutis, *RG* 34. The concept is particularly clear in Pliny, *NH* II. 154: 'etiam monimenta ac titulos gerens nomenque prorogans nostrum et memoriam extendens contra brevitatem vitae' (relating, it is true, in the first instance to grave-monuments); also Pliny, *NH* XXXIV. 17; XXXVI. 42; Horace,*Carm.* IV. 8. 13 ff. Note the (exceptional) counter-instance of Sex. Iulius Frontinus, Pliny, *Ep.* IX. 19. 1 ff., with Pliny's typical reference to *gloria*. Cf. *AE* 1948, 77: 'sumsit per statuam dimissum in saecula nomen'. In general also H. Häusle, *Das Denkmal als Garant des Nachruhms* (1980), 110 ff. The fact that inscriptions attracted the attention of both contemporaries and later generations is clear from, for example, Cic. *Att.* VI.1. 17; Pliny, *NH* XXII. 13; Juvenal X. 143 ff.; Aul. Gell. *NA* IX. 11. 10; cf. esp. A. Stein, op. cit. (n. 24), *passim*.

26. For other possibilities cf. n. 16.

27. The pregnant phrase of Syme, *Roman Papers* I. 269.

28. *CIL* VI. 31705, an inscription for L. Considius Gallus, speaks of a 'titulus magni monumenti marmorei', without however making clear that the reference is to a tomb, see Lanciani, *NSc* 1883, 420; *Bull. com.* 1883, 223.

29. *PIR*² L 125 regards as possible the identification of Tib. Latinius Pandusa, *IV vir viar. cur.*, *CIL* XIV. 2166 (Aricia), and Latinius Pandusa, *legatus* in Moesia in AD 19. However it is clear from the brief report in Lanciani, *NSc* 1883, 173, that it is not a matter of a building erected by Tib. Latinius Pandusa as *IV vir viar. cur.*, but of a monument in his honour. It can however hardly have been erected until after his death, since it is scarcely conceivable that so young a man could have performed during his life a service which evoked such a monument.

30. In the case of quite a few complete texts, and above all with fragmentary ones, no closer precision is possible. One criterion, accepted here, of the funerary context of an inscription is its location outside the walls and beside a *via publica*. It

is also normally indicative of a funerary inscription if the lines are significantly wider than the total height of the text (e.g. *CIL* VI. 1402–3; 1406; 1414; 1428; 1442; 1449; 1460; 1521–2). Compare also, e.g., *CIL* VI. 1541, regarded until now as a public building-inscription. In fact it is a funerary inscription for two persons, see M. G. Granino Cecere, in *Epigrafia e ordine senatorio, Roma, 1981* (printing).

31. e.g. *CIL* VI. 1337; 1381; 1537; 1544; 1487 = 31665; 31679–31682; 31715; 31746; 31754; 31769–70. Urns: VI. 1380; 1399; 1462; 1524; 1535–6; 31700; 31721 ff.; 31755. Outside Rome also many sarcophagi of senators are attested, cf. W. Eck, *ZPE* 43 (1981), 127, n. 2. See in general G. Koch and H. Sichtermann, *Handbuch der Archäologie: Römische Sarkophage* (1982), 22 ff.

32. e.g. *CIL* VI. 31721 ff.

33. *CIL* VI. 1344–5; 1376; 1413.

34. Tombs were not in general accessible for entry, not even the grave of the Scipios, although A. Degrassi, *Inscr. Ital.* XIII. 3, p. X seems to presume, in dealing with the inscriptions, that they were. But compare the tomb of the Salvii in Ferentium, where accessibility, and legibility of the inscriptions, was excluded, see A. Degrassi, *Scritti vari* III (1967), 158. Similarly, the inscriptions of the Plautii may have been placed internally, *Inscr. Ital.* IV. 1. 122 f.

35. Cf. L. R. Taylor, *MAAR* 24 (1956), 27. The same purpose was served by the acephalous *titulus Tiburtinus*, *CIL* XIV. 3613 = *ILS* 918 = *Inscr. It.* IV. 1. 130; most recently R. Syme, 'The Titulus Tiburtinus', *Akten des 6. Kongr. Griech. u. Latein. Epigraphik* (1973), 585.

36. *CIL* IX. 2845–6 = *ILS* 915; see H. Brandenburg, *JdAI* 93 (1978), 280. An incorrect explanation of this phenomenon is found in G. Koch and H. Sichtermann, *Handbuch der Archäologie: Römische Sarkophage* (1982), 25, with n. 3. An inscription of which the occasion was a man's death can be found in Rome also, in the case of P. Paquius Scaeva, *CIL* VI. 1483. One would normally conclude from that that he was buried in Rome!

37. *AE* 1972, 174 ff.; improvements by W. Eck, *Hermes* 100 (1972), 461 and S. Panciera, in *Volusii*, 83 ff. Also deriving from a *lararium* perhaps *CIL* VI. 31684 and 31737.

38. e.g. *CIL* VI. 1358; 1365; 1467. Cf. Pliny, *NH* XXXIV. 17; XXXV. 6; E. F. Bruck, *Über römisches Recht im Rahmen der Kulturgeschichte* (1954), 97 ff.

39. Pliny, *Ep.* I. 17. 1.

40. It does not seem possible to find an unquestionable example of this in the epigraphic material from Rome.

41. Mommsen, *Staatsrecht* I, 450 ff., esp. 451, n. 2. His remarks are ignored by J. P. Rollin, *Untersuchungen zu Rechtsfragen römischer Bildnisse* (1979), 105 ff.; cf. also R. Düll, 'Zum Recht der Bildwerke in der Antike', in *Studi E. Betti* III (1962), 129; F. Musumeci, 'Statuae in publico positae', *SDHI* 44 (1978), 191.

42. For inscriptions put up by cities see e.g. *CIL* VI. 1382; 1400–1; 1508; 1526; 1578; 31801; 37064. On statues of senators in private houses compare Lahusen, *Ehrenstatue*, 39, n. 277 (incomplete). Also probably from the private sphere *CIL* VI. 1474; 1490; 1739–41; 31632; 31685; 31752 ff.; 37094.

43. *CIL* VI. 1450 = *ILS* 2935; 1451; 1453; VI. 1452 = *ILS* 2936 probably also belongs here. The residence of the Aradii in Rome can also be securely identified by the same means, see *CIL* VI. 1687–95 (including *tabulae patronatus*). We still lack a collection of the evidence for the location of senatorial houses in Rome; it would have to be based largely on epigraphic material. The methodological problems involved are multiple, as is evidenced by the relevant remarks of G. Lugli, *Fontes ad topographiam veteris urbis Romae* (1957), libri XII ff., 95 ff.; 275 ff.; 386 ff. His conceptions are often problematic and dubious.

44. *CIL* VI. 31742; 31743 = *ILS* 911; similar *trapezophora* for L. Cassius Longinus, cos. A.D. 30, dedicated by the Sextani Arelatenses, G. Mancini, *Bull. com.* 56 (1928), 318 = *AE* 1930, 70. Similarly for P. Plautius Pulcher in Ciciliano, R. Paribeni, *NSc* 1932, 126 f. = *AE* 1933, 151. For their erection in the private sphere, compare E. Simon, in W. Helbig, *Führer durch die öffentlichen Sammlungen klassischer Altertümer in Rom* II⁴ (1966), 486, no. 1700.
45. Above all *AE* 1972, 174; *CIL* VI. 1377 = *ILS* 1098; *CIL* VI. 1386 = *ILS* 1023; 1599 = *ILS* 1326; 1549 = *ILS* 1100 (add VI. 1497 = *ILS* 1094); 31293 = *ILS* 984; 37087; *NSc* 1933, 508, no. 233; Suet. fr. 290, 10 ff. (Roth); Tac. *Ann.* IV. 15; XV. 72. 1; Dio LXIX. 7. 4; Suet. *Otho* 1. 3. A statue erected in the Temple of Vesta is probably referred to in *CIL* VI. 37090 (cf. VI. 31719, found in this temple). Uncertain: VI. 31781; 31809; 37088. For the erection of statues on the Palatine see W. Eck, *Hermes* 100 (1972), 472. M. Taliaferro Boatwright, in *Volusii*, 9 ff., has recently tried to explain these in all cases by the fact that the honorands had taken part in the discovery of a conspiracy. This is indeed attested for Nerva and Tigellinus and also for Otho. But this interpretation collapses in the case of Volusius Saturninus, in the light of the fact that the statue was first erected in AD 56, after his death, while the *ornamenta triumphalia* that he is supposed to have won in AD 42 for his role in the suppression of the revolt of Furius Camillus Scribonianus are not actually attested, but are restored without adequate grounds in the inscription, see *Hermes* 100 (1972), 464 ff. Moreover it is most unlikely that Nero would still in 56 have reverted with such an honour to the events of 42. In any case why should Claudius, who had in fact awarded Otho such an honour, not already have recorded his gratitude in the same way to Volusius also? For a text which lends in support of this critique see R. M. Sheldon in *Epigrafia e ordine senatorio*, Roma, 1981 (printing).
      The Capitol is never mentioned as a site for the erection of honorific statues for senators; *CIL* VI. 31748; 31791; 31818, found during the construction of the Victor Emmanuel monument, may equally have stood in private houses (VI. 31748 at any rate was erected privately – 'amico optimo'). Augustus had cleared away some statues of *viri illustres* from the *area Capitolina* (Suet. *Cal.* 34. 1), although the monument of the Claudii Marcelli remained intact (*AE* 1978, 658). As regards findspots, especially in the case of very fragmentary pieces, it is admittedly necessary to take displacement into account, since hardly a single text has been found in *situ*. Cf. e.g. E. A. Stanco in *Epigrafia e ordine senatorio* (printing) on a text possibly deriving from the Forum Traiani.
      One of the statues of Volusius Saturninus was erected in the Porticus Lentulorum near the Theatre of Pompey. Although the Porticus has not been located, it is possible to surmise why this site was chosen. Saturninus was married to a Cornelia (*PIR*² C 1476), the daughter of an L. Cornelius Lentulus (*PIR*² C 1384). It is probable that the site was chosen to demonstrate the connection with this family. On the various sites for the erection of statues see now Lahusen, op. cit. 7 ff. (not quite complete). For a historically interesting special case see now the illuminating hypothesis of F. Coarelli, 'La statue de Cornélie, mère des Gracques, et la crise politique à Rome au temps de Saturninus', in *Le Dernier Siècle de la République romaine et l'époque augustéenne* (*Journées d'étude – Strasbourg, 15–16 février 1978*) (1978), 13.
46. From the Forum Romanum: *CIL* VI. 31293 = *ILS* 984; 31719; 31785; 37070; 37085; 37087. Forum Augusti: *NSc* 1933, 468 ff., nos. 93–4; 97–9 = *AE* 1934, 155 (belonging together, cf. G. Alföldy, *Fasti Hispanienses* (1969), 38 ff.); nos. 95; 100–1. Forum Traiani: *CIL* VI. 1377 = *ILS* 1098; 1497 + 1549 = *ILS* 1094 + 1100; 1566; *NSc* 1928, 343 = *AE* 1929, 158 (uncertain).
47. So A. N. Sherwin-White, *The Letters of Pliny* (1966). 153.

48. It is particularly striking that late-antique inscriptions from the various Fora are more frequent than those from the first three centuries (cf. e.g. Pietrangeli, *NSc* 1933, 455 ff. and n. 136 below). We may perhaps take it as a presupposition that the numerous fires in Rome also caused the destruction of statues and inscriptions in the Fora. Moreover we can conceive of many other reasons, for example the re-use of statue-bases in Late Antiquity, e.g. *CIL* VI. 37107; 37109–10. Cf. also H. Blanck, *Wiederverwendung alter Statuen als Ehrendenkmäler bei Griechen und Römern²* (1969), 65 ff. (incomplete). For an example of a statue-base, probably erected in a public place, which was later re-used as a column-capital, see *CIL* VI, 31801. G. Lahusen, 'Zur Funktion und Bedeutung der Ehrenstatue für Privatpersonen in Rom,' in *Römisches Porträt. Wege der Erforschung eines gesellschaftlichen Phänomens. Wissensch. Konferenz Berlin 1981, Wiss. Zeitschr. der Humb.-Univ. zu Berlin, Ges.-Sprachw. Reihe* 31 (1982), 239 ff. assumes that from Marcus Aurelius onwards only Emperors and their relatives were honoured with statues in Rome during their lives, and that even for dead persons honorific statues were erected only in exceptional cases. Both points as stated seem to me incorrect, since they do not take sufficient account of the survival-rate of inscriptions.

49. This is ignored for instance in Gordon, *Veranius*, 305.

50. This distinction is necessary although in the case of senators it is not easy to speak of 'einer eigentlichen Trennung von öffentlichem und privatem Bereich', Löhken, *Ordines dignitatum*, 19.

51. See p. 133 of the essay and n. 137 below.

52. One can demonstrate this *exempli gratia* for the inscriptions for senators in *CIL* X and XI, where the proportion of funerary inscriptions is smaller compared to honorific inscriptions for living persons, above all in comparison to Rome.

53. Tac. *Ann*. III. 72. 1. The significance attached to the naming of persons in inscriptions on public buildings is visible for instance from the relevant late-antique restrictions, Löhken, *Ordines dignitatum*, 75.

54. *CIL* VI. 896 = *ILS* 129. Similarly *CIL* VI. 1275 = *ILLRP* 377.

55. Cf. e.g. the *inscriptiones aquaeductuum*, *CIL* VI. 1243 ff. and numerous texts among the imperial inscriptions, *CIL* VI. 872 ff.

56. *CIL* VI. 1314 = *ILLRP* 367; 1313 = 368.

57. *CIL* VI. 1265 = *ILS* 5937. Cf. also *CIL* VI. 1263; 1264 = *ILS* 5938; 1266 = *ILS* 5939; 1267a–b.

58. *CIL* VI. 1384–5. Cf. VI. 1539, the building inscription for the Carcer Mamertinus, of AD 21.

59. *CIL* VI. 37068 = *AE* 1968, 24; on this P. Romanelli, in *In Africa e a Roma* (1981), 827: perhaps of *c*. 10 BC. Cf. also *CIL* VI. 1278.

60. *CIL* VI. 1235; 31541; cf. J. Le Gall, *Le Tibre, fleuve de Rome dans l'Antiquité* (1953), 152 ff.; cf. *AE* 1951, 182a.

61. *CIL* VI. 1234; 31540; 37025–8; Le Gall, op. cit. 150 ff.

62. *CIL* VI. 1236; 31542; Le Gall, op. cit. 154 ff.

63. *CIL* VI. 31540 l; 31541 o and s; 31542s; 31543; 1237 = 31544; XIV. 4704. Le Gall, op. cit. 156 ff.

64. *CIL* VI. 31545; Le Gall, op. cit. 157.

65. *CIL* VI. 1238 = 31546; 31547–52. Le Gall, op. cit. 158 ff.

66. *CIL* VI. 31553; cf. 1241 = 31554.

67. In Late Antiquity this pattern changed, in that quite frequently *praefecti urbis* appear as 'builders' on inscriptions; cf. Löhken, *Ordines dignitatum*, 76 f.

68. E. de Ruggiero, *Lo stato e le opere pubbliche in Roma antica* (1925), 21 ff.; 112 ff.; I. Shatzman, *Senatorial Wealth and Roman Politics* (1975), 90 ff.; P. Veyne, *Le Pain et le cirque* (1976), 375 ff.; C. C. Vermeule, *Roman Imperial Art in Greece and Asia Minor* (1968), 15.

69. Tac. *Ann.* III. 72. 1. If ἔργον in Dio LX. 25. 3 means exclusively 'a public building' then we could reckon with the continuation of such activity under Claudius.
70. Sen. *Contr.* IX. 14. 18; the baths were probably situated in the immediate vicinity of Domitius' house (*CIL* VI. 2037 = 32352; 2039; 2041 = *ILS* 229). See G. E. Rickman, *Roman Granaries and Store Buildings* (1971), 164 ff.; Panciera, in *Volusii*, 90 ff.
71. Tac. *Ann.* III. 72. 1; Suet. *Aug.* 29. 4 ff.
72. See e.g. Cic. *de Prov.* 29; *Pis.* 56 ff., 59; *Planc.* 61; *Marc.* 28; Polyb. VI. 15. 8. On the related ideology of victory, see G. Ch. Picard, *Les Trophées romains* (1957), 138 ff. Cf. also F. Coarelli, *DdA* 4/5 (1970/1), 262, speaking of 'ideologia trionfale'.
73. *Inscr. Ital.* XIII. 3, nos. 10; 12; 13; 17; 24; cf. nos. 61; 65; 71. The significance of the entry of a victorious general into Rome, even when not in the form of a triumph, is visible from the negative example in Tac. *Agric.* 40. 3.
74. *Fasti Triumphales Capitolini, Inscr. Ital.* XIII. 1, pp. 86 ff.
75. Cf. A. Degrassi, *Scritti vari* I (1962), 239 ff.; P. Zanker, *Forum Romanum. Die Neugestaltung durch Augustus* (1972), 15 ff.; most recently J. Johnson, *Augustan Propaganda. The Battle of Actium, Marc Anthony's Will, The Fasti Capitolini Consulares and Early Imperial Historiography* (Diss. Univ. Calif. Los Angeles, 1976), 130 ff.
76. See *Inscr. Ital.* XIII. 1, p. 86, fr. xli.
77. *CIL* VIII. 16456 = *ILS* 120. Also a coin from Africa: L. Müller, *Numismatique de l'ancienne Afrique* (1874; repr. 1968), Suppl. 43, no. 39.
78. Vell. Pat. II. 116. 2; Dio LV. 28. 4; Syme, *RR*, 401, n. 4; on the extra name see *PIR²* C 1380.
79. *AE* 1940, 68 = *IRT* 301.
80. Tac. *Ann.* III. 74. 4.
81. V. A. Maxfield, *The Military Decorations of the Roman Army* (1981), 104 ff.
82. Dio LIV. 11. 6; 24. 7 ff.
83. Dio LIV. 31. 4.
84. In general for building activity up to 44 BC see F. Coarelli, in *Hellenismus in Mittelitalien*, ed. P. Zanker, I (1976), 29 ff.; also the numerous buildings bearing the name of the senator who built them, see B. Platner–Th. Ashby, *A Topographical Dictionary of Ancient Rome* (1929); I. Shatzman, *Senatorial Wealth and Roman Politics* (1975), 90 ff.; F. W. Shipley, 'Chronology of the Building Operations in Rome from the Death of Caesar to the Death of Augustus', *MAAR* 9 (1931), 7 ff.; Syme, *RR*, 241; F. Bona, 'Sul concetto di "Manubiae" e sulla responsabilità del magistrato in ordine alla preda', *SDHI* 26 (1960), 105 ff.; I. Shatzman, 'The Roman General's Authority over Booty', *Historia* 21 (1972), 177; further I. Calabi Limentani, 'I fornices di Stertinio e di Scipione nel racconto di Livio', in *Politica e religione nel primo scontro tra Roma e l'Oriente* (1982), 123 ff. Note the significant remark of Dio XLIV. 5. 2 that the objective was to prevent the continued attachment of the name of Sulla to the Curia. On the public exhibition of spoils see G. Waurich, 'Kunstraub der Römer: Untersuchungen zu seinen Anfängen anhand der Inschriften', *JRGZ* 22 (1975), 1 ff.; Pape, *Kunstwerke aus Kriegsbeute, passim*. In general on Augustus' building activity P. Gros, *Architecture et société* (1978); idem, *Aurea templa* (1980); and Kienast, *Augustus*, 336 ff. For the significance of buildings both for the public and for those who had them erected see A. Demandt, 'Symbolfunktionen antiker Baukunst', in *Palast und Hütte* (1982), 49 ff.
85. R. Seager, *Pompey* (1979), 131; F. Coarelli, 'Il complesso pompeiano del Campo Marzio e la sua decorazione scultorea', *RPAA* 44 (1971/2), 99 ff.

86. *CIL* VI. 1316 = *ILS* 41; cf. X. 6087 = *ILS* 886. According to Fittschen, *JdAI* 91 (1976), 210, the temple was first dedicated after Actium: 'Zum Dank für diese wichtige Unterstützung *durfte* er den . . . Tempel am Forum vollenden oder überhaupt erst in Angriff nehmen.' The verb 'durfte' in this context is however too strong.
87. *PIR²* A 1241.
88. Pliny, *NH* XIII. 53; XXXVI. 28; cf. Fittschen, *JdAI* 91 (1976), 209, referring to the dedication on the birthday of Augustus.
89. Suet. *Aug.* 29. 5; *CIL* VI. 29844, 2. In *CIL* VI. 4305 = *ILS* 1732 an 'aedituus Dianae Cornif(iciae)' is named. Cf. the personnel of the Amphitheatrum Statili Tauri, *CIL* VI. 6226–8. This is closely comparable to the organization of a fire brigade by Egnatius Rufus or to the *familia* which Agrippa set up for the maintenance of the aqueducts built by him. For further examples see F. W. Shipley, *MAAR* 9 (1931), 7 ff., and T. P. Wiseman, *PBSR* 42 (1974), 7; 11.
90. *RG* 20; cf. Suet. *Aug.* 30, 1.
91. W. Eck, *Die staatliche Organisation Italiens in der Hohen Kaiserzeit* (1979), 28 ff. According to F. W. Shipley, *MAAR* 9 (1931), 36, the triumphators of 28 and 27 BC, C. Carrinas, L. Autronius Paetus, and M. Licinius Crassus, will also have participated; there is however no direct evidence. Dio LIII. 22. 2 makes this unlikely.
92. *CIL* X. 6895; 6897–900; 6901 = *ILS* 889; *AE* 1969/70, 89. Outside Italy there is so far as I know only one known milestone from the reign of Augustus, which was put up by the proconsul (named in the nominative) without reference to the *princeps*, *AE* 1955, 40. All other milestones, even as early as Augustus' reign, name the Emperor. Domitius Calvinus, according to E. Bormann, *Festschrift für Benndorf* (1898), 283 ff., also dedicated the calendar in the grove of the Arvales.
93. Suet. *Aug.* 29. 5; Pliny, *NH* XXXVI. 60; Tac. *Ann.* III. 72. 1; Dio LIV. 25. 2; LXVI. 24. 2. On the site cf. G. Gatti, *MEFRA* 91 (1979), 237 ff.
94. *PIR²* L 253; E. Nash, *Pictorial Dictionary of Ancient Rome* II (1962), 467.
95. Tac. *Ann.* III. 72. 1. The obligation on the part of descendants to maintain temples built by their forbears, attested in Dio LIII. 2. 4, relates to the years immediately after Actium. Cf. e.g. Cic. *Verr.* II. 4. 79.
96. Tac. *Ann.* III. 72. 2; cf. II. 49. 1 ff.
97. For this reason the explanation given by Mommsen, *Staatsrecht* I³, 451, n. 3 is not adequate by itself.
98. See the evidence in W. Eck in *Studien zur antiken Sozialgeschichte. Festschrift Fr. Vittinghoff* (1980), 295 ff.
99. *AE* 1957, 220; *CIL* X. 1423.
100. *CIL* XI. 7746.
101. *AE* 1939, 110 = *Corinth* VIII. 3, 306. On competition for prestige via building in the provinces, e.g. V. M. Strocka, in *Proc. Xth Int. Congr. Class. Arch., 1978* II, 899.
102. *RG* 19–21.
103. Cf. the remarks in Dio LIII. 23. 3 ff. on the attitude of Agrippa, who showed no φθόνος of Augustus. Cf. also Schmitthenner in *Augustus*, ed. W. Schmitthenner (1969), 461 ff. Moreover the outcome of the debate in the Senate in AD 70 on the rebuilding of the Capitol in the absence of the new *princeps* (Tac. *Ann.* IV.9) is significant for the conceptions which were from now on current as regards the allocation of responsibilities in this area. On the Forum Romanum as a 'theatrum gentis Iuliae', see Fittschen, *JdAI* 91 (1976), 208.
104. There did not however develop any comprehensive formalization of types of representation, as in Late Antiquity, cf. Löhken, *Ordines dignitatum*, 73 ff.
105. Similarly in the sphere of the various annual games, restrictions were introduced under Augustus, which limited the hitherto unrestrained competition for pub-

licity on the part of some senators, cf. e.g. G. Ville, *La Gladiature en Occident des origines à la mort de Domitien* (1981), 121 ff.; H. Galsterer, *Athenaeum* 59 (1981), 414; Kienast, *Augustus*, 93.

106. Mommsen, *Staatsrecht* I³. 465 ff.; Gordon, *Veranius*, 305 ff.; V. A. Maxfield, *The Military Decorations of the Roman Army* (1981), 105 ff.; A. Abaecherli-Boyce, 'The Origin of ornamenta triumphalia', *CP* 37 (1942), 130 ff.

107. List in Gordon, *Veranius*, 305 ff. including the *statuae triumphales*.

108. Mommsen, *Staatsrecht* I³, 466. *Dona militaria* were always granted to senators directly by the Princeps as the holder of the auspices. The award of *ornamenta triumphalia* and *dona militaria* to the same senator is only once attested: *CIL* VI. 1444 = *ILS* 1022. On the identification of the person C. P. Jones, *JRS* 60 (1970), 93 ff. and recently I. Piso, *AMN* 19 (1982), 39 ff., against which see W. Eck, *ZPE* 52 (1983), 151 ff.

109. *CIL* XI. 5743 = *ILS* 273.

110. Suet. *Aug.* 31. 5. P. Zanker, *Forum Augustum* (1968), 14 ff. On the statues see most recently S. R. Tufi, *Dial. di Arch.* 3 (1981), 69. For the surviving fragments of the *elogia* see Degrassi, *Inscr. Ital.* XIII. 3, nos. 1 ff. For a new restoration of the inscription on the base for Drusus, see A. Vassileiou, *ZPE* 51 (1983), 213 ff., already correctly restored by R. Paribeni, *NSc* 1933, 460 ff. There is little new in L. Braccesi, *Epigrafia e storiografia* (1981).

111. Vell. Pat. II. 104. 2; Degrassi, *Inscr. Ital.* XIII. 3, p. 8, relates this to the *decretum in acta senatus relatum.* Cf. e.g. Cic. *Phil.* XIII. 9.

112. Suet. *Aug.* 38. 1; Gordon, *Veranius* 315 ff; *AE* 1972, 174 for L. Volusius Saturninus; cf. *AE* 1969/70, 96–7 (cf. 1971, 91) and 1978, 132 and 134 for Cn. Sentius Saturninus (cf. n. 176 below).

113. Tac. *Ann.* XV. 72. 1; cf. on this W. Eck, *Hermes* 100 (1972), 479 ff. with references to other irregular awards of military decorations.

114. *AE* 1972, 174; the restoration of 'ornamenta triumphalia' in the text is improbable; cf. W. Eck, *Hermes* 100 (1972), 464 ff.

115. Cf. on the distinction between bronze and marble statues, Tuchelt, *Denkmäler*, 86 ff., esp. 87, n. 120.

116. Cic. *Att.* VI. 1. 17.

117. Cf. n. 41 above. For the concurrence of the Senate see also e.g. *AE* 1953, 251: '[statuam posuit equester o]rdo et populus Romanus consentiente senatu.'

118. Cf. in this connection the references in Tac. *Ann.* IV. 15. 1 ff.; *Hist.* IV. 47; Pliny, *Ep.* II. 7. 3; *HA, v. Marc.* 13. 5; 22. 7; for Late Antiquity e.g. Symm. *Rel.* III; *CIL* III. 214 = *ILS* 738; VI. 1727 = *ILS* 1275; 1784 = *ILS* 1284.

119. H. von Roques de Maumont, *Antike Reiterstandbilder* (1958), 79; idem, 'Inschriftlich bezeugte Reiterstandbilder der römischen Kaiserzeit', in *Festschrift E. v. Mercklin* (1964), 122. Contra, e.g. H. B. Siedentopf, *Das hellenistische Reiterdenkmal* (1968), 27 ff.; W. Eck, *Hermes* 100 (1972), 471; cf. also Tuchelt, *Denkmäler*, 92 ff.

120. e.g. *CIL* VI. 1377 = *ILS* 1098; VI. 1540 = *ILS* 1112; cf. VI. 1599 = *ILS* 1326 for M. Bassaeus Rufus. K. Fittschen, *BJ* 170 (1970), 544; also Lahusen, *Ehrenstatue*, 51 ff.

121. Cf. the material collected by H. v. Roques de Maumont, in *Festschrift E. v. Mercklin* (1964), 122 ff.(often incorrectly interpreted).

122. H. von Roques de Maumont, *Antike Reiterstandbilder* (1958), 80; but cf. Fittschen, *BJ* 170 (1970), 543, who also draws attention to the very small number of surviving equestrian statues of Emperors. On the statue of M. Nonius Balbus see *AE* 1947, 53 and L. Schumacher, *Chiron* 6 (1976), 171 (perhaps even two such monuments).

123. See the examples given by W. Eck, *Hermes* 100 (1972), 471, n. 3.

124. *Forsch. in Ephes.* V. 1², 62, nos. 2–3.

125. *CIL* V. 1878 = *ILS* 931. Described in the Corpus just as 'basis magna'; correctly recognised by G. Alföldy, *Aquileia nostra* 51 (1980), 274. Other examples given there.
126. *IG* II/III². 4174; cf. H. B. Siedentopf, *Das hellenistische Reiterdenkmal* (1968), 30, 142; on pp. 28 and 36 he refers to an equestrian statue of M. Maecilius Rufus, *Inschr. v. Olympia*, 334. From around the middle of the first century BC there is a surviving group of seven equestrian statues from Lanuvium, which is to be brought into relation with the activities of L. Licinius Murena and Lucullus in the Third Mithridatic War, see Siedentopf, op. cit. 73 ff.; cf. recently M. L. Gualandi, 'Il gruppo equestre rinvenuto nell'area del santuario di Giunone Sospita a Lanuvio', *SCO* 30 (1980), 69, and in detail F. Coarelli, 'Alessandro, i Licinii e Lanuvio', in *L'Art décoratif à Rome à la fin de la République et au début du principat. Table ronde organisée par l'École Franç. de Rome (Rome, 10–11 mai 1979)* (1981), 229.
127. Possibly *CIL* IX. 2637 = *ILS* 894 was the base for an equestrian statue ('ingens basis'), similarly IX. 414. The case is certain with *I. Cret.* IV. 292. Alföldy, *Aquileia nostra* 51 (1980), 273 ff., like Siedentopf before him, has noted that the inscriptions on the bases of equestrian monuments were normally placed on one of the shorter sides, that in front. That raises the question of what will have stood on those bases where the text occupied one of the longer sides, e.g. *CIL* XI. 1432 = *Inscr. Ital.* VII. 1. 16; X. 408 = *ILS* 1117 = *Inscr. Ital.* III. 1. 18 (according to Bracco probably an equestrian statue). Compare *CIL* VI. 1401 = *ILS* 412 = H.-G. Pflaum, *Sodales Antoniniani* (1966), 94 ff.; *CIL* XII. 2452–3; *AE* 1897, 19 = *ILS* 8975 (for restorations see G. Alföldy, *Fasti Hispanienses* (1969), 81 ff., and for dimensions Chr. Hülsen, *Röm. Mitt.* 11 (1896), 252; and the new text from Volsinii, P. Gros, *MEFRA* 92 (1980), 977 (with an overall width of *c.*4 m) = *AE* 1980, 426. It may be that one should suppose that the monument was a biga or quadriga. Bigae were of course erected for Sejanus, see Juv. X. 58 ff. Cf. also Apul., *Flor.* p. 29, 15 ff. (Helm): all provinces expressed the desire to erect four- or six-horse chariots in honour of Aemilius Aemilianus. The inscription of C. Fufius Geminus, recently published by L. Gasperini, *Ottava Misc. Greca e Romana* (1982), 285, is either a building inscription (height 0.86 m; width over 3 m) or must have belonged to a monument of which the side for display was the longer one.
128. *AE* 1972, 231.
129. Pietrangeli, *NSc* 1933, 508, no. 233: '[---]que in rostris e[questrem? --- in] aede divi Iuli et [in---] saeptis Iul[iis---ponen]das ei c[ensuit?].' The base of an equestrian statue, reused for an inscription in honour of Stilicho, was found near the Rostra, Henzen, *Bull. Inst.* 1880, 169. On the significance of the Rostra for the erection of a statue, see Cic. *Deiot.* 34; 'nullus locus est ad statuam quidem rostris clarior.'
130. But cf. Fittschen, n. 122 above.
131. *AE* 1972, 174; W. Eck, *Hermes* 100 (1972), 469 ff. On *statuae consulares* cf. *CIL* VI. 32346 and J. Scheid, *MEFRA* 92 (1980), 236. A sort of catalogue of honours in the form of statues and monuments is provided by the *s.c.* passed after the death of Drusus, *CIL* VI. 31200. In general on the different types of statue, Lahusen, *Ehrenstatue*, 45 ff.
132. Statues, portraits, and relief sculptures which can be related to senators whose names are known for certain are extremely rare; indeed up till now hardly any have been identified. The following examples may be listed: L. Iulius Ursus, *cos.* III AD 100, G. Daltrop, *Die stadtrömischen männlichen Privatbildnisse traianischer und hadrianischer Zeit* (1958), Abb. 11; T. Caesernius Statianus, G. Daltrop, *Münch. Jb. bildend. Kunst* 22 (1970), 7 ff. (see also n. 23 for references to a possible portrait of Sex. Vetulenus Civica Pompeianus); for the possible senators on

Trajan's Column cf. W. Gauer, *Untersuchungen zur Traianssäule* (1977), 60 ff.;
also P. Zanker, in *Eikones. Festschrift Jucker* (1980), 196 ff.; Herodes Atticus,
T. Lorenz, *Galerien von griechischen Philosophen- und Dichterbildnissen bei den
Römern* (1965), 30 ff.; also G. Treu, *Die Bildwerke von Olympia in Stein und
Thon* (1897), 260 ff.; L. Baburius Iuvenis and C. Baburius Herculanius,
H. Manderscheid, *Die Skulpturenausstattung der kaiserzeitlichen Thermenanlagen*
(1981), 121, nos. 468–9 (*AE* 1958, 137–8); Ti. Iulius Celsus Polemaeanus(?),
K. Stemmer, *Chronologie und Ikonographie der Panzerstatuen* (1978), 101 ff.
(hardly a single one of the *statuae loricatae* collected by Stemmer can be attributed
to an identifiable person). For the statue of a *femina consularis* see Fr. Sartori,
'Statua di moglie o figlia di consolare', *Mem. Accad. Patavina, Cl. sc. mor., lett. ed
arti* 70 (1957/8); for portrait busts of members of the Licinii (not individually
identifiable), see V. Poulsen, *Les Portraits romains* I (1962), 101 ff., nos. 67, 73.
For statues or portrait busts of M. Nonius Balbus and his wife, of Domitius
Corbulo, of Seneca and of L. Iunius Rusticus see J. J. Bernoulli, *Römische
Ikonographie* I (1882), 269 ff. For statues of members of the Volusii family see
M. Moretti – A. M. Sgubini Moretti, *La villa dei Volusii a Lucus Feroniae* (1977),
38 ff., plates LV ff. Admittedly in quite a few of these cases an exact attribution
to nameable persons is not possible.

133. Compare, for the provincial sphere, G. Alföldy, 'Bildprogramme in den
römischen Städten des Conventus Tarraconensis – Das Zeugnis der Statuen-
postamente', *Rev. de la Univ. Complutense Madrid* 38 (118), 1979, 177.

134. Panciera, in *Volusii*, 83 ff.

135. See the evidence collected in Gordon, *Veranius*, 305 ff.; cf. Suet. *Aug.* 38. 1. It is
possible that *CIL* VI. 1386 = *ILS* 1023 derives from such a base. Some later
statues conferred for this reason are attested as coming from the Forum Augusti
or Traiani: *ILS* 1098; 1094 + 1100; *NSc* 1933, 468 ff. = G. Alföldy, *Fasti
Hispanienses* (1969), 38 ff.

136. From this period e.g. *CIL* VI. 1658c, d; 1679; 1721; 1725; 1727; 1729; 1731; 1764;
1783; 1789; 31883f; 31886 = 37105 and n. 48 above.

137. Cf. nn. 45 ff. above. *CIL* VIII. 24583 = *ILS* 8963; Pliny, *Ep.* II. 7. 3; Tac. *Ann.*
IV. 15. 2; *Hist.* IV. 47; *ILS* 984 = *CIL* VI. 31293; Dio LVII. 21. 3; LXVIII. 15. 3;
HA *v. Marc.* 13. 5; 22. 7, cf. Friedländer, *Sittengeschichte* III⁹. 73 ff.; C. Braschi,
Diz. epigr. II. 2100 ff. Cf. also H. Jordan, *Topographie der Stadt Rom im Altertum*
I. 2 (1885), 446, 465, and G. Lugli, *Fontes ad topographiam veteris urbis Romae
pertinentes* VI (1965), 4 ff.; 24 ff.; 59 ff.

138. Cf. Friedländer, *Sittengeschichte* III⁹, 65 ff. on the frequency of such statues; on
the monotony of the types cf. e.g. those erected in the forum in Pompeii, Mau,
Pompeji in Leben und Kunst² (1908), 44 ff., showing at least eleven bases for
equestrian statues on the west side of the forum. On the average size of the
statue-bases see also G. Barbieri, *Epigraphica* 19 (1957), 106 ff.

139. The same applies also to the cities of the Empire. Thus for example among the
very numerous inscriptions of Ephesus one can obviously establish the character
only of those honours which consisted of a standard base with a *statua pedestris*. It
is almost never possible to grasp the architectural context in which in many cases
the statues will have been placed and on which they may in part have depended
for their effect. Inscriptions on *clipei*, e.g. *CIL* V. 6977, and A. Albertini,
Commentarii dell'Ateneo di Brescia per l'anno 1971, 88 = *Archeol. e storia a Milano e
nella Lombard. or.* (1980), 262–9; on *vascula*, *CIL* V. 6978; 6985–6. A *sella curulis*
in the theatre, *AE* 1947, 53; cf. L. Schumacher, *Chiron* 6 (1976), 176 ff. On the
concept of a *statua pedestris* see *CIL* VI. 31781.

140. During the Republic the monuments had been, for instance, in the East, of a
more variable character (see Tuchelt, *Denkmäler, passim*). In Rome a number of
triumphal arches, though not many, had been erected (Kähler, *RE* VIIA. 377 ff.,

nos. 1–6). From the reign of Augustus onwards this is no longer attested for private persons, and not in the provinces either. Kähler, 470, supposes that governors were honoured with such arches in Ephesus and Patara. However the inscription in *Forsch. in Eph.* III. 214. 222, is much too fragmentary to allow a definite decision; in Patara by comparison it is probable that there was originally an inscription in honour of Hadrian, as has been shown by G. W. Bowersock, *Bonner Historia Augusta Colloquium 1982* (printing). According to G. Alföldy, *Aquileia Nostra* 51 (1980), 274, it is possible that *CIL* V. 8661 is the remains of the attic of a triumphal arch. The monumental nymphaeum in Miletus, long regarded, on the basis of the reconstructed text of *ILS* 8970, as an honour for M. Ulpius Traianus, *procos. Asiae* 79/80, was in fact built by Titus '. . . [per M. Ulp]ium Traianum' (B. Kreiler, *Die Statthalter Kleinasiens unter den Flaviern* (Diss. Munich, 1975), 32 ff.). On triumphal arches cf. Lahusen, *Ehrenstatue*, 61 ff.

141. e.g. for Volusius Saturninus after his death; compare also the large number of statues for P. Memmius Regulus in Achaia, *PIR*² M 468.

142. That naturally does not imply that there was no differentiation, perhaps corresponding to status within the Senate or to other informal criteria, in the forms of representation, cf. n. 131. That question must however be reserved for a separate investigation.

143. G. Marchetti Longhi, *Bull. com.* 71 (1943/5), 67 ff. = *AE* 1948, 93; cf. G. Alföldy, *Fasti Hispanienses* (1969), 5 ff. and Wiegels, *Gnomon* 1974, 191.

144. *NSc* 1906, 205 = *CIL* VI. 37058. Cf. Wiegels, *Gnomon* 1974, 191.

145. Marchetti Longhi, *Bull. com.* 71 (1943/5), 69. But see n. on p. 167 below.

146. It is admittedly not certain that we should imagine all the inscriptions as being laid out in a single line. They might, for example, have run round a large quadrangular base. A. Degrassi, *Scritti vari* I, 483.

147. *CIL* VI. 1508 = Moretti, *IGUR* I. 71.

148. Th. Mommsen, *Ges. Schriften* VIII, 175 ff.

149. C. Bosch, *Die kleinasiatischen Münzen der römischen Kaiserzeit* II. 1 (1935), 82, n. 60; *PIR*² C 6; D. Magie, *Roman Rule in Asia Minor* II (1950), 1400.

150. In September 1978 I was able to check the text. Proposed in the mean time by L. Moretti, 'A proposito di Pirro Ligorio e di IGUR 71', in Φιλίας χάριν, *Miscellanea in onore di E. Manni* V (1980), 1582 ff.

151. Cf. W. Eck, *Chiron* 14 (1984) (printing).

152. Pietrangeli, *NSc* 1933, 462 ff.: just 6.5 m; this width approximately equals that of the monument on which the colossal inscription for L. Caesar, *CIL* VI. 36908, was placed (illustration in E. Nash, *Pictorial Dictionary of Ancient Rome* II (1962), 244, no. 993). According to P. Zanker, *Forum Romanum* (1972), 16 ff., two inscriptions were inscribed on the attic, of which one was VI. 36908.

153. *CIL* VI. 36908 (cf. n. 152); the height of the letters in line 1 is 24.5 cm. The dimensions of the letters on the Arch of Drusus and Tiberius in the Forum Augusti: line 1, 16 or 13 cm (Pietrangeli, *NSc* 1933, 461). On the monument for one (Petronius) Persa, which according to Alföldy (cf. n. 127) may have been a triumphal arch, the letters in line 1 were 18 cm. high. Particularly large letters obviously attracted attention; cf. Cic. *Verr.* II. 154: 'huic etiam Romae videmus in basis statuarum maximis litteris incisum', and HA *Trig. Tyr.* 33, 4: 'grandes litterae.'

154. Cf. Kähler, *RE* VIIA, 465 ff.

155. 3.4–3.8 cm.

156. Phlegon, *de mirab.* fr. 13 (*FGrHist* 257, fr. 36, 13). Degrassi, *Scritti vari* I, 438; Degrassi presumes that each city erected a separate statue for the proconsul Rufus, which is unlikely. Admittedly we cannot exclude the possibility that some form of large chariot with horses, for example a *quadriga*, was erected.

However this supposition seems less probable in view of the separate enumeration of the individual cities. See also now C. Vermeule, 'The Basis from Puteoli: Cities of Asia Minor in Julio-Claudian Italy', in *Coins, Culture and History: Studies in Honour of B. Trell* (1981), 85. On *bigae* and *quadrigae* as honorific monuments cf. n. 127 above. There is a possible reference to a *quadriga* erected in Rome in honour of a senator in *CIL* VI. 37088.

157.   So L. Moretti, op.cit.(n. 150), 1591.

158.   That an argument could be based on the size, number, and place of erection of monuments and statues is shown for example by Tac. *Ann.* I. 74. 3: in the case against Granius Marcellus a certain Hispo gave evidence that 'statuam Marcelli altius quam Caesarum sitam'; cf. Tac. *Ann.* II. 57. 4; 83. 3; Cic. *Verr.* II. 4. 90. Under Septimius Severus accusations were brought against Plautianus to the effect that his statues were larger than those of the Emperors and not only outside Rome, but in it, Dio LXXVII. 14. 6 ff. (LXXVII. 16. 2: his statues more numerous). This gives us an important pointer: outside Rome the possibilities were greater than in the capital; the effects of competition were felt much more sharply in Rome. Tac. *Ann.* XIV. 52. 2 refers to Seneca's 'ingentes et privatum modum evectas opes' and 'quodque studia civium in se verteret, hortorum quoque amoenitate et villarum magnificentia quasi principem supergrederetur.'

159.   The distinction between the Emperors and private persons could on occasion also be expressed in the location of statues, cf. those of Augustus, Claudius, Agrippina, and Nero located opposite the equestrian statues of other persons in the forum of Pompeii; see R. Etienne, *Pompeii* (1974), 120 ff., with a plan. Compare also *Die Bildnisse des Augustus, Herrscherbild und Politik im kaiserzeitlichen Rom*, ed. K. Vierneisel, P. Zanker (1979), 34 ff. Compare also A. Cameron, *JRS* 72 (1982), 140: 'it was not prudent for a private citizen, however rich, to make the same sort of bid for popular favour in Constantinople as was customary in Rome. No emperor would tolerate that sort of competition.' Distinctive statue-bases put up by Herodes Atticus for the imperial family are to be found in the *exedra* at Olympia (*Inschriften aus Olympia*, nos. 612–28). It is possible that their type was determined by architectural considerations. For possible differentiation in the specific form of statues cf. e.g. Fittschen, *Madr. Mitt.* 15 (1974), 172 ff. Whether particular materials were reserved for statues of the Emperor remains in dispute: Th. Pekáry, 'Goldene Statuen der Kaiserzeit', *Röm. Mitt.* 75 (1968), 144 ff.; idem, 'Das Bildnis des römischen Kaisers in der schriftlichen Überlieferung', *Boreas* 5 (1982), 124 ff., esp. 129 ff.; G. Lahusen, 'Goldene und vergoldete römische Ehrenstatuen und Bildnisse', *Röm Mitt.* 85 (1978), 385 ff.; Th. Pekáry, *Das Bildnis des römischen Kaisers in Staat, Kult und Gesellschaft, dargestellt auf Grund der schriftlichen Überlieferung* (1983) (printing) and G. Lahusen, *Ehrenstatue*, 45 ff. In general the evolution towards clear hierarchical distinctions and externally visible formalization progressed at a different pace in different spheres, cf. Löhken, *Ordines dignitatum*, *passim*.

160.   Bibliography in W. Eck, *ZPE* 43 (1981), 127,n. 2.

161.   F. Engesser, *Der Stadtpatronat in Italien und den Westprovinzen des römischen Reiches* (Diss. Freiburg, 1957), 55 ff.

162.   *ILLRP* 309 ff.; the earliest entirely complete example is no. 316. See D. R. Stuart, *Epochs of Greek and Roman Biography* (1928), 201 ff. According to S. Mazzarino in *Antico, tardoantico ed èra costantiniana* II (1980), 289 ff. the concept of the *cursus honorum* was taken over from the Etruscans.

163.   Cf. Pliny, *NH* VII. 139; see A. Lippold, *Consules* (1963), 75; W. Kierdorf, *Laudatio Funebris* (1980), 10 ff.; 71 ff. It is fully intelligible, for this reason also, that additional honorific epithets are lacking in such sepulchral inscriptions, while elsewhere they are entirely normal; cf. S. Smitt, *De defunctorum virtutibus in carminibus sepulcralibus Latinis laudatis* (1916). The *cursus* was declaration enough.

164. S. Mazzarino, op. cit. (n. 162), 289, speaks of the *cursus honorum* '. . . dalla biografia del defunto in funzione, per così dire, *p u b b l i c a.*'

165. Examples of inscriptions set up after a person's death, *ILLRP* 316; 391; 402; 436; 440; 443. No. 438 is not a sepulchral inscription, but a building-inscription from Volsinii. *CIL* I² Supp. (printing) does not offer any further examples (H. Krummrey has been kind enough to place the proofs at my disposal). The same observation is valid furthermore also for inscriptions honouring municipal office-holders. The remark of J. Deininger, *ANRW* I. 1, 987, referring to Roman *cursus honorum* 'die in der späten Republik allmählich auch auf Ehreninschriften vermehrt erscheinen', is thus incorrect. In none of the examples which he cites in n. 25 is its character as an honorific inscription (for a living person) demonstrable.

166. e.g. *ILLRP* 324, 337; 344; 349; cf. further the numerous items of evidence in Tuchelt, *Denkmäler*, 135 ff.; *ILS* 865 ff. In isolated cases a priesthood also appeared; as it was held for an unlimited period it could be recorded as a further means of characterising the individual concerned. This is shown by a still unpublished inscription from Buthrotum, for example, set up to Cn. Domitius Ahenobarbus, *cos.* 16 BC, as patron of the town. His rank is defined only by mention of the consulate and pontificate (previously unknown). (Information kindly given to me by H.Freis, Saarbrücken.) For other examples see *ILS* 893a; 894; 900 (which all belong in the early Augustan period).

167. *ILLRP* 351–2; 354–6. Cf. n. 166. For general treatments of the evolution of honorific inscriptions (not always dealing with the exact date of any one honour) see e.g. H. Dessau, in A. Gercke – E. Norden, *Einleitung in die Altertumswissenschaft*³ I (1927), 10; 12 ff.; E. Sandys, *Latin Epigraphy*² (1927), 93 ff.; I. Calabi Limentani, *Epigrafia latina* (1968), 235 ff.; I. Kajanto, *Epigraphica* 33 (1971), 3 ff.

168. M. Nonius Balbus *CIL* X. 1426–34; *AE* 1979, 177–8. On the dating, L. Schumacher, *Chiron* 6 (1976), 165 ff.

169. *CIL* V. 6974–87.

170. See the evidence in *PIR*² I 507. R. Harder, *Kleine Schriften* (1960), 3 ff.

171. Pliny, *NH* XXXIV. 17 provides what can hardly be regarded as a fully accurate account of its historical evolution.

172. *CIL* III. 551 = *ILS* 928; *AE* 1919, 1 = *Corinth* VIII. 2, 54. E. Groag, *Die römischen Reichsbeamten in Achaia bis auf Diokletian* (1939), 15 ff.

173. *CIL* XI. 7553 = *ILS* 916; see G. Paci, *Scritti in memoria di M. Zambelli* (1978), 261 ff.; *CIL* X. 5059; 5060 = *ILS* 930; 930a; *CIL* V. 1878 = *ILS* 931; *NSc* 1886, 108 = *AE* 1888, 24 = *ILS* 931a, see G. Alföldy, *Aquileia nostra* 51 (1980), 286; *CIL* VI, 3835 = *ILS* 911. It is possible that the *Ignoti* of *CIL* V. 879 and XI. 1837 are also Augustan; but this remains uncertain.

174. *Inscr. Ital.* XIII. 3, nos. 17 and 83; 14 and 80; 84.

175. So however L. Braccesi, *Epigrafia e storiografia* (1981), 32.

176. *AE* 1969/70, 96–7;1978,132; 134. As in three texts the *praenomen* 'Cn.' seems to be preserved (although, as has been proved, many readings in the wax tablets from Murecine are very dubious), the senator should be identified with the consul of AD 41, whose role in the conquest of Britain is attested by Florus VII. 13; cf. A. R. Birley, *Fasti of Roman Britain* (1981), 360 ff.

177. Suet. *Aug.* 31. 5.

178. See n. 46 above.

179. Cf. Panciera in *Volusii*, 87 ff.

180. See nn. 172 ff. above.

181. *CIL* X. 832 = *ILS* 898. The extent to which the *nomen* alone, especially in the early Principate, could function as a social marker is evident from the nomenclature of many freedmen of senators, who indicate the patronage-relationship not in the normal form, by giving the *praenomen* of their *patronus*, but either with

the latter's complete name or at least with the *cognomen*. In that way they were able to gain a share in the public standing of their *patronus*; cf. G. Fabre, *Libertus* (1981), 116 ff. and W. Eck in *Actas del coloquio 1978, Colonato y otras formas de dependencia no esclavistas* (*Mem. de Historia Antigua II*) (1978), 45 ff.

182. R. Bartoccini, *Autostrade July–August, 1963*, 12 ff. = *AE* 1978, 304. Whether this text might possibly belong to the base of an equestrian statue in the Forum cannot be decided on the basis of the reports. On this type compare also, e.g., G. Alföldy, 'Cnaeus Domitius Calvinus, Patronus von Emporiae', *AEA* 50/51 (1977/8), 47 ff.

183. On the changes which took place in the concept of the honorific inscription in Late Antiquity cf. e.g. R. Laqueur, 'Das Kaisertum und die Gesellschaft des Reiches', in *Probleme der Spätantike* (1930), 1 ff., esp. 33 ff.; L. Robert, *Hellenica* IV (1948), 107 ff.

For the inscriptions of L. Aelius Lamia (p. 146 above) see now I. Kajanto, *L'area sacra di Largo Argentina* (1981, app. 1983), 112 ff.

VI. AUGUSTUS AND THE EAST: THE PROBLEM OF THE SUCCESSION

GLEN BOWERSOCK

The eastern part of the Augustan Empire had been, for a short but dangerous season, the preserve of Antonius. Through judicious compromise and the diplomatic arts of well placed partisans, Augustus swiftly managed to ensure the smooth incorporation of Antonius' realm into the larger Roman world, but vestiges of hostility remained. It was not only that many had to bear the burden of public adherence to a vanquished cause: the Greeks had been obliged to endure the depredations of Roman soldiers, who used Greece as their base for the three greatest battles in the civil wars of the late Republic. At the battle of Actium in 31 BC, only Mantinea and Sparta had had the foresight – or perhaps, it must have seemed at the time, the folly – to come to the aid of the future Augustus.[1] In Asia Minor Octavian had his Zoilus at Aphrodisias, but Antonius commanded the loyalty of the rich family of Pythodori from Tralles, the progenitors of kings in Pontus.[2]

It is well recognized that Augustus' success in administering the Antonian portion of his Empire was due in large measure to the winning of allegiance from the affluent and well placed citizens of those regions. In two major missions to the East, Augustus' general, Marcus Agrippa, brought the message of the Augustan peace, and between the years 21 and 19 BC, Augustus himself journeyed from Greece to Syria. But even then, ten years after Actium, the Athenians were not ready to welcome the new ruler; and he, for his part, passed a winter on the island of Aegina instead of in the great city of Athens, in order to show his indignation.[3] The Hellenized East had entered the Empire of Augustus as defeated nations. This created a problem that required constant watching, as Augustus recognized. It offered a potential for any rival with sufficient personal eminence and audacity to exploit it. Before Antonius' failure Sulla had confronted the masters of Italy with the support of the Greek East behind him. But Sulla, unlike Antonius, had prevailed.

After the visits of Augustus and Agrippa to the East, the next member of the royal house to be present in those parts was Augustus' own stepson, Tiberius Claudius Nero. Setting forth from Rome in 6 BC and endowed with the tribunician power,[4] which represented to the whole world his position as the heir of Augustus, Tiberius began a diplomatic trip to negotiate with the Parthians over the throne of Armenia in repetition of his success in dealing with comparable issues in 20 BC. But instead of proceeding to the banks of the Euphrates, Tiberius settled down on the island of Rhodes and devoted himself to the academic pleasure of attending lectures on Greek culture by noted professors.[5] The mystery of Tiberius' alleged retirement to the island of Rhodes has beguiled scholars across the centuries and will serve as the central point of the investigation that follows.

Tiberius, stepson of the Emperor and philhellene, in residence on a Greek island from 6 BC to AD 2, cannot fail to have some bearing on our understanding of Augustus and the East. The issues become most sharply defined after 2 BC, that is, after the expiry of the five-year grant of Tiberius' tribunician power. For in the ensuing years, 1 BC, AD 1 and AD 2, Tiberius continued to reside on Rhodes with only the vague title of *legatus*.[6] He had no meaningful position in respect to Rome apart from his familial relationship to the Emperor. His sojourn on the island is often described as self-imposed or voluntary exile,[7] and yet Suetonius is explicit in telling us that Tiberius remained on Rhodes 'contra voluntatem' and that he often asked to return to Rome during these last years but was expressly forbidden to do so.[8] He was not to go home unless and until Augustus' grandson and now his adopted son, Gaius Caesar, so permitted.[9]

It was just as Tiberius' tribunician power was coming to an end that the Emperor dispatched Gaius to the East to undertake negotiations with the Parthians, in a project not all that unlike what had been proposed for Tiberius five years earlier. The presence of Gaius together with Tiberius in the East

between late 2 BC and AD 2 generated a tension that has left
clear traces in our sources. The role of Tiberius, while Gaius
set forth on his tour of the region as the new heir of Augustus,
is a central part of the drama Sir Ronald Syme has taught us to
call the crisis of 2 BC. In his important paper devoted to this
subject, in the *Proceedings of the Bavarian Academy of Sciences*,
Syme emphasized the importance of the testimony of Ovid in
the first book of the *Ars Amatoria* for the interpretation of
events in this crucial year.[10] The treatment of Ovid's evidence
was to be enlarged in Syme's later work, *History in Ovid*, and it
will be appropriate on this occasion to begin our examination
of Augustan policy for the East in 2 BC with Ovid's famous
account of the dedication of the temple of Mars the Avenger,
Mars Ultor, in May of that year.

With his customary fluency and enthusiasm, Ovid drew a
close connection between the dedication of the Mars temple
and the imminent departure of Gaius Caesar. He saw the
Parthians as about to pay at last the penalty for their destruction of the army of Crassus, and he declared that Gaius would
enlarge the realm of Rome to the limits of the eastern world:
'nunc, oriens ultime, noster eris', 'now, farthest east, you will
be ours.' 'Parthe, dabis poenas', 'Parthian, you will pay the
penalty.'[11] Young Gaius is described as himself an avenger,
ultor, and is hailed as the favoured child of Mars and Augustus.[12]
It was not without good reason that Ovid forged this link
between Gaius' mission and the dedication of the temple of
Mars Ultor. An important part of the ceremonies had been the
solemn installation in the new temple of those legionary
standards which had been recovered from the Parthians in 20
BC as a step toward the rehabilitation of the Roman name after
the defeat of Crassus.[13] Augustus was proud to have recovered
the standards by diplomacy, and he boasted of his success in
the *Res Gestae*, of which the first draft appears to have been
written in the very year of the dedication of the new Mars
temple.[14] By all of this publicity, Augustus and Ovid were
proclaiming the strength of Rome against the barbarian and
the identification of the young Gaius Caesar as a new avenger
in the struggle with Parthia.

But the celebration of Gaius and his mission was no merely
local affair for the delectation of Romans and the readers of

Ovid's elegiacs. All this publicity was designed to endow Gaius Caesar with an incontestable authority in the East itself. The poet Antipater of Thessalonica composed two epigrams within a year of Ovid's verses, to make much the same point: 'Be on your way to the Euphrates, son of Zeus', wrote Antipater. 'To you already the Parthians in the East are deserting apace. Be on your way, my prince; you shall find their bows unstrung through terror, Caesar. Rule in accord with your father's precepts. Be yourself the first to certify to the rising sun that Rome is bounded by the ocean on all sides.'[15]

Ῥώμην δ᾽ Ὠκεανῷ περιτέρμονα πάντοθεν αὐτός
πρῶτος ἀνερχομένῳ σφράγισαι ἠελίῳ.

Here in the elegant contortions of the Greek Anthology we have the equivalent of Ovid's 'nunc, oriens ultime, noster eris'.

In another poem, obviously of about the same date, Antipater of Thessalonica hailed Gaius as favoured by no less than four divinities – Athena, Aphrodite, Alcides, and Ares.[16] It is the last which again calls to mind the tribute of Ovid. The association of Gaius with Mars in connection with the opening of the new temple at Rome is eloquently attested at Athens in an inscription from the theatre of Dionysus in which Gaius is proclaimed νέος Ἄρης, the new Ares.[17] This Hellenized version of Roman propaganda fits into a substantial tradition of Athenian honours, whereby a benefactor, past or prospective, is declared to be a new incarnation of a famous figure, divine or otherwise, from the past. Automedon, another contemporary poet included in the Greek Anthology, provides clear evidence of the frequency with which the Athenians were given to offering these honorific epithets.[18] If you can offer a pig to the Athenians, you will be declared, according to Automedon, no less than another Triptolemus. If you supply cabbage stalks, lentils, or snails, you may take on the names of Erechtheus, Cecrops, Codrus, or anybody you like. Nobody cares at all: οὐδεὶς οὐδὲν ἐπιστρέφεται. Obviously Automedon's satire makes its point because people did care, and the designation of Gaius as new Ares can have been no accident.

'Marsque pater Caesarque pater, date numen eunti': the adopted son of Augustus left Rome in the guise of a new

Mars.[19] When he arrived in Athens as the new Ares, he confronted an extraordinary spectacle, undoubtedly in his honour. A fifth-century-BC temple of Ares in Acharnae had been systematically dismantled and moved (or was conceivably then in the process of being moved) stone by stone into the agora at Athens, where it was reconstructed.[20] The excavators in the agora have tended to associate this bizarre operation with the progress of Gaius' military expedition in the East and therefore to date the reconstruction to the first years of the first century AD. But in doing this they consistently failed to recognize the importance of Mars Ultor at Rome in 2 BC and the dispatch of Gaius from Rome as a new Mars. In reviewing the evidence for the rebuilding of the Ares temple at Athens, a recent scholar has acutely observed 'it should be (but has not been) irresistible for the excavators to date this reconstruction in close proximity to the building of the temple of Mars Ultor in the Forum of Rome.'[21] To be sure, Parthia and the eastern campaign were important, but as a future prospect rather than a current event. An issue of Roman imperial gold and silver, persuasively dated to 2 BC, depicts Gaius Caesar on a galloping horse with a sword in his right hand and a shield in his left, and behind him an eagle between two legionary standards. These standards undoubtedly represent those that were transferred to the temple of Mars Ultor, reminders of Augustus' past success in dealing with the Parthians and portents of the mission to come.[22]

The Athenians carried out with distinction the dissemination in their own city of the publicity for Gaius that had been started in Rome. Not only Gaius himself but his companions, L. Domitius Ahenobarbus and M. Lollius, were honoured in inscriptions as they reached the city by way of the lower Danube in the late summer or autumn of 2 BC[23]. Caesar Augustus had clearly found friends in Athens whom he had lacked during his own visit two decades earlier. The good offices of M. Agrippa in the interim may be invoked in explanation of this changed attitude in the Greek capital, and before we are done it will even be possible to identify the principal mover in organizing the honours for Gaius.

But first it is worth observing that Athens appears not to have been the only Greek city to have recognized the new heir of Augustus. Messene in the Peloponnese had been among the conspicuous supporters of Antonius during the final phase of the civil war and, like so many other Greek cities in the region, had been strengthened in its allegiance to Antonius because Sparta, hated as a tyrannical city, had conspicuously espoused the cause of Augustus.[24] But it is clear from two new inscriptions that by the time of the mission of Gaius Caesar Messene was solidly behind the regime in Rome. In one text dated to AD 2 the Messenians can be seen publicly expressing their loyalty to Gaius and their gratitude for the good news that he is in sound health, despite perilous campaigns in the distant East.[25] Another inscription, which, because of its proximity to the first in the excavation, ought to be close in date, records donations for the repair and reconstruction of many of the city's older buildings, and this is being done explicitly as a tribute to the Romans and the emperor Augustus.[26] The donors are praised for their εὔνοια toward the people of Rome and Caesar Augustus ὑπὲρ τᾶς πόλιος φροντίδος.[27] As at Athens there seems to be some kind of self-conscious, deliberate association of the monuments of the classical Greek past with the new dynasty in Rome.

The large number of buildings involved in the restoration project at Messene can be compared not only with the removal of the Ares temple to Athens but with two other unusual operations at about the same time: the removal of parts of temples at Thorikos and Sunium and their redeployment in buildings of the agora at Athens.[28] Augustus and Gaius emerge as the patrons, even the defenders of the great classical traditions of Greece.

And there is more to be said about Rome's cultivation of the Greek past at this time. Athens' finest hour had undoubtedly been the dramatic repulse of the Persian forces at Salamis in 480 BC. In the Augustan age the home of the Persians was now under the sway of a Parthian monarchy, which represented no less a threat to the Hellenized world in those days as the Persians in the past. If the government at Rome were interested in presenting itself as the defender of Hellenic traditions, nothing would be more compelling than the celebration of Rome as protector of the Greeks against the present menace in the Iranian heartland. From what we have already seen of

operations in Greece for the visit of Gaius Caesar and the close
linkage of observances in Rome and in Athens, it should come
as no surprise to discover that the parallel with the victory at
Salamis was made explicit in 2 BC.

Introducing his panegyric of Gaius on the eve of the expedition to the East, Ovid describes a great sea battle that was
artificially contrived at Rome in connection with the celebra-
tions of the consecration of the new Mars temple:[29]

> Quid, modo cum belli navalis imagine Caesar
>   Persidas induxit Cecropiasque rates?

> What of the mock naval war in which the Emperor
> recently displayed Persian and Greek ships?

This alludes to the sensational *naumachia* of which Augustus
himself speaks with such pride in the *Res Gestae*.[30] He devotes
an entire section to a grand naval battle which was enacted in
an excavated site across the Tiber. He mentions a fleet of
warships, including thirty triremes or biremes, and says that
3,000 men participated in the exercise. Several centuries later
Cassius Dio noted that there were still remains of this great
naumachia to be seen in his own time, and he states that the
conflict between the navies of Athens and Persia ended as
history prescribed – with a great victory for the ships of
Athens.[31] In his paper on the crisis of 2 BC, Syme observed:
'This piece of pageantry advertised Rome as the champion of
Hellas against the Orient.'[32] It did indeed. The event was
staged not merely as an entertainment for the Romans but as a
great statement of purpose and propaganda for the Greeks.

We can scarcely wonder, therefore, that the inscriptions of
Athens have revealed a great benefactor of the city in the
Augustan age, who was honoured, according to the style so
ridiculed by the poet Automedon, as a new Themistocles.[33]
This person was a Syrian by origin who possessed both the
Roman and the Athenian citizenships. His name was C. Iulius
Nicanor, and we know from a remark in Dio Chrysostom a
hundred years later that one of his most magnificent benefactions to the city was nothing less than the purchase of the island
of Salamis on behalf of the Athenians.[34] Nicanor's magnificent
gesture, putting an end to the dispensation of Sulla, who had
deprived the city of its island, must certainly be seen in the

context of the great *naumachia* at Rome. We have once more in
the repossession of Salamis a Greek echo of the events at Rome
in 2 BC. The benefaction of Nicanor appears to have suffered
some kind of tarnish in later years, for his title of new
Themistocles, and, in addition, another title which he received
from the Athenians – that of new Homer, doubtless for poetical achievements of some kind – were systematically erased on
Athenian inscriptions.[35] Before long we shall be able to suggest
why the Athenians chose to dishonour their great benefactor,
but at this point it will suffice to identify C. Iulius Nicanor as
the man who played the most conspicuous part at Athens in
representing Gaius Caesar as the Greeks' protector against the
barbarian.

Writing of the mission of Gaius Caesar, Syme observed: 'It
was advisable to display the heir apparent to provinces and
armies which had seen no member of the syndicate of government since Agrippa, the vicegerent, departed from the East
twelve years before.'[36] When Tiberius had left Rome in 6 BC,
he might well have appeared to be a member of the syndicate
of government. After all, he had the tribunician power and
was destined for some kind of negotiations concerning
Armenia. But the fact of the matter was that he never carried
out his mission, did not visit provinces and armies, and,
although his tribunician power continued to the end of its
five-year term, was clearly perceived as isolated from the
central government. Yet, for all that, he remained the stepson
of the Emperor Augustus, and he was not altogether unnoticed
in the Greek world. He had friends and clients in the area.
Among them was the cultivated family at Mytilene which had
provided Pompey with his great confidant, Theophanes, and
Tiberius himself with a man identified as one of his most
intimate friends in the early years of his imperial rule. This was
Cn. Pompeius Macer, whose son, Q. Pompeius Macer, was
the first eastern senator under the principate.[37]

In Sparta the family of Tiberius' father had a *clientela* of long
standing, which made it possible for his mother, Livia, to take
him there for refuge when the two of them fled from Italy after
the defeat of L. Antonius in the Perusine War.[38] Historians
have perhaps not adequately appreciated the extent to which
Augustus owed the allegiance of the Spartans to their devotion

to Livia and her husband. As we have seen, Sparta was almost the only city in the entire Peloponnese not to support Antony: how could it when it had sheltered a refugee who had become the wife of Octavian? The dynast of Sparta, C. Iulius Eurycles, must therefore have been numbered among the old friends of Tiberius and his mother as he settled into his Hellenic life on Rhodes.[39] If Tiberius' isolation soon became apparent to the friends of Augustus, the potential for this philhellene as a leader of the Greeks will have been equally apparent to the friends of Tiberius. In 1 BC, after the actual termination of Tiberius' tribunician power, we find a priest in the city of Nysa, near Tralles in Asia Minor, with the title of priest of Tiberius Claudius Nero for life.[40] Nearly twenty years ago I surmised that this document showed just how ignorant a city in Asia Minor could be of the facts of Roman politics.[41] But the truth of the matter seems to me now to have been quite different. The people of Nysa could not fail to have been aware of what was going on in the East, of the conflict between Tiberius, not far away off the coast, and a new claimant to the role of defender of the Hellenes, namely Gaius Caesar, who had supplanted Tiberius as heir of Augustus.

The Greeks were constantly reminded of Tiberius' presence in their area and of his sympathy for their way of life. It was not merely his attendance at the lectures of their professors or his donning of their forms of dress that made this plain. It was, in addition, his dispatch of chariots to compete in the great Greek games at Olympia, as well as the games at Thespiae.[42] He cannot fail to have been in touch with his friends on Mytilene, and the ancestral connection with Sparta must also have been important. In fact, we know from the testimony of Josephus that Augustus' man in Sparta, C. Iulius Eurycles, behaved very oddly in the last years of the first century BC[43]. He caused trouble throughout the cities of Greece, provoking civil strife, and, in Josephus' words, 'stripping' (περιδύειν) the cities. The situation became so bad that Augustus felt obliged to banish Eurycles.

It has always seemed peculiar, to say the least, that Augustus' own nominee should have given him such trouble. It seemed even more peculiar that, after the banishment of Eurycles, he and his family were somehow rehabilitated to such an extent that a cult in his honour was conjoined with the celebration of the imperial cult at Gytheum in the early years of the reign of Tiberius.[44] Over twenty years ago it was possible to demonstrate by an analysis of the texts of Strabo and Josephus that the stasis which Eurycles stirred up in Greece and the banishment which resulted from it occurred between the years 7 and 2 BC, in other words, in exactly the period of Tiberius' residence on the island of Rhodes.[45] Furthermore, we have already seen that a city such as Messene, which had once been hostile to the victor at Actium, principally because Sparta had supported him, turns out to be a bastion of Augustan sympathizers by the end of the first century BC. By then Augustus had taken firm action against the tyrant at Sparta, and, no doubt in the process, won the goodwill and support of all those cities that had formerly viewed the *princeps* with suspicion. The obvious implication of all this is that Tiberius' old friend in Sparta had supported Augustus when the fortunes of the two Romans had been linked. But when the two men went their separate ways Eurycles opted for Tiberius, and Augustus had to wipe him out. At the time no one could have told that Tiberius himself would be rehabilitated under the force of sheer necessity and reinstated again in AD 4, with Gaius and Lucius Caesar both dead, as Augustus' successor. The fact that Tiberius did return to favour and ultimately succeeded his stepfather on the throne of the Caesars is undoubtedly the explanation of the rehabilitation of Eurycles' family in Sparta. Eurycles' son, Laco, took over the dynastic position from which his father, now deceased, had been expelled.[46]

In the subsequent generation, the eastern friends of Tiberius are drawn even closer together. The grandson of Eurycles married into the Mytilenean family of Pompeius Macer, taking as his wife the daughter of Tiberius' intimate, the man whom Strabo describes as among the foremost friends of the Emperor Tiberius in the early years of his reign.[47] This visible nexus of the Mytilenean and Spartan friends of Tiberius and the elevation of both families during the reign of Tiberius must have taken its origins in the political atmosphere of the long sojourn on Rhodes. In short, some Greeks expected at that time that their future lay with Tiberius and not with Augustus or the new heir Gaius Caesar. Others calculated differently and, in the event, unwisely. C. Iulius Nicanor, who cast his lot conspicuously with Gaius by orchestrating the commemorations of 2–1 BC at Athens, learned later that this display had cost him dear when Gaius was in his grave and Tiberius returned to favour. The subsequent ascendancy of Tiberius and his ultimate rule as Emperor constitute the best explanation of the public *damnatio* which C. Iulius Nicanor suffered as new Themistocles. Nicanor as Themistocles was a visible evocation of Nicanor, the partisan of Gaius.

One might well go on to ask why the Athenians, out of deference to Tiberius either as heir or as Emperor, saw fit to delete, in addition, the title of new Homer, which they had also bestowed upon Nicanor.[48] The answer is less clear, but it probably had something to do with another of Tiberius' eastern clients. His friend, Pompeius Macer, was, among other things, a notable poet, who is mentioned by Ovid as a writer in the Homeric tradition. Among his themes was the anger of Achilles.[49] Ovid calls him, in one of the poems from his Pontic exile, Iliacus Macer, 'Macer of the *Iliad*'.[50] It seems that we have at least two notable Homeric poets flourishing at the end of the first century BC, one a partisan of Tiberius and the other a partisan of Gaius Caesar. With the admission of Pompeius Macer's son into the Senate at Rome and the disgrace of Nicanor at Athens, the adulators of Tiberius would have had good reason to remove their praise of Nicanor as a poet no less than their gratitude to him as a Themistocles. The Athenians would have known that Tiberius had a long memory and did not forget those who slighted him during the difficult time of Gaius' ascendancy. It is recorded that a man he once defended, King Archelaus of Cappadocia, in an action before Augustus himself, had so miscalculated the future as to slight him in favour of Gaius during the years of residence on Rhodes. This was something which, as Cassius Dio says, Tiberius did not forget.[51] A smouldering resentment drove Tiberius as Emperor to summon Archelaus to Rome for trial on a charge of revolution, and the outcome would have been death, had not the king's old age proved a more efficient executioner.

The tension between Tiberius and Gaius as rival heirs of Augustus is well documented in the pages of Suetonius' biography of Tiberius. Someone even offered to execute the older man in order to please Gaius.[52] The two rivals had an uneasy meeting at Samos or Chios, but for reasons of protocol conspicuously not at Rhodes.[53] Augustus' concern is evident in his determination that Tiberius not be allowed to return to Rome without the explicit permission of Gaius Caesar. It was stipulated further that when the return took place, Tiberius was to have no part whatever in the government.[54] It was even suggested to Augustus that Tiberius was plotting a revolution, but Tiberius strenuously and perhaps truthfully denied this.[55] Tiberius was too cunning. What he saw happening (and presumably encouraged) was the gradual building up of support in the Greek East, so that when the moment of succession to Augustus should occur, his claims would be so strong in that part of the Empire that they could not be ignored. Accordingly, the effort to establish Gaius Caesar as a friend and defender of the Greeks and as a victor over the Parthians was, in large measure, designed to counteract the increasing support for Tiberius.

The ultimate recall of Tiberius in AD 2 seems not to have been altogether fortuitous. It may be wondered why, after Tiberius had remained for three years of continued residence on Rhodes without a renewal of the tribunician power, Augustus finally decided to authorize a return when Gaius was still alive. From the evidence of Suetonius we may presume that Gaius himself concurred in this decision, although he was at the time far away, on the eastern frontier. To be sure, Gaius was expected back in the Greek provinces very soon, as the enthusiastic inscription from Messene attests. But what appears to have made the removal of Tiberius a particularly urgent matter was the fact that, after long years of waiting, the Greek supporters of the exile had taken a bold step. They had declared outright their firm expectation that Tiberius would succeed Augustus. This is incontrovertibly established by a passage in Suetonius, taken in conjunction with a precious epigram of Apollonides in the Greek Anthology. Shortly before the recall of Tiberius, says Suetonius, an eagle – a bird never before seen on Rhodes – took up its place on the roof of Tiberius' house.[56] There are ample parallels to prove that the appearance of an eagle above a potential ruler was presumed by the Greeks to be a certain portent of succession.[57] It scarcely matters whether or not an eagle was actually obs rved on the roof of Tiberius' house. It was quite sufficient for someone to have said that the bird was there. And that someone said it is clear not only from Suetonius but from the epigram of Apollonides:[58]

> The holy bird, in former days no visitant of
> Rhodians – the eagle, in former days a mere
> fable to the sons of Cercaphus – just then I
> arrived, borne aloft on high-flying wings through
> the broad sky when Nero held the island of the
> Sun (Ἡλίου νῆσον ὅτ᾽ εἶχε Νέρων).
> And in his house I lodged, tame to the ruler's
> hand, not shrinking from the future Zeus (οὐ
> φεύγων Ζῆνα τὸν ἐσσόμενον).

This poem confirms Suetonius' report of the portent of the eagle at Rhodes. From the words 'when Nero held the island of the Sun' (Ἡλίου νῆσον ὅτ᾽ εἶχε Νέρων), scholars have reasonably judged the poem to have been written after Tiberius' departure from Rhodes.[59] Such an interpretation is made the more likely by the chronology in Suetonius, according to which the eagle appeared shortly before Tiberius' recall. But these verses cannot have been written very long after the report of the eagle. Tiberius is still called by the name Nero, which he abandoned in AD 4 upon his adoption as Tiberius Iulius Caesar. While it is true that historians of a subsequent age, such as Velleius Paterculus and Tacitus, felt free to use the name Nero in describing the career of Tiberius under Augustus, there is no evidence whatever that this name was perpetuated at the time,[60] and there was every reason for Tiberius and his friends to parade the imperial name of Caesar from the moment of his adoption. The Athenians, for example, upon learning the news in AD 4, promptly erected a monument celebrating the Emperor's new heir as Tiberius Caesar, even though they had honoured him in at least five earlier inscriptions as Tiberius Claudius Nero.[61]

It must also be remembered that the Greek poets of the *Anthology* often composed occasional poetry. Those who consorted with members of the imperial house regularly wrote their slight, but graceful, commemorative epigrams soon after the occasion they were celebrating. In the case of Apollonides we have good reason to believe that he lived in the general area of Greek Anatolia and that he had been at least a visitor on Rhodes. One of his most inconsequential poems celebrates the beauty of a youth who lived on that island, described as the most blessed of islands, 'lit by such a sun'.[62] It would be reasonable therefore to see in Apollonides one of the cultivated Greeks who had seen Tiberius on Rhodes. His epigram on the eagle would have been a natural and appropriate tribute to the man he believed to be the future Zeus (Ζῆνα τὸν ἐσσόμενον), the next Augustus.[63]

The suggestion of Gow and Page, in their commentary on the poems of the *Anthology* in Philip's Garland, that Apollonides composed his eagle epigram soon after the adoption of Tiberius cannot be supported.[64] Those scholars supposed that Apollonides was writing before it became generally known that Tiberius, on acquiring his new name, had abandoned the names of Claudius and Nero. It should be clear enough from what has already been said that Tiberius had too many intimate friends in the East for such ignorance to prevail, least of all in the circle of those with whom he had associated on Rhodes. And it is inconceivable that news of the adoption was spread without news of the change of name. In short, Apollonides' epigram stands as precious testimony of the aspirations of Tiberius' Greek adherents in the uncertain period just after his departure from the East.

When Tiberius returned to Rome he took with him a scholar well versed in Greek philosophy and, more importantly, in the science of astrology. In a walk along the cliffs of Rhodes Tiberius had tested Thrasyllus' skills of prediction and found them so impressive that he was willing to share his inmost thoughts with him.[65] Thrasyllus foretold Tiberius' rise to power and thereby provided the exile of Rhodes with the encouragement he needed to wait and to dissemble until his hour should come. Among the other Greeks whom Tiberius learned to cherish in the East was, as we have already seen, the descendant of Theophanes, Cn. Pompeius Macer, the noted Homeric poet. Since Macer appears as chief librarian at Rome in the latter years of Augustus and remains to be named by Strabo as one of Tiberius' most intimate friends after the accession,[66] it is likely that Tiberius also prevailed upon Macer to join Thrasyllus in going to Rome in AD 2.

Along with his most precious Greek friends Tiberius took back to Italy his memories of the exile, memories which he stored up in characteristic fashion for future use. He nourished a deep loathing for M. Lollius, who had accompanied Gaius Caesar in the opening phase of his travels; and, as can be seen in Velleius and Tacitus, much of Tiberius' resentment over the Rhodian episode was deflected, in later years, away from Augustus and Gaius to the malign figure of Lollius.[67] By contrast P. Sulpicius Quirinius had treated Tiberius with respect during Gaius' mission. When Quirinius died in AD 21 Tiberius, then Emperor, requested a public funeral for this good man and eulogized him fulsomely in a speech that included a bitter attack on Lollius as the evil genius of Gaius Caesar.[68] Nor, as we have seen, did Tiberius forget the offence of the king of Cappadocia. In addition, among his memories back in Rome after AD 2 was probably the hypnotic and attractive figure of a strong young man whom he must have met in the entourage of Gaius, L. Aelius Sejanus.[69] Ambitious and immoral, crafty and patient, Sejanus, who had already exploited the sexual weaknesses of the rich old Apicius,[70] must have spotted the vulnerability of Tiberius. What Syme has called so perceptively Tiberius' 'infatuation' with Sejanus, 'a delusion more than intellectual',[71] may already have begun in the lifetime of Augustus. It may partially explain the sudden rise to prominence of Sejanus' father as Prefect of the Guard in the year of Augustus' death.[72] All within Tiberius' very first year as Emperor, Sejanus himself was named a colleague of his father in the guard prefecture, only to become sole prefect when his father was swiftly transferred to the prefecture of Egypt.[73]

Upon returning to Rome Tiberius was without a wife. His second wife, Julia, Augustus' daughter, had been banished three years previously after scandalous revelations about her private life.[74] From the list we possess of her alleged lovers a suspicion naturally arises that these men were more active in political conspiracy than in the bedroom.[75] Their misdemeanours had contributed to the urgency of the crisis of 2 BC, but inasmuch as Tiberius had never really been happy with

Julia he is unlikely to have had any role in her machinations during his absence. Furthermore Tiberius was much too clever to involve himself in a sordid and desperate scheme. Hesitation and dissimulation, the hallmarks of his character as Emperor, may be presumed to antedate his accession. Everything about his sojourn on Rhodes and his immersion in Hellenic culture shows his willingness to wait as he carefully prepared himself and his eastern clients for the time Thrasyllus had told him would surely come. In the two years of uncertainty after leaving Rhodes Tiberius must have been delighted not to have Julia beside him. His mother, Livia, had taken the place of a wife.

In the end Augustus' plan to entrust his Empire to Gaius Caesar collapsed, and Tiberius was waiting. The competition between these two rivals was rooted in the Greek East, where divided loyalties inherited from the age of Antonius gave ample scope for political manipulation. The growing support for Tiberius demanded counter-measures, which Augustus supplied through the mission of Gaius. Friends in Athens, such as Nicanor, together with the enemies of Sparta, joined forces to welcome the heir-apparent as he passed toward Parthia, a new Ares. But as he waited on the island of Rhodes Tiberius continued to consolidate those resources of personal allegiance which were, in the fullness of time, to serve him well. The house of Eurycles would be rehabilitated, and Nicanor disgraced. Thrasyllus and Pompeius Macer would join him in Rome, and the son of Macer would attain the praetorship in AD 15, leading the way for later generations of Greek senators. And perhaps more telling than anything else was the celebration of Tiberius' own son Drusus at Athens, early in his reign, as a new Ares.[76] Less than two decades had elapsed since the last one.

It is ironic that in Tiberius' final years on the throne he turned against many of those upon whom his career had depended. The treachery of Sejanus had perhaps unhinged him to some degree, even though he had proved himself the cleverer man. The family of Pompeius Macer fell into disgrace in AD 33, and with it a grandson of the great Eurycles. One wonders whether the nexus of Greek supporters from the days of the Rhodian exile had not disintegrated in the ruin of the

irresistible Sejanus, upon whom Tiberius had perhaps first
pinned his hopes, as upon the families of Macer and Eurycles,
in the aftermath of the crisis of 2 BC.

NOTES

1. Paus. IV. 31. 1 (Sparta); VIII. 8. 12 and VIII. 9. 6 (Mantinea).
2. For Zoilus, see J. Reynolds, *Aphrodisias and Rome* (1982), 156–64; on the
   Pythodori, G. W. Bowersock, *Augustus and the Greek World* (1965), 8 and 53.
3. G. W. Bowersock, *CQ* NS 14 (1964), 120–1, discussing [Plut.], *Mor.* 207 E.
4. Dio LV. 9. 4; Suet. *Tib.* 10. 2; Vell. Pat. II. 99. 2.
5. Suet. *Tib.* 11. 1–3. Tiberius' decision not to proceed reflected his recognition that
   Augustus had chosen to prefer the young Gaius to him. Augustus' new choice
   became apparent with the designation of Gaius as *princeps iuventutis* in 5 BC (Dio
   LV. 9. 9). Later Tiberius said that he had not wanted to get in the way: Suet. *Tib.*
   10. 1–2; Vell. Pat. II. 99. 2.
6. Suet. *Tib.* 12. 1. Livia is said to have been instrumental in obtaining the title *ad*
   velandam ignominiam.
7. e.g. H.-G. Pflaum, *Les Carrières procuratoriennes équestres* III (1961), 957 ('son exil
   volontaire à Rhodes').
8. Suet. *Tib.* 12. 1.
9. Suet. *Tib.* 13. 2.
10. R. Syme, *Sitzungsber. der Bay. Akad. der Wiss.*, Phil.-Hist. Klasse, 1974. 7.
11. Ovid, *Ars Amat.* I. 178–9. Cf. R. Syme, *History in Ovid* (1978), 8–10.
12. Ovid, *Ars Amat.* I. 181 and 203.
13. Augustus, *Res Gestae* 29. On Dio LIV. 8. 3, see F. E. Romer, *TAPA* 108 (1978),
    192–3.
14. Cf. Syme, op. cit. (n. 10 above), 13.
15. *Anth. Pal.* IX. 297 (Gow–Page, Antipater no. 47). In addition to Parthia and
    Armenia, Gaius had business in Arabia: G. W. Bowersock, *Roman Arabia* (1983),
    56.
16. *Anth. Pal.* IX. 59 (Gow–Page, Antipater no. 46).
17. *IG* II². 3250, cf. p. 349, and *Hesperia* 16 (1947), 68–9.
18. *Anth. Pal.* XI. 319 (Gow–Page, Automedon no. 5). On this poem and the form of
    honour it mocks, see the important analysis by L. Robert, *REG* 94 (1981),
    338–61.
19. Ovid, *Ars Amat.* I. 203.
20. W. Dinsmoor, *Hesperia* 9 (1940), 49–50; H. A. Thompson and R. E. Wycherley,
    The Agora of Athens (1972), 163. Cf. P. Graindor, *Athènes sous Auguste* (1927), 51,
    whose views influenced the subsequent writers on this matter.
21. Romer, op. cit. (n. 13), 202 n. 35. Mars also figures in the great inscription of
    Nicopolis on the site of the victor's camp at Actium. It is usually assumed that this
    text belongs to the years immediately after the battle: J. H. Oliver, *AJPh* 90
    (1969), 178–82; J. M. Carter, *ZPE* 24 (1977), 227–30. But it is clear from Dio LI.
    1. 3 that the first structure on the camp site was an open-air platform dedicated to
    Apollo. The temple dedicated to Neptune and Mars on the same spot cannot be
    the same structure (cf. Suet. *Aug.* 18. 2 and 96. 2 with the inscription fragments
    [*Nep*]*tuno* [*et* *Ma*]*rt*[*i*]). A date for this temple *c.*2/1 BC would be worth
    considering. One fragment of the inscription has the letters *VL*, conventionally
    restored [*cons*]*ul*. But, as I suggested in *Augustus* (n. 2), p. 95, n. 5, *ul*[*tori*] would
    be attractive.
22. Romer, op. cit. (n. 13), 187–202. The coins appear in Mattingly–Sydenham,
    Roman Imperial Coinage, I. *Aug.* (1923), as nos. 348–9.

23. *IG* II². 4239, 4140 (Lollius); 4144 (Domitius). On the journey through the Balkans, Dio LV. 10. 17, with the comments in Romer, op. cit. (n. 13), 202, n. 36.

24. For the date of summer, 2 BC, for Gaius' departure for the East: Romer, 200–1.

25. Paus. IV. 31. 1; Αύγούστω γὰρ βασιλεύοντι 'Ρωμαίων ἐπολέμησαν 'Αντώνιος, γένει καὶ οὗτος 'Ρωμαῖος · καὶ οἱ τῶν ἐν τῇ 'Ελλάδι ἄλλοι τε καὶ οἱ Μεσσήνιοι προσέθεντο, ὅτι ἐφρόνουν Λακεδαιμόνιοι τὰ Αὐγούστου. (I am grateful to Christian Habicht for drawing my attention to this important text.) On the reaction to Sparta's allegiance, see also Paus. VIII. 8. 12: all Arcadia except Mantinea supported Antonius at Actium ὅτι... ἐφρόνουν οἱ Λακεδαιμόνιοι τὰ Αὐγούστου.

25. *SEG* XXIII. 206 (cf. J. and L. Robert, *Bull. épig.* 1966, 201).

26. *SEG* XXIII. 207 (cf. *Bull. épig.* 1966, 200). For the inscription *in situ*, A. K. Orlandos, Πρακτικά 1959, 169 fig. 10.

27. *SEG* XXIII. 207, lines 36–7. The expression ὑπὲρ φροντίδος presumably represents *pro cura* in Latin.

28. H. A. Thompson, *AJA* 66 (1962), 200.

29. Ovid, *Ars Amat*. I. 171–2.

30. Augustus, *Res Gestae* 23. Cf. Dio LV. 10. 7. A. E. Raubitschek mistakenly tried to transfer the whole *naumachia* to Athens: *Hesperia* 23 (1954), 317–19, on which see the criticism in *Bull. épig.* 1955, 79.

31. Dio LV. 10. 7.

32. Syme, op. cit. (n. 10), 15.

33. *IG* II². 1069 (line 6), 1723 (line 4), 3786–9. See further the new fragment of *IG* II². 1723 in M. Mitsos, *Arch. Eph.* 1972, 55–7, and the discussion of it in C. P. Jones, *Phoenix* 32 (1978), 227–8.

34. Dio Chrys., *Or.* XXXI. 116. On Nicanor, see L. Robert, *Stele*, Festschrift Kontoleon (1977), 14–16, and C. P. Jones, op. cit. (n. 33), 222–8.

35. Erasures in *IG* II². 3786, 3788, and 3789.

36. Syme, *RR*, 428.

37. On the descendants of Theophanes,Tac. *Ann.* VI. 18, erring in the number of generations down to Q. Pompeius Macer: cf. Syme, *Tacitus* (1958), 748–9, and *History in Ovid* (n. 11), pp. 73–4. On Cn. Pompeius Macer, Strabo XIII. 2. 3 (618 C): καὶ νῦν ἐν τοῖς πρώτοις ἐξετάζεται τῶν Τιβερίου φίλων. See further, Pflaum, op. cit. (n. 7), I. 11, and H. Halfmann, *Die Senatoren aus dem östlichen Teil des Imperium Romanum bis zum Ende des 2. Jh. n. Chr.* (1979), 100.

38. Suet. *Tib*. 6. 2: 'Lacedaemoniis publice, quod in tutela Claudiorum erant, demandatus'.

39. On the evidence for Eurycles, especially Strabo VIII. 5. 5 (366 C), see G. W. Bowersock, *JRS* 51 (1961), 112–18.

40. *SIG*³ 781, reprinted as no. 69 in R. K. Sherk, *Roman Documents from the Greek East* (1969). An inscription at Pergamum shows another priest of Tiberius Claudius Nero, but the precise date – sometime before AD 4 – cannot be determined: *Ath. Mitt.* 32 (1907), 321 (*IGR* IV. 454), with the acute observations of D. Magie, *Roman Rule in Asia Minor* II (1950), 1297.

41. Bowersock, *Augustus* (n. 2), p. 118, n. 4.

42. *SIG*³ 782 (Olympia); *BCH* 82 (1958), 159 (Thespiae), as interpreted in *Bull. épig.* 1959, 184, p. 194. At Olympia Tiberius is called Τιβέριος Κλαύδιος Τιβερίου υἱὸς Νέρων; at Thespiae the formula is the same except for the absence of Νέρων.

43. Jos. *BJ* I. 531 (ἐπὶ τῆς στάσεως ἐμπλῆσαι τὴν 'Αχαΐαν καὶ περιδύειν τὰς πόλεις); also *AJ* XVI. 310.

44. S. B. Kougéas, 'Ελληνικά (1928), 16, reprinted in *AE* 1929, 99 and in E. Kornemann, *Neue Dokumente zum lakonischen Kaiserkult* (1929).

45. Bowersock. op. cit. (n. 39), 116.

THE PROBLEM OF THE SUCCESSION 187

46. Ibid.
47. C. Julius Argolicus, grandson of Eurycles, married Pompeia Macrina: Tac. *Ann.*
    VI. 18. For the generations of the family at Mytilene and Strabo's comment on
    Cn. Pompeius Macer, see above, n. 37.
48. The title of 'new Homer' appears alongside that of 'new Themistocles' in *IG* II².
    3786–9, and where the erasures occur (i.e. in 3786, 3788, 3789), they cover both
    titles. Jones, op. cit. (n. 33), 224, excludes from the honours to Nicanor the
    statue-base inscribed Ἰλιὰς ἡ μεθ' Ὅμηρον ἐγὼ καὶ πρόσθεν Ὁμήρ[ου] / πάροστατις
    ἵδρυμαι τῶι με τεκόντι νέω[ι], published by H. A. Thompson, *Hesperia* 23 (1954),
    62–5. Jones follows Thompson in believing that the base for a statue of the
    personified *Iliad* (which survives) stood on one side of a statue of Homer himself,
    and a statue of the *Odyssey* (which also survives) on the other side. The inscription
    on the *Iliad* base alludes to the ancient opinion that Homer wrote the *Iliad* when he
    was young (τῷ με τεκόντι νέῳ) and the *Odyssey* when he was old. In other words,
    νέος here means 'young' rather than 'new'.
49. Ovid, *Amores* II. 18. 1–3: 'carmen ad iratum dum tu perducis Achillem /
    primaque iuratis induis arma viris, / nos, Macer, ignara Veneris cessamus in
    umbra'. Cf. *Amores* II. 18. 35. See also Syme, *History in Ovid* (n. 11), 73.
50. Ovid, *Ex Pont.* IV. 16. 6.Cf. *Ex. Pont.* II. 10.
51. Dio LVII. 17. 3–5.
52. Suet. *Tib.* 13. 1.
53. Suet. *Tib.* 12. 2, says the two met on Samos, whereas Dio LV. 10. 19 puts the
    meeting on Chios.
54. Suet. *Tib.* 13. 2.
55. Suet. *Tib.* 12. 3.
56. Suet. *Tib.* 14. 4: 'ante paucos vero quam revocaretur dies aquila numquam antea
    Rhodi conspecta in culmine domus eius assedit'.
57. Cf., e.g., Plut. *Mor.* 340 C.
58. *Anth. Pal.* IX. 287 (Gow–Page, Apollonides no. 23).
59. Cf. A. S. F. Gow and D. L. Page, *The Garland of Philip* II (1968), 160.
60. For the proof, see K. Müller, *Die Epigramme des Antiphilos von Byzanz* (1935),
    14–21. Even Gow and Page, op. cit. (n. 59), p. 120, admit this in their discussion
    of Antiphilus' poem, *Anth. Pal.* IX. 178, which they believe must refer to the
    Emperor Nero.
61. *IG* II². 3254, part of a monument representing the adoptions of AD 4, with
    Tiberius, Germanicus, and Drusus: see Graindor, op. cit. (n. 20), 46–7. For the
    five earlier inscriptions: *IG* II². 3243–7.
62. *Anth. Plan.* B 49 (Gow–Page, Apollonides no. 28).
63. Gow–Page, op. cit. (n. 59), p. 160, oddly misunderstand Ζῆνα τὸν ἐσσόμενον as
    'the man who will be *Divus* some day'. By a familiar convention Zeus simply
    denotes the current ruler: C. P. Jones, *The Roman World of Dio Chrysotom* (1978),
    44, comparing in n. 83 on p. 174 R. Riewald, *Diss. Phil. Halenses* 20 (1912), 273–7
    and 287–96.
64. Gow–Page, op. cit. (n. 59), 160.
65. Suet. *Tib.* 14. 4; Tac. *Ann.* VI, 21; Dio LV. 11. 1–2. On Thrasyllus, see F. H.
    Cramer, *Astrology in Roman Law and Politics* (1954), 92–108.
66. Suet. *Jul.* 56.7: 'ad Pompeium Macrum, cui ordinandas bibliothecas delegaverat
    [sc. Augustus]'. For citation of Strabo, see n. 37 above. Pflaum, op. cit. (n. 7), III.
    957, seems to opt for placing Macer's library post as well as an Asian procurator-
    ship in the last decade of Augustus' rule, although there is no necessity to fix the
    Asian post 'vers l'année 5 ap. J.-C.'.
67. Vell. Pat. II. 102. 1; Tac. *Ann.* II. 48.
68. Tac. *Ann.* III. 48.

69. Tac. *Ann*. IV. 1: 'prima iuventa C. Caesarem, divi Augusti nepotem, sectatus'.
70. Tac. *Ann*. IV. 1: 'non sine rumore Apicio diviti et prodigo stuprum veno dedisse'. Cf. Dio LVII. 19. 5.
71. R. Syme, *Historia* 23 (1974), 488.
72. Tac. *Ann*. I. 7.
73. On Sejanus' appointment to the guard: Tac. *Ann*. I. 24 and VI. 8; Dio LVIII. 19. 6. His father, L. Seius Strabo, is already in Egypt in AD 15: Dio, loc. cit., and Pliny, *NH* XIX. 3, together with the fact that Seius' successor, C. Galerius, (*PIR²* G 25) is in office in AD 16. The ascription of *ILS* 8996 to L. Seius Strabo has been persuasively challenged by G. V. Sumner, *Phoenix* 19 (1965), 134–45.
74. Cf. Syme, *Sitzungsber. Bay. Akad.* (n. 10), 18–24.
75. Vell. Pat. II. 100. 4–5. Cf. Tac. *Ann*. IV. 44 and Dio LV. 10. 15.
76. *IG* II². 3257.

VII. AUGUSTUS AND THE POETS: 'CAESAR QUI COGERE POSSET'

JASPER GRIFFIN

It is not every ruler who gives his name to a period of literature, still less to one which contains great masterpieces. It is of course worth remembering that the poets whom we call Augustan came, with the exception of Ovid, from the generation which had already grown up before the battle of Actium; they were not the creation of Augustus. Browning, Dickens, and Tennyson had all produced characteristic work before the accession of Queen Victoria; we call them 'Victorian', none the less, and feel that we make more than a merely chronological point when we do so. But only for Tennyson was personal contact with the monarch important, as in more or less degree it was not only for Horace and Virgil but also for Propertius.

In this chapter I discuss the problem which Augustus posed for the poets of that generation, and the different ways in which they tried to solve it. Little will be said of Ovid. The phrase in the title, 'Caesar qui cogere posset', comes from the only passage in the first book of Horace's *Satires* to refer to Octavian. Singers are all alike, says the poet; they won't perform when you want them too, and they won't keep quiet when you don't. Tigellius had that habit. If Caesar, who could have compelled him, begged him in the name of his own friendship and that of his father, he got nowhere . . . (*Sat.* I. 3 *init.*) 'Caesar, who could have compelled him'; the phrase is suggestive. He might have insisted, but he did not. Horace uses it in a mildly ironical context and manner, as he does again in the *Epistle to Augustus*. There he says that 'we poets are very unreasonable. Each of us imagines that as soon as you hear that he is a poet, you will send for him, order him to want for nothing, and force him to write' –

commodus ultro
arcessas et egere vetes et scribere cogas (*Epp*. II.1.228)

Again the tone of the passage is such that any idea of Augustus
really forcing a poet to write is evidently absurd.[1] The deftness
with which Horace plays with the thought – potentially an
alarming one – makes it a suitable motto for a discussion in
which questions of self-consciousness, and even of embarrassment, will loom large.

The question of dynastic patronage of poets carries us back a
long way. Greek tyrants and kings employed poets as one of
the traditional devices of self-aggrandizement and propaganda.
Hieron of Syracuse, in the 470s, is praised by Pindar as 'kindly
to the people, free from hostility to the nobles, to foreign
guests a wondrous father'. That did not prevent another tradition from remembering Hieron as 'grasping and violent and,
in general terms, utterly without simplicity or nobility'.
Archelaus of Macedon, the king who first began the rise of his
country to power, invited Euripides and half a dozen other
poets and artists to his court. Euripides obligingly provided
the king with an ancestor in the mythical period and wrote a
tragedy, the *Archelaus*, about him: that cut no ice with Plato,
who regarded Archelaus as a mere thief and murderer.[2] Later
Greeks liked to tell the story of Archelaus inviting Socrates to
share in guilty splendour, and the philosopher nobly refusing;
discreditable reasons were invented for Euripides' trip to
Macedon, and it gave satisfaction to moral readers to be told
that he met a grotesque death there.[3]

By the fourth century the whole question of the patronage
of intellectuals by rulers was a familiar one. For the literary
man, there is the terrible problem of servility, *adulatio*, and the
embarrassment, for a sophisticated person, of dealing with a
man of commanding power. The Seventh Epistle of Plato
contains a passionate meditation and self-defence for having
been associated with the tyrant Dionysius of Syracuse. 'When
I thought of leaving,' says the great philosopher, 'he implored
me to remain; and we know that the requests of tyrants contain
an element of compulsion'. It is interesting to find Cicero
quoting this very passage in the year 49, in the context of his
decision to join Pompey against Caesar in the Civil War:

Caesar looks so formidable that Cicero fears that, unless he himself makes it impossible, Caesar will induce him to take his side, by a mixture of persuasion and compulsion.[4] What Cicero feared but avoided was experienced by the sixty-year-old mime writer Laberius in 46. Caesar induced him to act in person at his games, promising an enormous fee. Laberius duly performed, but expressed in a moving prologue his bitterness at being forced to stoop to appearing as an actor. Macrobius, who preserves the story, says that Laberius was 'invited' by Caesar, but the old poet evidently felt that he could not refuse; and Macrobius himself observes that 'power does compel, not only if it invites but even if it beseeches'.[5] By contrast with Caesar's high-handed action, which Laberius' response made highly invidious to him, we find M. Brutus being ostentatiously careful to treat a professional actor with respect. Anxious to secure the services of Canutius, a popular actor, for his games after the assassination of Caesar, he wrote to the man's friends asking them to persuade him, 'for no Greek could properly be compelled to appear'.[6]

The question of compulsion is of course a very tricky one, and there is no simple answer to it. Sir Ronald himself has observed that 'no despot can compel a poet to compose an elogium in epic verse'[7]; but he would agree that a request from Augustus was a different thing from a request from anybody else. I shall be returning to this subject, and to the Horatian phrase of my title. For the moment we observe only that the question of compulsion, and of loss of freedom, was vividly present in men's minds in the generation of Caesar. Augustus and the poets his contemporaries will not have been less mindful of it. It is tantalizing to find that Cornelius Gallus broke with the Neoteric tradition by writing verse in praise of Caesar, and to know nothing of the circumstances or the details.[8]

The question of gifts was also very delicate. To ask for a reward was painful: Theocritus in his sixteenth *Idyll* addresses an appeal for patronage to Hieron II of Syracuse, doubtless hoping that he would emulate the spectacular patronage exercised by earlier Syracusan rulers. The poet is clearly embarrassed by his task, and his poem is a brilliant medley of ingenious devices for stating it without loss of dignity. Hieron was unresponsive, and we next find Theocritus in the eastern end of the Mediterranean, praising Ptolemy II for his lavish generosity to any poet who comes to Egypt: 'and those mouthpieces of the Muses sing of Ptolemy in return for his benefactions', adds the poet with a *naïveté* that for a moment lifts the curtain on the economic facts of poetic life (XVII. 115).

At Rome the question was no less pressing. All four of the first generation of 'Augustan' poets – Virgil, Horace, Tibullus, Propertius – seem to have been impoverished in the triumviral proscriptions.[9] Horace and Virgil were certainly enriched by the patronage of Maecenas and Augustus; the situation with the elegiac poets, gentlemen by birth, is less easy to read. Horace, the only one to be explicit on these matters, makes it clear that the receipt of the largesse which made him a small landowner (we ought to speak of Horace's 'Sabine estate', not of his 'Sabine farm': there were five small farms on it),[10] was constantly in his mind as a real or potential embarrassment. In the seventh *Epistle* of the First Book he asserts his willingness to give it all up, if necessary, to maintain his freedom of movement; in other poems of that collection he writes sardonically of the obligations entailed by a career as a dependent of the great. And in the *Epistle to Augustus* he finds opportunity to say, with some emphasis, that the generous gifts which Augustus has made to the poets Virgil and Varius have conferred great credit on the giver (II. 1. 246). Virgil has not, in the *Eclogues*, made clear what exactly happened about his own inheritance. My guess is that having lost his land near Mantua he was compensated by those in power with an estate near Naples, the place where we later find him resident; this essentially unpoetical transaction lies behind the cryptic first and ninth *Eclogues*, which leave it unclear whether the poet was ejected or restored, grateful or embittered. We read in the Donatus *Life* of Virgil that he was offered by Augustus the property of a man in exile, but refused to accept it. Whatever the truth of that edifying anecdote, both Horace and Virgil were handsomely enriched by Maecenas;[11] and it would hardly do to enquire closely into the source of Maecenas' colossal wealth. If one were to have the cruelty to press the question, the answer would surely be that much of it must have come from the profits of the proscriptions and the evictions. At whatever remove, the largesse of the great patron must have had its roots in violence. The poets present him as the scion of a hundred kings – 'Maecenas atavis edite regibus' – which was not only flattering but enabled the real origin of the money to stay out of sight.

It has often been remarked that the poetry of the 30s BC makes surprisingly little allusion to Octavian. He is not named in the *Eclogues*, and he barely appears in the first book of the *Satires*; those collections were published before the battle of Actium. Even works appearing soon after that decisive event may have little to say of him – his name is absent from the poems of Tibullus and occurs only once, and then in an invidious context, in the first book of Propertius. It is true that Horace has composed an *Epode* on the battle and given it the central position in that collection, and that Virgil has devoted several grandiose passages of the *Georgics* to Octavian's praise. Already Virgil is prepared to write of him as a superman, destined for heaven, the one possible saviour of a tottering world. Other poets found that note harder to strike; and we observe an absence of personal intimacy of the sort which would have made the process easier. This point has, I think, some importance.

Only shattered fragments survive of what was once a rich tradition about the royal dynasty of Ptolemies and the resident scholars and poets whom they subsidized at Alexandria. Eratosthenes is quoted for a remark made to him by Queen Arsinoe III, which he recorded in one of his prose works: 'What a sordid party', said the queen,[12] going on to complain of her husband's unselective entertainments. P. M. Fraser cites the story as evidence for the 'intimacy in which in the third century the intelligentsia lived' with the court. The second Ptolemy, the greatest patron of poets, was a man of gallant life, who made no secret of his amours and filled Alexandria with statues of his mistresses. Theocritus, in a poem which recommends to discontented men that they should enlist in Ptolemy's service, gives a catalogue of the king's merits. He declares that he is 'kindly, cultured, a ladies' man, as agreeable as can be'.[13] That note of manly comradeship was inconceivable for a Roman poet writing about Augustus. In the next reign, Callimachus allows himself an arch piece of risqué humour at the expense of the young queen. She wept profusely when her brother-husband went off to the wars: are we to believe that it was just the departure of her *brother* which called up the tears? We know young brides better than that! As for the king, he went off, Callimachus tells us, 'bearing the delicious traces of nocturnal warfare, in which he had triumphed over her maidenhood' (fr. 110 = Catullus 66). Imagination fails to call up a poem in such terms on the departure to the wars of Augustus, or even of one of the young princes. Augustan poetry is not court poetry in that sense: the great ladies do not appear in it. And, on the other hand, Augustus was too concerned with his dignity to encourage intimate glimpses of his private life – despite the improper verses which he wrote himself in the turbulent 30s. A generation earlier, Cicero had alleged that the Greek poet Philodemus, a protégé of L. Piso, wrote at Piso's request scandalous poems about his patron's love life; but Cicero cannot quote any, and doubtless they never existed.[14] A Roman grandee, even if he was not Augustus, did not countenance that sort of thing.

The absence of erotic insinuation is only one aspect of the absence of informal relationships between Augustus and his poets. Despite the much fuller extant evidence, we do not find in life such episodes as that between King Antigonus and the poet Antagoras, when he came upon him making fish soup, and the two exchanged banter;[15] and in poetry this is part of the importance of the role of Maecenas. Horace could versify scenes in which he and Maecenas appear in unbuttoned mood. Thus he can rally his patron on his fear of death, describe the small talk between the two of them as they travel in Maecenas' carriage,[16] and even, in the *Epodes*, complain to Maecenas of his own difficult love affair, and go on to say 'I am as deep in love as old Anacreon was with Bathyllus. You are in love yourself: the object of your flame is as fair as that who burned Troy'. The spicy underlying hint is of Maecenas' scandalous intrigue with an actor named Bathyllus. Horace slyly introduces the name, but as if it were only that of the beloved of a long-dead Greek poet. Maecenas' sweetheart is compared to Helen – or perhaps to Paris;[17] we observe that the poet has succeeded in avoiding any word whose gender would have been unambiguous. That is not to say that a tactful poet would

talk like that about Maecenas' wife. The only appropriate
appearance of that lady in verse is at the bed-side of her dying
husband,[18] and some will deny credence to the idea that it was
she whom Horace extols for her erotic arts in *Odes* II.
12 – her
shining eyes, her burning kisses, her prowess in the dance:
such a description related not to a Roman matron, however
sprightly she may have been in reality, but to a professional.[19]

The relationship with Maecenas could serve the poets as a
smoked glass, as it were, between them and the naked glare of
the sun of Augustus. Virgil refers to his *Georgics* as 'your
exacting command, Maecenas', 'tua, Maecenas, haud mollia
iussa'; that was more agreeable than ascribing a command to
Octavian ('Caesar qui cogere posset'), for a command from
him would look like a different, a more real, a less agreeable
thing. Conversely Propertius tells Maecenas that 'if only I had
the divine inspiration necessary for heroic verse, I should
certainly tell of the wars and achievements of your Caesar
('bellaque resque tui memorarem Caesaris', a notably chilly
epithet)[20] – Mutina, the disastrous civil war of Philippi, the
retreats of the war in Sicily, the ruin of the ancient people
of Etruria' (II. 1. 25). That catalogue of Octavian's career,
invidiously singling out episodes of disaster or discredit,[21] was
easier to address to a recipient other than the *princeps* himself.
So too Propertius finds an urbane formula for declining to
compose panegyric of the *princeps*, when he says to Maecenas
that his modesty in not venturing beyond the limits of his
talent is an emulation of Maecenas' own modesty in declining
public office: 'I excel you in your own line' (III. 9. 22).

Maecenas could provide a welcome nuance of personal
intimacy to a poet's relationship with the regime, and he
could, as we see, serve as a device enabling a poet to evade
tackling full-scale encomium of Augustus. Not only Propertius
but also Horace made deft use of it. 'If you want Caesar's wars
written up', he tells Maecenas, 'you will make a better job of it
yourself in a prose history': 'tuque pedestribus/dices historiis
proelia Caesaris,/Maecenas, melius' (*C.* II. 12). The humour
of that suggestion is lost when commentators omit to observe
that we know what Augustus thought of Maecenas' prose: 'He
constantly attacked his style for its affectedness', we read, 'and
imitated and made fun of what he called his "perfume-

drenched lovelocks".'[22] Both Maecenas and Augustus were meant to read Horace's poem in the light of that: of all styles for the narration of the great man's military career, that would be the least appropriate or acceptable.

As with the glance at Maecenas' love life in the fourteenth *Epode*, Horace's touch is light and discreet; not everybody was meant to understand fully. That showed tact. On the other hand, such writing, like Horace's way of life, carried an implication of intimacy with the great; and that was likely to breed jealousy and resentment. Horace dwells repeatedly on the envy which people felt for his intimacy with Maecenas, and Propertius addresses him as 'Maecenas nostrae spes invidiosa iuventae', 'the hope on whom my youth relies, source of jealousy in others'.[23] Privileged persons with no position of responsibility always risk being unpopular. Kipling spoke of 'power without responsibility, the prerogative of the harlot throughout the ages'. In the light of that aphorism one finds particular point in the fact that Horace uses the image of the *meretrix* in both of a pair of *Epistles* on the subject of dependence. 'If you are taken by the great man as a travelling companion on a trip to Brundisium or Surrentum, don't complain of your expenses and losses: that is like a kept woman constantly pleading that she has lost a bracelet or a dog' (I. 17. 52). 'If you set up as a friend of the great, you will be anxious not to be a mere sponger – the difference is as great as that between a matron and a meretrix' (I. 18. 3). In these two poems Horace warns his ambitious addressee not to recite his poetry to a patron who is anxious to do something else, not to be aggressive and insist on losing his temper with his patron in an argument about the merits of a couple of gladiators, not to ask for presents on a trip to Brundisium. We see the deep and lasting sensitivity of the poet on these matters, when we reflect that all these points relate at least as much to Horace himself as to his addressees. He is anxiously careful that his own poems shall not be obtruded at an unseasonable moment on Augustus; he discusses the form of a couple of gladiators with Maecenas; he describes being taken as a travelling companion on a trip to Brundisium.[24] In the light of these passages we are perhaps justified in thinking that Horace is not unmindful of himself when he advises his friend, in the same poem, 'Yield to your

mighty friend's gentle commands' – 'tu cede potentis amici/
lenibus imperiis' (*Epp.* I. 18. 44).

The Brundisium poem is worth lingering on, as it shows us
Horace's skill and evasiveness at work. In the year 37 BC the
peace between Octavian and Antonius, always fragile, was on
the point of breaking down. That would have meant civil war,
as in the end it did; but in the event friendly relations were
restored, and the Roman world had another six years of uneasy
peace. Antonius came to Italy and met Octavian.[25] Trusted
negotiators from both sides made the journey, among them
Maecenas, who took along some of his poets, including Virgil
and Horace. Horace produced an amusing poem about his
journey, dwelling on his own discomforts: indigestion, sleep-
less nights in noisy hostelries, the time the kitchen nearly
caught fire, a girl who stood him up on a date. It is not until
line 27 that we discover that the journey has a background of
high and exciting politics, the reconciliation of estranged
'friends'; only at line 33 do we find the name of Antonius,
introduced innocently ('Fonteius Capito, second to none
among Antonius' friends'); that of Caesar never appears at all.
The poem has been compared to 'an evening with slides',[26]
produced for those who took part in the trip. The image is a
pleasing one, but we must add that Horace did include the
poem among his published works. What impression does it
make on a reader who was not one of the party? That question
brings out the evasiveness of the poem. Many people would
have liked to hear about such exciting political matters, and
Horace says just enough to let us see that he could have told us
about them; but with ironical elegance he prefers to give us
instead nothing but an account of a purely personal set of
experiences. He crowns it all by saying, in the very last line of
the poem – line 104! – that he only went as far as Brundisium.
'Brundisium is the end of my paper and my journey: both are
long.' But, as we know from the historians, Antonius was in
fact prevented from landing at Brundisium and went on to
meet Octavian and his retinue at Tarentum instead. It was
there that the great political crisis was resolved. And Horace?
Horace, it seems, was not there . . . Reluctance to come clean
can hardly be carried further: any secrets Horace knew were
clearly quite safe. As he was to observe himself in one of the

Roman Odes, 'loyal silence, too, has its reward', 'est et fideli tuta silentio/merces'.[27]

The urbane evasiveness of that Horatian performance is not to be forgotten when we ask the question how far the poets, and in particular Horace, were in the secrets of the regime. Naturally scholars have wanted to know whether, for instance, when Horace says that Rome must march against Parthia, or that Caesar is about to attack the remote Britons, the last people in the world ('serues iturum Caesarem in ultimos/orbis Britannos',*C.* I. 35. 30), that is to be taken as representing the real policy and intention of Augustus. Or is it, perhaps, the deliberate propaganda of Augustus, to conceal his real intentions? Or may it be an attempt by the poet to influence Augustus? Or is it simply – if 'simply' is an appropriate adverb here – Horace's own fantasy or rhetoric? For, after all, Augustus never did march on Parthians, or on Britons either. Part of the explanation, I think, lies in certain facts. Caesar's heir must by definition be a great commander: one thinks of the legacy, ultimately disastrous, of Bonapartist militarism to Napoleon III. But his great victory of Actium was not a satisfactory subject for military narration, both because propaganda had distorted the whole nature of the war, and also because in the actual battle there seems to have been very little fighting. Poets were driven to tackle Actium in symbolic or indirect ways; and to compensate, perhaps, by cheap fantasies of easy conquests of exotic peoples, British or Asiatic, at the ends of the world. The campaign in Spain, all too real and familiar, failed to excite the poets. Rhapsodies on the subjugation of Britain, the lost conquest of Caesar, and of the Parthians, the target of Caesar's last, doomed campaign, no doubt gave special pleasure to a *princeps* sensitive on the subject of military glory and inevitably compared with his irresistible parent.

Horace has kindly given us what appears to be a definitive answer to such questions. In *Satires* II. 6 he gives us a vivid vignette of his conversations with Maecenas, which are strictly limited to sport, the weather, 'and topics which can safely be entrusted to a leaky ear'. '. . . quae rimosa bene deponuntur in aure' (46). Everyone expects the poet to know the secrets of high policy: ' "Have you heard anything about the Dacians?"

"No, not a word. . ." "Where does Caesar plan to settle the
veterans, in Sicily or in Italy?" I assure them that I know
nothing, and they just regard me as a miracle of discretion and
secretiveness: but it is true.' What are we to make of this?
Gilbert Highet was sufficiently enraged to snort 'Horace simply
lies':[28] he *must* have known a lot about high political problems.
That perhaps is rather deficient in subtlety. We remember that
this is the Horace who assures a possibly jealous lover that he
need have no fear of the poet becoming a rival: 'Do not suspect
a man who is forty years old' (*C*. II. 4. 22). Only those who
regard the age of forty as a real, or a plausible, end of love-
making will take that utterance literally, whether as a truth or
as a lie; Horace, of course, has his tongue in his cheek. So he
does, too, I think, in his denial of inside information about
politics; he would have been chagrined to be taken literally,
astonished to be attacked as a liar. Already in the Hellenistic
world we find a celebrated anecdote – Plutarch uses it three
times – about King Lysimachus and the poet Philippides, his
friend. 'Which of my possessions shall I share with you?' asked
the King. 'Anything you like, except your secrets', replied the
astute poet.[29] But that did not prevent him from using his
influence with the King to get great benefactions for Athens,
his fatherland. Like Philippides Horace claims to know no
secrets; but he turns the denial in a more openly flattering
direction, when he makes his imagined questioners say 'You
must know all about it, since you are so close to the gods' –
'deos quóniam propius contingis'. So the poet finds an in-
offensive way of claiming an enviable status for himself
('Everyone comes to me for the inside story, I can't think
why'), and also of introducing a compliment to Maecenas and
Augustus (to seem close to them is to seem close to the gods).
And he gives nothing away. We are reminded of the cardinal
importance of the ability to keep secrets; it was to be Maecenas'
indiscretion in sharing one with his wife which led to his
exclusion from power.[30] Horace, capable of an apparent open-
ness which yet revealed nothing, was offered by Augustus a
position as his secretary; that is a considerable compliment.
Behind that smooth facade it is as hard to speculate on Horace's
'real' motives as it is to know exactly what he means when he
says that he is not as sexually attractive as his rival, or that he

was simply hopeless as a soldier, or that he has not a big
enough talent to write epic poetry.[31]

We see in Horace the difficulty of finding a form for eulogy:
in another self-conscious period W. H. Auden ended his poem
for W. B. Yeats: 'Teach the free man how to praise.'[32] I give
another example, from *Epistles* I. 16. Starting by saying to his
addressee 'I hope you don't take the word of public opinion for
your own condition, flattering as it is', he goes on to say 'If you
were to hear yourself addressed as the supreme general and
darling of Rome, you would know that such praise belonged
not to you but to Augustus' (I. 16. 25). Again the poet has
contrived to slip in a handsome slice of eulogy as if in a natural
manner, rather than committing himself to set out on a crudely
straightforward paean of praise. His most successful poems of
eulogy are, I think, those in which he has managed to marry
praise of the ruler with characteristic attributes of his own
personality; rather than the unmixed panegyric of a poem like
Odes IV. 14, the more subtly blended praise of one like *Odes*
III. 14, in which Horace combines the triumphant return of
Augustus from the Spanish wars and his state reception, by
way of the motif of celebration, with the idea of a typical
Horatian party. That, of course, means typical Horatian drink,
so bring out a vintage of the days of the Social War, if the
ravages of Spartacus have spared any; it also means a typical
Horatian girl: so – hurry up and fetch Neaera. But if her
concierge makes a delay – we expect the poet to say 'Knock
him down'; instead, he says 'Let it go. My hair is turning
white, I'm not so keen on a row as I was. I wouldn't have stood
for this in my fiery youth, when Plancus was consul'. In the
consulship of Plancus, 42 BC, Horace was indeed fighting – at
Philippi, on the wrong side; now we have peace, no more
Social Wars and no more Spartacus. That is something to
celebrate, at the triumphant return of the man who guarantees
our safety. I take it that *Odes* I. 37, 'Nunc est bibendum', is an
attempt at the same thing. The lyric poet, by definition at
home in the symposium, addresses himself to the downfall of
Cleopatra by treating it as the death of a personal enemy. The
comparative failure of the poem, which despite striking
passages seems to me not to cohere in the same successful way
as III.14, is not unconnected with the fact that Horace makes us

believe that he really wanted and valued peace, but not that he cared all that much about the defeat of one dynast by another. To put it another way, he makes a desire for peace and security a coherent part of his whole poetical persona, while the exultation over the victory of Actium has been overstated in a way which is out of harmony with that persona, and which therefore suggests hollowness. Antonius, the real opponent, is of course ignored; that fact, which makes the poem fit exactly with Augustus' propaganda, must strengthen our reluctance to suspend our disbelief.

Let us look at the whole business from Augustus' point of view. Patronage of poets has its difficulties, not only for the poet but also for the patron. Augustus could not help knowing that the great Alexander made a fool of himself by patronising Choerilus of Iasus, a poet proverbially awful, and giving him enormous rewards for his bad verses. In case he has forgotten, Horace reminds him in the *Epistle to Augustus*, contrasting Choerilus' 'ridiculum poema' for Alexander with the distinction which Augustus has earned by his generous and enlightened patronage of Virgil and Varius.[33] Cicero's attempts to extort panegyrical verse on his own achievements, and his eventual disastrous decision to write the poem himself, were a standing joke in Cicero's own lifetime. Horace indeed expresses the fear that poetical panegyric, in unskilful hands, may actually discredit the subject – 'modesty restrains me from impairing the glory of Caesar through lack of talent' ('culpa detere ingeni', *C.* I. 6. 12). Augustus took the possibility seriously, and we read that he 'was angered if works of literature were written about him except in a serious style and by the best writers; he warned the praetors not to allow his name to become hackneyed at the games'[34] (Suet. *Aug.* 89). Alexander and his bad poet stood as a notorious warning; and yet, conscious of it as they were, the Augustan poets found themselves, in their full-dress panegyrical utterances, echoing the language of Alexander's flattering rhetoricians and poets.[35] The parallel forced itself on the encomiast, however self-conscious.

Augustus himself certainly did not lack self-consciousness. We see a notable sophistication in the different sorts of style and content which he found suitable for different forms of

propaganda. On coins, for instance, the Emperor took credit
to himself for such matter-of-fact achievements as the repair of
highways, QUOD VIAE MUNITAE SUNT; and on the
other hand struck many coins with the image and title of
Apollo of Actium, APOLLINI ACTIO.[36] The *Res Gestae*
contain claims similar to that on the subject of the remaking of
the roads, but do not refer to Actian Apollo. Augustus' own
autobiography, his *Commentarii de vita sua*, laid great emphasis
on miraculous dreams and portents. The poets are again different. They do not talk of road repairs: they do talk of Actian
Apollo. Propertius indeed uses the god as the central point of
his deliberately baroque treatment of the battle of Actium
(IV. 6).

The *Res Gestae*, it has been observed, do not mention the
poets at all: the claim 'I celebrated the Secular Games' makes
no reference to Horace's *Carmen Saeculare* (§ 22), and in the
context of theatrical performances we find only the demotic
forms – gladiators, wild-beast shows, naval battles – not the
Thyestes of Varius, for which Augustus gave the favoured poet
a million sesterces.[37] Nor does the *Aeneid* itself appear in
Augustus' considered statement of his benefactions. It would
be wrong to infer from that silence that the *princeps* did
not regard the poets as important: the point is the self-
consciousness with which the different forms are kept
distinct.[38] No mere splash of unreflective panegyric would be
appropriate to satisfy this exacting taste.

That self-consciousness emerges yet more strikingly from
what we possess of Augustus' letters. He attempts to recruit
Horace as a secretary, and writes to Maecenas in these terms:
'So he shall pass from your table (that of a parasite) to mine
(that of a king), and help me with my correspondence' (*Ep.* 33
Malcovati). The one title even a Caesar could not take at Rome
was that of king; Augustus urbanely applies it to himself, in its
slangy sense of 'a great man in relation to his clients.'[39] If he is a
'king' in relation to Maecenas, then the superb millionaire
Maecenas is a 'parasite', a professional hanger-on, in relation
to him. The choice of these words, deliberately exaggerated, is
evidently meant to smooth the potentially embarrassing fact
that Augustus' unique power and position make a request
from him a special one. None the less Horace pleaded ill health

and declined. After that we find Augustus writing to the poet himself and saying 'Your name came up in conversation when Septimius was present: you can ask him what I said about you. Even though you are so proud that you have rejected my friendship, that does not make me haughty in my turn.'[40] He expresses 'be haughty in my turn' with a Greek word, seven syllables in length, whose portentous form and rarity underline the irony of the omnipotent Emperor speaking in such terms to a poet, the son of a freedman. Another letter to Horace says 'Let me tell you, I am cross with you', for not addressing Augustus himself in the poetical epistles of which Horace had published a book of twenty: 'Are you afraid that it will discredit you with posterity if you look like a friend of mine?' (39 Malcovati).

We have nothing of the letters which must have passed between the Ptolemies and their court poets; they would make a fascinating comparison.[41] What strikes us about these letters of Augustus is their sophistication, their self-awareness. We are not in the world of Stalin and the Writers' Union; there is no question of the bullet in the back of the head if the right sort of literature is not immediately forthcoming. The *princeps* is aware that a poet may find it awkward to get too close to a ruler, just as he is aware that hack work by pushy but untalented poets may do more harm than good to himself. We see also that Augustus could be informal, even charming – but only in private. We perhaps spare a sigh for the informal and human poems which his poets might, had his public persona been less rigorously exigent, have composed for him: in reality the poetical *Epistle* (II. 1) which Horace wrote in response to the Emperor's informal request begins 'Since you alone are supporting the business of the world, defending Italy with the army, adorning our morals and emending our laws, I should be sinning against the public interest, Caesar, if I were to take up your time with a lengthy address . . . We hail you as superhuman in your own lifetime . . . we give you the preference to all other rulers, Roman and Greek . . .' He goes on to develop the argument that the supreme honours and recognition given to Augustus in his own lifetime by everyone, perfectly justified, are exceptional: in the case of poets, the reading public underestimates living talent and admires only the dead. The poem then settles to the subject of poetry. We can see here that Horace has tried to work his *adulatio* into the texture of his poem, and to make it seem to arise naturally out of it; but the effort is none the less visible, and it is clear that he did not find it a possibility to write to Augustus, in a poem for public consumption, in a tone other than that of ostentatious and humble respect.[42]

Yet it is natural for Augustus to think in terms of posterity reading Horace's poems, and to want his name to go down to posterity in them. He accepts, that is, the poets' own claim for their work.[43] He was himself a reader of poetry, we are told, and knowledgeable about it. 'What he looked for particularly, both in Greek and Latin writers, was precepts and instances which could be edifying in public or private life: he used to copy them out and send them to members of his family and to governors of the armies and provinces . . . if they seemed in need of admonishment.'[44] That strikes us as an unsophisticated use to make of literature; we perhaps see an example of it in practice, when we read of his irritation at the sight of crowds of citizens in the Forum not dressed up in the toga: hot and inconvenient, but ancestral and Roman. Indignantly he repeated a line of the *Aeneid*: 'Look at them, "Romans, lords of the world, the people of the toga" ', 'en Romanos rerum dominos gentemque togatam': and he made it the business of the aediles to see that nobody should appear in or near the Forum except in the toga.[45] We perhaps catch another echo of this tenet of the Emperor in the insistence of Horace, in his later works, that the original function of poetry was to inculcate morality. Scholars who trace that idea to earlier philosophers and theorists seem to neglect that possibility, which surely is a natural one when we find Horace saying, in the *Ars Poetica*, that music and poetry first taught men 'publica privatis secernere, sacra profanis,/ concubitu prohibere vago, dare iura maritis' – 'to distinguish public from private property, to forbid random sexual intercourse and impose the laws of marriage' (390 ff.).[46] We hear the echo of cherished ideas and laws of the Emperor.

There are many other places where we can see the poets making use of Augustan themes, adapting them to the poetical persona which each of them has made his own. War comes most naturally into their poetry in the form of a victory celebration, whether grandiose, as in *Georgic* III and *Odes* IV. 2, or intimate, as in *Odes* III. 14, or subversive, as in *Ars Amatoria* I. 205–28. Peace, eminently Augustan, is a congenial theme to the poets. It can appear as a desperate prayer, or a cheeky squib, or a complacent sigh of relief (*Georgic* I. 500; Propertius III. 5; *Odes* IV. 5: 'condit quisque diem collibus in suis' etc.). The moral exhortation to which Augustus attached importance appears no less. Virgil, Propertius, and Horace all deplore the *avaritia* and *luxuria* of the age. These things are bad for the production of soldiers (*Georgic* II. 167; *Odes* III. 2; III. 6), bad for the looks of young men (*Odes* I. 8) – and bad for amorous poets who cannot compete with the high prices paid by rich debauchees (Prop. I. 8, II. 16, etc.). With face more or less straight Propertius denounces fancy cosmetics (I. 2, II. 18), immoral paintings (II. 6), even wine itself (II. 33. 27); we find him praising the institutions of Sparta, and deploring the infidelity of wives (III. 14, III. 13. 23). At times indeed the relation between the Augustan ideal and its poetic expression looks like burlesque, as when it turns out that Propertius praises Sparta because you can get closer to girls there, or when the elegists proclaim undying fidelity in love, but to a mistress, not a wife. The poetry of married love, slimmest of volumes of all times, received little addition from the poets of Caesar Augustus. But the recurrence, in whatever form, of ideas to which he attached importance, is not to be forgotten when we estimate his significance for poetry.

Augustus' most direct commission, presumably, was the *Carmen Saeculare*, which Horace composed for the Secular Games of 17 BC. That poem has not evoked much enthusiasm in scholars of the recent age.[47] Deficient, after a striking opening, in sublimity, and naturally not rich in humour, it is content to pray for a continuation of practical benefits received, in agriculture, in the birth-rate, in peace and prosperity. One stanza echoes and endorses the recent marital legislation; another asks for 'virtuous morals for tractable youth, peaceful rest for old age'. A comparison with Kipling's *Recessional*, also produced at a moment of imperial jubilee, suggests the less complacent notes that might have been sounded; so does the *Aeneid*. Although not mentioned in the *Res Gestae*, this poem

was – uniquely among the works of the Augustan poets –
recorded on marble, in the official inscription which recorded
the Secular Games: 'Carmen composuit Q. Horatius Flaccus'.
The *Carmen Saeculare* found full favour with Augustus. Its
freedom from ambiguity probably weighed with him when he
urged Horace to compose another collection of *Odes*, and this
time to include straight-forward glorifications of the victories
of Drusus and Tiberius over Alpine tribes. It is not unreasonable to suppose that these poems give us an idea of what
Augustus would have liked Augustan poetry to be; and to feel
grateful that this was an area in which even he could not fully
have his way.

I have dwelt on Horace particularly, because he is the one
among the poets who does speak on the subject of relations
with Augustus, and also the one to whom we have revealing
letters from the Emperor. It remains to see how the views and
attitudes which have emerged from that enquiry can be made
to apply to the other poets.

The First Book of Propertius shows no acquaintance either
with Octavian or with Maecenas. The poet has friends rather
than patrons, and writes about the life of love.[48] The one
incidental allusion to Octavian is far from friendly.[49] Yet in
the first poem of the Second Book Propertius is addressing
Maecenas as his patron and explaining that he is unfortunately
unable to compose panegyrical verse on Augustus' achievements. As we have seen, he spells out those achievements in a
way which cannot have been much to the ruler's liking. In the
tenth poem of that book, after eight love poems, he announces
that he will now change his note and sing of the battles and
campaigns of 'my leader':

> iam libet et fortis memorare ad proelia turmas
> et Romana mei dicere castra ducis.[50]

No sooner are these words out than the poet recedes from
them: all that, it turns out, is for his old age: 'Let my youth sing
of love, my old age of war'. Four couplets are given to
Augustus' future triumphs over Parthians, Indians, and
Britons. 'I shall write about all that, if I live long enough', says
Propertius; meanwhile, I can sing only of love.

These curious poems surely put it beyond doubt that the

appearance of Propertius' First Book led to an acquaintance
with Maecenas and encouragement by him to write systematic
works of panegyrical narrative about the *princeps*. That may
seem a surprising reaction to a collection of antipolitical love
poems; but we see just the same thing with Virgil. The
mannered and exquisite verse of the *Eclogues* might not naturally seem to suggest that the author was a born epic poet, but
with him, too, we find that his next publication contains, at
the beginning of the third *Georgic*, an elaborate account,
addressed to Maecenas, of his hopes of writing a martial epic
on Augustus. Clearly Maecenas put the idea to any poet he
thought talented, however little evidence he had given of a
turn for epic. Even Horace finds himself waving away the
laborious honour. That Tibullus never mentions Augustus or
Maecenas, and never explicitly lends his supporting voice to
any aspect of imperial policy, is a tribute to the self-contained
nature of the circle of Messalla. One thinks of the delightful
letters with which the Prince Regent's secretary tried to induce
Jane Austen to write royal panegyric: 'Any historical romance,
illustrative of the history of the august House of Cobourg,
would just now be very interesting . . .' Her reply to this
fantastic suggestion was as urbane as that of Horace.[51]

At the end of Book II Propertius greets the inception of the
Aeneid, with joy and (dare one say?) with relief. At last Virgil is
at work on it: and he will sing of the battle of Actium and the
heroic fleet of Caesar (II. 34. 61). Like Augustus himself,
Propertius no doubt expected an epic primarily concerned
with the recent rather than the heroic past. As we shall see,
Virgil himself either shared or encouraged that hope at the
beginning of the third *Georgic*. With Virgil actually producing
the longed-for masterpiece, Propertius felt free to amuse himself, in his Third Book, with the theme of Augustus and his
wars. We have seen him make the frivolous point that in
declining ambitious forms of poetry he was only emulating
the modesty of Maecenas in declining public office (III. 9). In
two other pairs of juxtaposed poems he shows similar, barely
concealed levity. In III. 4, 'Arma deus Caesar dites meditatur
ad Indos', he describes Augustus' projected conquest of the
East as a looting expedition:[52] the Indies are opulent, even the
sea is full of pearls; they will come back loaded with booty.

Good luck to them! For Propertius' part, all he wants is to watch the rich procession with his arm round his girl. Maliciously he follows it with a poem opening 'Love is a god of peace' (whereas Caesar is a god of war), which contrasts useless wealth and conquest with the simple delights of love. And when one is too old for love, one turns to philosophy and science; those are the subjects to which the poet will devote his mature years. 'As for you who prefer fighting, you can bring home the standards of Crassus':

> vos, quibus arma
> grata magis, Crassi signa referte domum.

In II. 10 Propertius spoke of turning, when love-poetry ran dry, to write of Caesar; that pious intention is now annulled. However long he lives, he will not do it. And the great patriotic expedition to humble the Parthians and retrieve the lost standards of Crassus is either a race for loot, or else it simply shows a taste for fighting. Finally, in the eleventh poem of Book III he does address himself to the Battle of Actium; but not in a way to give unmixed satisfaction to Augustus. 'You are shocked that my life is at the mercy of a dominant woman. There have been lots of formidable women in myth: Medea, Omphale, Semiramis. Look at Cleopatra, for that matter . . .' The last part of the poem contains flattering lines, but the conception of the whole, that Cleopatra was a magnified version of Cynthia, is remarkable rather for its wit than for its tact. Nor has Propertius been able to resist following it with a poem which reproaches a man for going off to Augustus' Parthian wars, at the price of leaving his poor wife in tears. 'Was any glory to be won by looting the Parthians worth it, when your Galla kept imploring you not to go?' (III. 12. 3 ff.) Greed for plunder must be the motive, or the man must be mad ('vesane', 7).

In his Fourth Book Propertius tackles Roman themes, but most of them are antiquarian and remote from the practical interests of Caesar Augustus. In the central poem alone he offers an extended and ambitious treatment of the battle of Actium. This time he has at least denied himself the pleasure of making some frivolous connection with his own love life; but in the quest for a new and unhackneyed approach to the battle he has exploited ingenious poems of Callimachus and Theocritus, and imagined virtually all the fighting as done by the god Apollo. Also some sophisticated visual effects: the two half moons formed by the two hostile fleets, the water coloured and glittering with the reflected armaments (25 ff.). After fifty lines of this highly eccentric account, Propertius is unable to conceal his boredom: 'I have sung of fighting long enough: now Apollo turns to the peaceful music of a party', ('bella satis cecini', 69). The wine will flow, and poets at table will improvise verse, about Augustus' past and future victories. 'And I shall keep the party up all night', concludes the poet.[53]

Like Horace, Propertius attempts to make the Imperial theme fit with his own general poetical persona. The resemblance goes further: both make the triumphs of Augustus the occasion for a party. Because the poetical persona of Horace is more urbane and accommodating, he can in his best poems make the combination a harmonious one. By contrast, the more reckless persona of Propertius, which defines itself by explicit rejection of the respectable values of marriage and soldiering,[54] produces more discordant and bizarre effects when the theme of Actium or of conquest is brought in. Exactly how far this is deliberate is hard to say. But Maecenas, one imagines, was able to appease any discontent which may have been felt by the Princeps. When Maecenas was gone, lack of respect, and lack of contact, brought the last heir of the elegiac tradition to ruin.

In Virgil's first published collection the name of Octavian, like that of Maecenas, did not appear; his persona lurked behind the word 'iuvenis' in the first *Eclogue*. That poem presented, in bucolic dress, an episode from the contemporary evictions. Meliboeus is dispossessed, driven out with his flock by the incursion of brutal soldiers; Tityrus has contrived to save his land by a timely trip to Rome. Apparently both old and a slave, he has gone to Rome to buy his freedom; although only his own master could free a slave, it was a superhuman 'young man' in Rome who 'was the first to' give the response 'Feed your flocks as before, boys, yoke your oxen.' 'Lucky old man', replies Meliboeus, 'so your land will remain yours'. As a narrative this makes little sense. Buying one's freedom from slavery, a great change in status: keeping one's land – and slaves did not own land – an escape from a change of status, and a carrying on 'as before'. The careful juxtaposition 'Carry on, boys': 'Lucky old man.' Virgil has spared no trouble to make it clear that his poem is not a documentary account of current events. And yet it is an echo of them. Real and shocking political happenings intrude jarringly into the timeless world of pastoral. They can be presented only in a transfigured form, the definiteness of their outline blurred and shimmering. It was Octavian who supervised the evictions, who sent the 'godless soldiers' in: Octavian was also, we infer, the marvellous youth who can at will exempt favoured individuals from the suffering he inflicts. Virgil's response is complex in a sense in which that of Horace, for all his sophistication, is not: to the difficulty of finding a form, to the awkwardness of addressing an autocrat, is added a moral scruple about the nature of power itself. The most moving lines are given to Meliboeus, ejected and embittered, with no timely saviour.

As for hopes for the future, these in the *Eclogues* can appear only in more or less mythical form. The dead herdsman Daphnis is now a god, and he will grant peace and plenty to the countryside; he is given features that hint at the assassinated dictator Julius, but which fall far short of identity (*Ecl.* 5). We observe in passing that this allusive technique will be developed on a far grander scale in the *Aeneid*, allowing the reader at times to see Augustus through the figure of Aeneas, and Cleopatra through that of Dido.[55] In the fourth *Eclogue* we can hope only for a miraculous new age, compounded of oracles, poetry, fantasy, hints from the East, Messianic speculations. I can do no more than state my view that this most elusive of poems was not written to celebrate the Pact of Brundisium in the autumn of the year 40, but at the end of 41, to greet the consul Pollio on 1 January, the day when a consul's year begins and his 'mighty months' begin to roll; that it is not a political poem written to glorify a political event which promised well for peace, but a Messianic poem written at a time of gloom, when politics seemed to offer no answer, and the mind turned away in despair to hopes and fantasies of another order.[56]

By the time of the publication of the *Georgics* Octavian was in sole power, and Maecenas was Virgil's patron. The *Georgics* is of course not a martial poem, but Virgil insists that it is wanted, urged even, by Maecenas ('tua, Maecenas, haud mollia iussa'). The theme of rustic virtues and industry, and of the restoration of peace, will no doubt have been in general terms acceptable to Octavian; but he will not have shared the fantasies of some moderns, that perusal of the work would lead to a flood of volunteer small-holders returning to the farms of their ancestors. The initial invocation of Octavian (G. I. 24 ff.) strikes an unexpected note. At the climactic end of a list of gods which includes Neptune and Minerva, he is addressed as a god who has yet to choose his sphere. Will he be a sea-god, induced to marry a mermaid by the offer of a dowry of all the waves? Will he join the signs of the Zodiac? Already the Scorpion is drawing in its pincers and leaving him more than his share of the sky.[57] At least he will not be a god of the dead – though it is true that Persephone is quite happy to stay in the Underworld. What is Virgil up to here? The combination of hyperbole and wit is an uneasy one, as though the poet were seeking a way to address his subject which would both be exceedingly flattering and also, if only because of its excess, allow a certain distance. Something similar may have been in Horace's mind when, in an *Ode*, he mooted the possibility that the god Mercury was dwelling on earth in Augustus' form (*C*. I. 2. 41); scholars have preferred to take Horace literally and rebuke him for servility.[58] Augustus was of course often addressed as a god. Can we guess what he and his intimates thought of it? He knew, as they knew, the celebrated retort of King Antigonus when addressed as 'Child of the Sun': 'The man who empties my chamber-pot doesn't think so'.[59] They knew about Ptolemy Theos Neos Dionysos Auletes, Ptolemy the God, New Dionysus, Fluteplayer, the disreputable father of Cleopatra; Antonius, too, had been a god. We have, I think, a hint. In a letter to Tiberius, Augustus tells him about the family games of dice over a holiday. 'I lost 20,000 sesterces on my own account, having been lavishly generous in the course of the game, as usual. If I had made everybody give me the stakes which I let go, or if I had kept what I gave to different people, I should have been a winner by about 50,000. But this is what I prefer: my generosity will raise me to the glory of heaven.'[60]

One is surprised to see that urbane sentence quoted as 'hardly the remark of a man who is habitually modest'.[61] Surely, like the reference to his 'kingly' table, it is a mildly ironical utterance – 'After all, you know, I'm going to be a god.'

In other passages of the *Georgics* Virgil extols Octavian's military feats. He is in Asia, doing marvellous things, thundering in war on the Euphrates while the poet is writing his poem (IV. 561),[62] driving back the unwarlike Indian from the Roman forts (II. 172). The *unwarlike* Indian? The epithet introduces, surely, a coolness in the midst of enthusiasm, which prepares us for the moment, 300 lines later, when Virgil glorifies the life of the rustic sage who knows the country gods. He cares nothing for the movements of the Dacians, nor for 'the power of Rome and kingdoms which pass away', 'res Romanas perituraque regna' (II. 498). The poet of those lines surprises us when, at the opening of Book Three, he makes a grandiose announcement of his intention to glorify Octavian. He will build a vast temple, with Octavian in its midst; he will celebrate games and bring offerings; he will represent all Octavian's conquests, including Britain but especially Actium, and the whole world subdued. His ancestors right back to Troy will be represented by statues in niches. 'Soon I shall be girding myself to tell of Caesar's fiery fights' (III. 10–48). The metaphor is elaborate and not entirely clear, but Octavian must have thought that the longed-for epic treatment of himself was promised at last. No wonder we find that he was impatient for the *Aeneid*'s completion, and anxious to be shown even a sketch of it or any section.[63]

I think that Virgil did contemplate writing it. Already in the *Eclogues* we find him expressing the wish that he may live long enough to eulogize Pollio (VIII. 6 ff.);[65] here, 'modo vita supersit', he will glorify the warlike career of Octavian. He had advanced in scale from the ten short *Eclogues*, poems of 100 lines or less, to a poem of more than 2,000 lines. That was far longer than anything contemplated by Horace, Tibullus, or Propertius. But as he tried to compose the Augustan epic, he came to see that it was an impossibility. The danger of mere *adulatio* was evidently enormous. The career of Augustus, impressive and important as it was, did not really offer a suitable subject for predominantly martial narrative: his wars, as wars, were evidently small by comparison with those of Caesar or even of Pompey, and his own role in some of them notoriously less than glorious. The problem of the gods would be terrible; how could contemporary history avoid becoming burlesque, if the gods were personally to be shown playing a large part in it? The same was true of the Homeric model which naturally suggested itself: was he to describe Octavian mowing down the enemy with his own strong right arm? Not least, to narrate his career in a direct manner would deprive Virgil of the ability to reflect upon it obliquely, or sensitively, or ironically. The pathos of loss and defeat which makes his Dido so haunting: that was simply not possible in a narrative about Cleopatra, the wicked opponent of Octavian and all Italy. In the second half of the *Aeneid* there is a vital tension between the divine mission and justification of Aeneas, and the terrible fact that these are Italians and an Italian prince whom he must kill; the civil wars of the recent past could not be represented in that manner, as the Augustan ideology had declared that the campaign against Antonius at Actium was not a civil war at all. And Aeneas himself, protégé of heaven, but personally unhappy and deprived of everything he values, ending the poem with the knowledge that he has killed Dido and Turnus, that he has failed to save Pallas, that he will not live to see the Rome for which he has done and suffered so much: he is presented by Virgil in a light which brings out both the triumph and the cost of Empire. It goes without saying that an *Augusteid* must have been a far more optimistic and positive poem. And so Virgil inverted the poem he announced in the third *Georgic*. Not, now, a poem on Augustus with glimpses back to the Trojan ancestors, but a poem on the Trojan ancestors with glimpses forward to Augustus.

We live in an age for which imperialism is a dirty word. Some are tempted to read the *Aeneid* as simply endorsing our modern emotions; others, to dismiss as anachronistic the idea that Virgil expressed any reservations about empire at all. Virgil presents the career of the imperialist as hard and self-denying; as Aeneas must give up Dido, the Roman must deny himself the arts and the sciences.[66] Left to himself, as he repeatedly tells us, Aeneas would never have left Troy. Yet he obeys his destiny and founds an Empire which will impose civilization on barbarism (*Aeneid* I. 264: 'moresque viris et moenia ponet'; VI. 853: 'pacique imponere morem'). Imperial might receives full description and endorsement: a conquered world queues to present its offerings to Augustus, 'incedunt victae longo ordine gentes,/ quam variae linguis, habitu tam vestis et armis' (VIII. 722), and the Empire knows no limits in time or space (I. 278). As for the *princeps* himself, at last he receives the praise which would live for ever, now that Virgil has found a way of creating sufficient distance to see him not as a contemporary but as a figure in a long historical perspective. Aeneas, who embodies the Homeric heroism of Odysseus and Achilles, who recalls at moments Heracles and Jason, is also a pattern of Augustus. When he celebrates games at Actium (III. 274) or delights in the Troy game (V. 556), the audience is given obvious hints; but when Aeneas prefers to spare the conquered, when he imposes 'mores', there, too, cherished claims of Augustus show through the mythical dress. And Augustus himself can be presented, in prophetic glimpses: the bringer of peace (I. 291), the indefatigable worker (VI. 801), the triumphant embodiment of Italian civilization against the bestial deities and barbaric glitter of the East (VIII. 685, 698). At last the battle of Actium finds a fitting presentation, not as a pretext for a drinking party, as in Horace, nor as a more or less frivolous parallel to Propertius' own difficulties with a dominant woman; but we observe that Virgil has found it necessary to avoid narrative and present it as the prophetic decoration of a shield in the heroic past, a work of art within a work of art, removed in time and form from contemporary experience. Only thus could Augustus be praised by a great poet: through abstraction from the details of his biography, and the presentation of a quasi-symbolic image, seen *sub specie aeternitatis*. We recall that Augustus' portraits in sculpture, too, were stylised, heroic, ageless. He was no stranger to such a mode of representation.[67]

Augustus was pleased with the *Aeneid*. How much he saw in it, we do not know. The line we saw him quoting comes, it may not be merely facetious to observe, early in the first Book. But the desire of the Emperor for straight-forward panegyric was not satisfied, and the pressure becomes more direct. In the First Book of the *Epistles* Horace writes to an officer on the staff of Tiberius on his Eastern campaign: 'Quis sibi res gestas Augusti scribere sumit?' (I. 3. 7) '*Who* is writing up Augustus' achievements?' The question has almost a look of desperation; or perhaps of levity. The Fourth Book of the *Odes* contains set pieces on victories by the princes of the imperial house, and straight-forward glorifications of the ruler (IV. 4; 5; 14; 15). The Fourth Book of Propertius contains his attempt at a full-dress treatment of Actium. These poems, like the *Carmen Saeculare*, have done less for Augustus' memory than those in which the poets allowed their own personality more freedom. Maecenas' influence declined, the Emperor grew older and more imperious, the poets who had grown up before Actium passed away. The rise and fall of Ovid, the only great poet to have grown up in Augustus' reign, form a bitter coda to the story. 'Caesar qui cogere posset': he could exact more and more direct adulation, he could banish a poet to the ends of the earth; but even he could not silence his voice. Posterity can find a fearful symmetry in the events. In the centre stand some of the greatest masterpieces of Latin literature, above all the *Aeneid*, but in the first part stands the ruin of the poet Cornelius Gallus, driven in the end to death by Augustus' insistence on a monopoly of glory: at the end the ruin of the poet Ovid. The disasters as well as the triumphs form part of the theme of Augustus and the poets; and still, as in Tacitus' account of his funeral, the *prudentes* find it hard to know how to judge him.[68]

NOTES

1. C. O. Brink, *Horace on Poetry* III (1982), 243, finds a slightly different nuance.
2. Pindar, *Pythian* 3. 71: Diodorus XI. 67; Plato, *Gorgias* 470 d.
3. M. Lefkowitz, *The Lives of the Greek Poets* (1981), 96.
4. Plato, *Epistle* VII. 329 d: τὰς τῶν τυράννων δεήσεις ἴσμεν ὅτι μεμειγμέναι ἀνάγκαις εἰσίν quoted by Cicero, *Ad Atticum* IX. 13. 4 (the word he uses of Caesar is πειθανάγκη). Cicero was anxious about falling into κολακεία if he published a political epistle addressed to Caesar, ibid. XIII. 27. 1; XIII. 51. 1.
5. 'Sed potestas non solum si invitet sed etiam si supplicet cogit', Macrob. *Sat.* II. 7. 2. The awkwardness involved in accepting presents was of course also familiar: e.g. Seneca, *De beneficiis* V. 6. 6–7; P. Veyne, *Le Pain et le cirque* (1976), 229.
6. Plutarch, *Brutus* 21. 6.
7. R. Syme, *History in Ovid*, 176.
8. First publication by R. D. Anderson, P. J. Parsons, and R. G. M. Nisbet, in *JRS* 69 (1979), 125–55. Caesar knew a lot of poets and had some on his staff; but I doubt if Gordon Williams is right, 'Phases in Political Patronage of Literature in

Rome', in *Literary and Artistic Patronage in Ancient Rome*, ed. B. K. Gold (1982), 12, to infer that he 'deliberately gathered the most distinguished writers of his time around him to foster a climate of opinion that would benefit him politically'. He seems to have regarded with apathy the prospect of being the subject of verse by either of the Cicero brothers: *Epp. ad. Q. fr.* II. 15; II. 16; III. 8; III. 9. III. 9.

9. Virgil, *G.* II. 198; Horace, *Epp.* II. 2. 49; Tibullus I. 1. 19; Propertius IV. 1. 127.
10. *Epp.* I. 14. 1–4.
11. Scholars in the first century AD claimed to know the details of Virgil's will: Pliny *NH* VII. 114; Gellius XVII. 10. 7; the ancient *Lives*. Maecenas and Augustus are named among his heirs. His fortune, we are told, amounted to nearly 10 million sesterces. Cf. N. M. Horsfall, *Poets and Patron* (1981), 4.
12. Eratosthenes, *FGrH* 241 F 16; P. M. Fraser, *Ptolemaic Alexandria* I, 310. On the intimacy of Antigonus Gonatas with Bion the Borysthenite, ('probably very much closer than written tradition gives us any idea of'), W. W. Tarn, *Antigonus Gonatas*, 234 f.
13. εὐγνώμων, φιλόμουσος, ἐρωτικός, εἰς ἄκρον ἀδύς. Theocr. XIV. 61.
14. Cicero, *In Pisonem* 58 f.
15. Plutarch, *Moralia* 182 F.
16. *Odes* II. 17; *Satires* II. 6. 42 ff.
17. It was Paris, not Helen, who was represented in myth as a firebrand which would destroy Troy. Perhaps Bathyllus had danced one of these roles? For his affair with Maecenas see Syme, *RR*, 342.
18. *Eleg. in Maec.* 153: 'moriens quaerebat amatae/coniugis amplexus oscula verba manus'.
19. Surprising is the hesitation of Nisbet and Hubbard ad loc: see *JRS* 52(1962), 36, n. 13.
20. One is sorry to see this cheeky line described as 'a palinode for 1. 22' (Reitzenstein), or 'a piece of literary opportunism' (L. P. Wilkinson in *Studi Castiglioni*, 1094).
21. Syme, *History in Ovid*, 184.
22. Suet. *Aug.* 86.
23. e.g. Hor. *Sat.* I. 6. 47; Propertius II. 1. 73: 'Maecenas nostrae spes invidiosa iuventae'.
24. *Epp.* I. 13. 3–5; II. 1. 220; *Sat.* II. 6. 44; *Sat.* I. 5.
25. Syme, *RR*, 225.
26. N. Rudd, *The Satires of Horace*, 60, 56.
27. *Odes* III. 2. 25–6. See the important discussion by C. O. Brink, op. cit. (n. 1), 523 ff.
28. *Hermes* 102 (1974), 333.
29. Plutarch, *Mor.* 176 c, cf. *SIG*³ 374.
30. Syme, *RR*, 342.
31. *Odes* I. 13; III. 9; IV. 11; II. 7; *Sat.* II. 1. 12; *Odes* I. 6, *Epp.* II. 1. 257.
32. *In Memory of W. B. Yeats.*
33. *Epp.* 2. 1. 231 ff.
34. Suet. *Aug.* 89.
35. On *Georgic* I. 34, cf. Q. Curtius VIII. 5; on *Aeneid* VI.791 ff., E. Norden, *Kleine Schriften*, 424. See below, n. 56.
36. Cf. L. Consiglieri, *'Slogans' monetarii e poesia augustea* (1978), 40, 82.
37. P. Veyne, *Le Pain et le cirque*, 486, refers to the 'saveur populaire et aussi républicaine' of Augustus' *Res Gestae*.
38. Tacitus observes of Augustus: 'Civile rebatur misceri voluptatibus vulgi' (*Ann.* I. 54).

39. *Oxford Latin Dictionary* s.v. 'rex', 8.
40. *Ep.* 8 Malcovati. ἀνθυπερηφανοῦμεν: the word, cited by LSJ only from this passage, occurs also in a letter, *P. Flor.* 367.
41. P. M. Fraser, *Ptolemaic Alexandria* I, 308. Letters were known in antiquity between Antigonus Gonatas and Zeno, Diog. Laert. VII. 7–9.
42. E. Fraenkel, on the other hand, thought 'the letter in which Horace responded to the request shows him perfectly at ease' (*Horace*, 383). See C. O. Brink, *Horace on Poetry* I (1963), 191 n. 3.
43. That seems to me to make the relationship of Augustus with the poets a special one, against the view of P. White, *JRS* 68 (1978), 76 and N. M. Horsfall, *Poets and Patron*, 9, that 'Horace and Virgil were, in short, clients . . . There is nothing special and peculiar about their status just because they are poets'. An ordinary client could not offer you immortal glory, nor would posterity have its eye on the nature of your relationship with him.
44. Suet. *Aug.* 89.
45. Ibid. 40, quoting *Aeneid* I. 282.
46. Cf. also *Epp.* II. 1. 128 ff.
47. H. P. Syndikus actually omits it from his two-volume *Die Lyrik des Horaz*. Very tepid is A. La Penna, *Orazio e l'ideologia del principato*, 108.
48. J. Griffin in *JRS* 71 (1981), 44.
49. Propertius I. 21. 7. On this poem and 1. 22 see G. Williams, *Tradition and Originality in Roman Poetry*, 172 ff.
50. 'Mei ducis' contrasts suggestively with 'tui Caesaris' at II. 1. 25.
51. See M. Lascelles, *Jane Austen and her Art* (1939), 122.
52. For another view of this poem ('unabashed admiration . . . the tone of the propemptikon is totally and directly encomiastic'), F. Cairns, *Generic Composition in Greek and Latin Poetry* (1972), 186.
53. A more positive view of Prop. IV. 6: C. Becker in *Hermes* 99 (1971), 451. On these Propertian poems, Syme, *History in Ovid*, 184.
54. e.g. Propertius I. 6; II. 6; II. 7; III. 4. The ingenious argument of F. Cairns, *Graz. Beitr.* 8 (1979), 185 ff., that II. 7 is really an encomium of Augustus, does not convince me.
55. J. Griffin, 'The Creation of Characters in the Aeneid', in *Literary and Artistic Patronage in Ancient Rome*, ed. B. K. Gold (1982), 118.
56. The other view is well put by R. G. M. Nisbet in *BICS* 25 (1978), 59–78.
57. Such things were said to Alexander: 'hi tum caelum illi aperiebant, Herculemque et Patrem Liberum et cum Polluce Castorem novo numini cessuros esse iactabant', Q. Curt. VIII. 5. Those who said them were regarded, then and later, as *adulatores*.
58. Nisbet and Hubbard ad loc. The mythical fantasy of the Tiber overflowing because of the death of Ilia, the fishes in the treetops, and so on, seems to me to have a family resemblance to the opening of the First *Georgic*.
59. Plut. *Mor.* 182 c.
60. Suet. *Aug.* 71. 3 = *Ep.* 7 Malcovati.
61. *Res Gestae Divi Augusti*, ed. P. A. Brunt and J. M. Moore (1967), 7.
62. G. IV. 559 ff. (on these lines, J. Griffin in *Greece and Rome* 26 (1979), 72 ff.); G. II. 171: 'qui nunc extremis Asiae iam victor in oris/imbellem avertis Romanis arcibus Indum.'
63. *Ep.* 36 Malcovati.
64. Despite the ingenious suggestion of G. W. Bowersock, *HSCPh* 75 (1971), 73; see R. J. Tarrant, *HSCPh* 82 (1978), 197.
65. In writing an epic on the foundation of the city, Virgil followed – no doubt consciously – a common practice of Hellenistic poetical panegyrists; see now

A. Hardie, *Statius and the Silvae* (1983), 23. That connection underlines the importance for the Augustan poets of the background of Hellenistic practice.
66. *Aeneid* VI. 847–53, cf. *Greece and Rome* 26 (1979), 65.
67. e.g. P. Zanker, 'Prinzipat und Herrscherbild', *Gymnasium* 86 (1979), 354. On the perspective of the *Aeneid*, see C. O. Brink, op. cit. (n. 1), 535.
68. *Annales* I. 9: 'at apud prudentes vita eius varie extollebatur arguebaturve'.

INDEX